THE
SISTER
QUEENS

THE
SISTER
QUEENS

ISABELLA & CATHERINE
DE VALOIS

MARY McGRIGOR

The
History
Press

To Caroline, Sibylla and Sarah, with all my love.

First published 2016

The History Press
The Mill, Brimscombe Port
Stroud, Gloucestershire, GL5 2QG
www.thehistorypress.co.uk

© Mary McGrigor, 2016

The right of Mary McGrigor to be identified as the Author
of this work has been asserted in accordance with the
Copyright, Designs and Patents Act 1988.

British Library Cataloguing in Publication Data.
A catalogue record for this book is available from the British Library.

ISBN 978 0 7509 6420 3

Typesetting and origination by The History Press
Printed in Great Britain

Contents

Acknowledgements

My deepest thanks to all those who have so kindly helped me with this book: Adrian Gibbs, Deputy CEO of the Bridgeman Library; Sian Phillips, Account Manager of the Bridgeman; Maria Cristina Pîrvu of the Bibliothèque nationale, Paris; Elizabeth Taylor of the National Portrait Gallery; Caroline Robot for translation; Sybilla McGrigor; Sarah McGrigor; Sophie Bradshaw, Naomi Reynolds and Katie Beard of The History Press; Rachel Bellery of Historic Scotland; Gemma Wright for images of Leeds Castle.

The Royal House of Valois

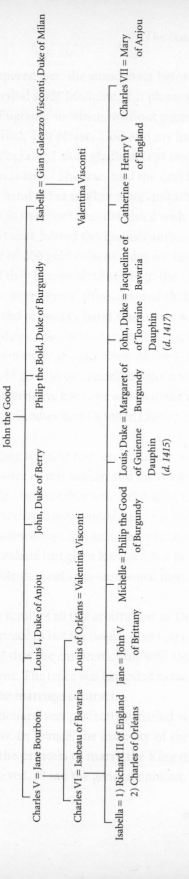

The House of Orléans

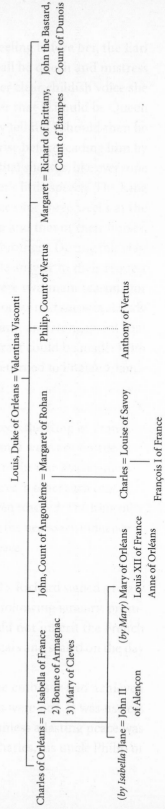

Family Tree Descendants of Edward III, King of England

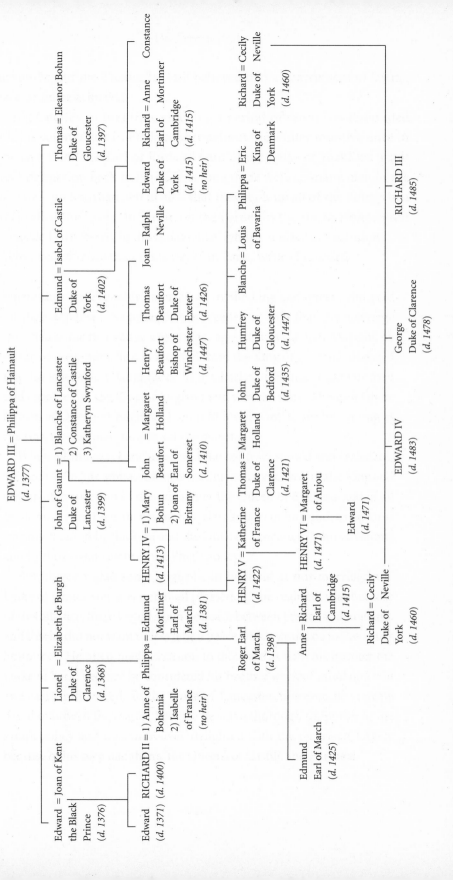

France after the Treaty of Troyes, 1420

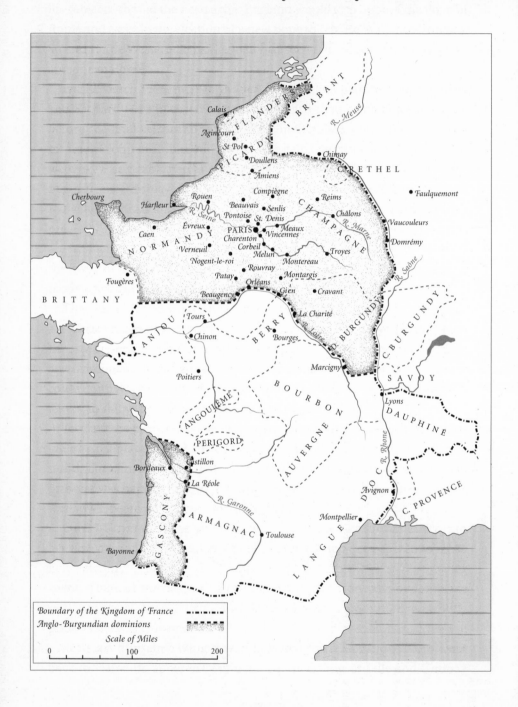

Calais
FLANDERS
BRABANT
R. Meuse
Agincourt
St Pol
PICARDY
Chimay
C. RETHEL
Doullens
Amiens
Faulquemont
Cherbourg
Compiègne
Reims
Harfleur
Rouen
Beauvais
Senlis
Châlons
Vaucouleurs
Caen
Évreux
Pontoise
St. Denis
CHAMPAGNE
R. Marne
Domrémy
NORMANDY
PARIS
Meaux
Vincennes
Charenton
Verneuil
Corbeil
Melun
Troyes
R. Saône
Nogent-le-roi
Rouvray
Montereau
Fougères
Patay
Montargis
BRITTANY
Beaugency
Orléans
Gien
Cravant
ANJOU
Tours
Cravant
D. BURGUNDY
C. BURGUNDY
La Charité
Chinon
BERRY
R. Loire
BURGUNDY
SAVOY
Bourges
Marcigny
Poitiers
Lyons
ANGOULÊME
BOURBON
DAUPHINÉ
PERIGORD
AUVERGNE
R. Rhone
Bordeaux
Castillon
La Réole
Avignon
C. PROVENCE
R. Garonne
ARMAGNAC
Montpellier
LANGUEDOC
GASCONY
Toulouse
Bayonne

Boundary of the Kingdom of France --·--·--
Anglo-Burgundian dominions

Scale of Miles

0   100   200

The Thrones of England and France
during the late thirteenth, fourteenth and fifteenth centuries

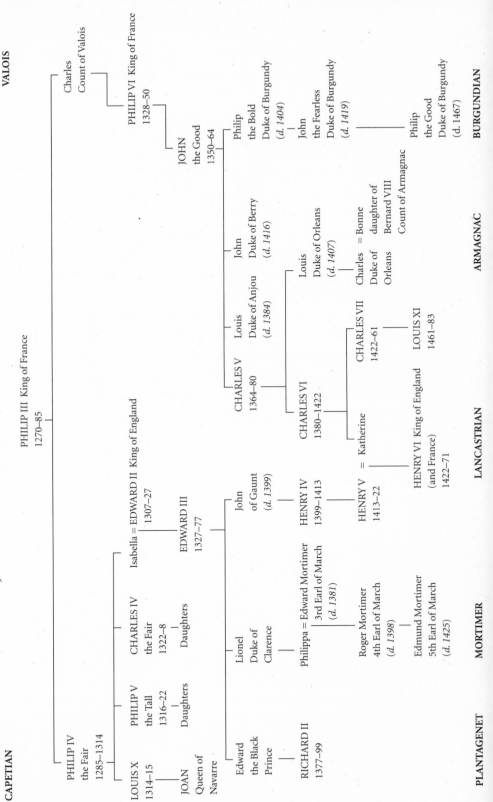

A Poet is Born

France 1394–1404

On 28 November 1394, at ten o'clock in the evening at the Hôtel Saint-Pol, Valentine, wife of Louis of Orléans, gave birth to a boy. He was not her first child. A previous son, called Louis after his father, had died when a few months old. Alarmingly, this infant seemed weak. Named Charles after the king, to whom as much he relied, his godfather and was greatly welcomed to be child of the King.

During the first two years of his life, the tension around the infant Charles increased as his mother's circumstances grew increasingly difficult. As the doctor's efforts to control the king's illness became ever more futile, it was rumoured that Valentine's soothing influence on him was sorcery.

Isabeau did not hesitate to use her authority. Knowing that her liaison with her brother-in-law, Louis of Orléans, was a source of widespread scandal, she connived to circulate the rumour that Valentine was in an adulterous relationship with her husband King Charles. Playing the outraged wife, Isabeau had the gentle and beautiful duchess summarily removed, not only from court but from Paris.

Deeply hurt by the accusations against her, Valentine nonetheless left the city in great state, her head held high. It was given out that she was going to visit one of her husband's castles, Asnières, in the county of

PART I

ISABELLA

1

The First Daughter

Paris 1389–93

Isabella was 3 years old when her father went mad.

Born in 1389, she was the third child and second daughter of King Charles VI of France and Isabeau of Bavaria, who herself was the eldest daughter of Duke Stephen III of Bavaria-Ingolstadt and Taddea Visconti of Milan. Paris was in a state of jubilation just previous to Isabella's birth. Her father, on reaching 20, had just come of age: his uncles' regency had ended, and he was the ruler of France.

Becoming king on the death of his father, Charles had been only 11 years old, so France had been ruled by his four uncles for eight years. On his father's side they were John, Duke of Berry; Philip, Duke of Burgundy; and Louis I, Duke of Anjou, the latter, being the kindest and wisest, having supervised the upbringing of both Charles and his brother Louis from the time of their father's death. On the distaff side was Louis II, Duke of Bourbon, the brother of Charles's mother, Jane of Bourbon.

Only 17 in 1385, Charles had still been underage when he met Isabeau, sent on approval as a possible bride when she was just 16. Delighted with her appearance (she had the dark skin and hair of her Italian mother and likewise her vitality), with typical spontaneity, Charles married her within three days. Since then Isabeau had lost a baby son and had a daughter who was a sickly child.

The queen's coronation and entry into her husband's capital was postponed for four years until Charles attained his majority. It finally took place on Sunday, 22 August 1389. By then there was a joint cause for festivity, for five days previously in Melun (the fortress town some 25 miles south-east of Paris on a higher reach of the Seine) the king's brother Louis, Duke of Touraine and Count of Valois and Beaumont, had married the beautiful Italian heiress Valentina Visconti, daughter of Gian Galeazzo, Duke of Milan. The king was devoted to his brother, with whom he had much in common – Louis was just as excitable, high spirited and addicted to pleasure as Charles. Soon, as the title became vacant, Charles would make him Duke of Orléans, granting him yet further estates.

Amongst the guests attending the ceremony was the King of England's uncle, Lionel Duke of Clarence, who came as the representative of his nephew Richard II, who, too occupied with trying to control his unruly kingdom, was unable to attend. With Clarence came an ecclesiastic, a chronicler of the times – Jean Froissart, or Sir John Froissart as he was known to the English. Born in Valenciennes, a town on the River Scheldt in Hainault, a province near the border of northern France and Flanders (Belgium in the present day), he was now in his fifties. His father, believed to have been a painter of armorial bearings, had no doubt wished his son to follow his career, but John, ambitious and perhaps bored with his home life, had contrived in his early twenties to obtain employment with Philippa of Hainault – herself born in Valenciennes – who had been married there by proxy to Edward III of England in 1327. Perhaps because he was a compatriot, or simply because she perceived his talent, the queen had encouraged the young clerk in her household to become the poet and historiographer of the court. Queen Philippa was now long dead, but thanks to the fame of his *Méliador*, a long Arthurian romance, Froissart now enjoyed the patronage of the Duchess of Brabant and other high-born ladies who believed him to be a genius of the age. That he was indeed greatly venerated is proved by the fact that he was ranked equal to the great Italian poet Francesco Petrarch and to the English Geoffrey Chaucer, the latter, by then at the advanced age of 67, being said to have been present at Charles and Isabeau's royal wedding.

On this occasion, even accustomed as he was to the great entertainments so beloved of medieval times, Froissart found that those following the wedding and the queen's coronation so surpassed all that he had previously seen as to astonish him. 'Never were such elaborate festivities seen in this realm,' he wrote, describing all that had taken place: 'There were so many people in Paris and round about that it was the most wonderful sight.'[1]

He goes on to describe how, in the town of Saint-Denis on the outskirts of Paris, an assembly of all the chief ladies of the nobility who were to accompany the queen and all the lords who were to escort the horse-drawn litters in which they sat, were gathered to form the procession which the frantically excited populace was waiting to see. 'There were 12,000 citizens of Paris, all mounted and ranged in the fields on either side of the route, dressed in tunics of green and scarlet brocade.'[2] First to appear was Jeanne the Queen Mother with her daughter, the Duchess of Orléans, borne in covered litters with an escort of barons. But they went no farther than the palace on the Île de la Cité, where they joined the king.

Then came the great moment when Queen Isabelle of France (as Froissart spells her name), set off with her ladies, headed by the wives of the king's uncles, the Duchess of Burgundy and the Duchess of Berry, with numerous other titled women following in order of rank.

The older ladies had similar litters, 'so richly ornamented that nothing could have been added'. Two of the younger ones, however, rode side-saddle (in those times, a contraption was used by which the lady, sitting sideways on the saddle, could rest both feet on a wooden platform below). One was Valentina Visconti, the new Duchess of Touraine. A tall and ele-gant girl of 19 mounted on a beautifully caparisoned palfrey, she was a joy to the public eye. The other was Jane of Boulogne, the 12-year-old second wife of the king's eldest uncle, the Duke of Berry – who at 49 was totally smitten with his young bride. Those gathered to watch had a splendid view as all proceeded at no more than a walking pace.

Amongst them was the king, who, in typical fashion, had decided it would be more amusing to mingle amongst the crowd. Unrecognised, he was beaten about the shoulders by officials before making a hasty escape for the safety of the old royal palace of Saint Louis on the Île de la Cité.

Interestingly, on foot beside the queen's litter was Louis, the king's brother, at that time the Duke of Touraine, although three years later he would become the Duke of Orléans, when his name would be linked scan-dalously with that of the queen. Other lords walked before and behind. The queen's litter was entirely open, as were those of most of the other ladies, whom the watchers cheered to distraction, marvelling at the dazzling display of jewellery and fine clothes.

At the outer gate of Saint-Denis (on the site of the modern Porte Saint-Denis) under a painted star-lit sky, children dressed as angels sang sweetly. Next there was a tableau of Our Lady holding in her arms a child playing with a windmill made from a large walnut. The upper part of the firmament was richly emblazoned with the arms of France and Bavaria, a golden sun set in its glory, which was the king's badge in the tournament to come.

When they had watched the tableau, they went on to where the fountain of Saint-Denis flowed 'with excellent claret and spiced wine',[3] and girls in gold caps sang tunefully as they held out golden cups and goblets offering drink to one and all.

Further on, in front of the Hospital of the Trinity, a wooden platform had been set up to bear actors portraying the battle with Saladin, Christians on one side, Saracens on the other. Above them a man, supposed to be the King of France, had the twelve peers of his kingdom around him, each wearing his own coat-armour.

As the queen in her litter passed under the inner gate of Saint-Denis, beneath a colourful sky where God sat in His Majesty, down came two angels, holding a golden crown richly studded with precious stones, which they placed very gently on her head as they sang in her honour. No magnificence was spared. Tableau followed tableau, wonderful contrivances of the artists and carpenters of the city which astounded the beholder's eyes.

But it was not a Parisian but 'a skilful man from Geneva'[4] who produced the final climax. Having attached a rope between the top of the highest tower of Notre-Dame and the tallest house on the Pont Saint-Michel, he sat astride it, and then worked his way the along the rope, singing loudly as he went, a wax torch in each hand because it was growing dark. Seen from one end of Paris to the other and from 2 or 3 leagues outside, his performance seemed nothing but a miracle to the watching crowd.

In the square in front of the great cathedral of Notre-Dame, the Bishop of Paris was waiting to greet the queen. Escorted through the church to the high altar, she knelt in prayer before making a gift to the cathedral's treasurer of four cloths of gold and the fair crown from the angels.

Crowned Queen of France by the Bishop of Paris, Isabeau returned with her ladies in their litters to the palace on the Île de la Cité, which was lit by 500 candles. The ladies, obviously exhausted, retired to their chambers, while the men, who must have included the king, 'did not return to their lodgings until after the dancing was over'. The entertainment then continued with several days of feasting and jousting and gift giving, before all the lords and ladies returned to their own provinces having bid farewell to the king and queen, who thanked them warmly for joining them at the festivities.

Not one of that gay crowd of people, who had so greatly enjoyed the hospitality of the young king and queen, could possibly have guessed what lay before them in the next three years. Three months after her coronation, the queen gave birth to a daughter, named Isabella after herself. This time the child survived.

2

Childhood of Fear

The French chronicler Jean Froissart, by then in his late fifties, gives a vivid account of what happened on another day, even hotter than that of the queen's coronation – 5 August 1392.

There had been some minor trouble in Brittany. Olivier de Clisson, the Constable of France, had survived an assassination attempt by a man called Pierre de Craon, who had been given asylum by Jean, Duke of Brittany. An infuriated King Charles, ignoring the advice of his uncles (the dukes of Burgundy, Berry and Anjou), led an army to punish Brittany. They delayed for some three weeks at Le Mans, deliberating as to what action should be taken.

Four knights were sent to the Duke of Brittany with a request to release de Craon into the hands of the king, and returned with an unequivocal reply. Always impatient, Charles said he would wait no longer in Le Mans but would lead his army into Brittany to see which barons and knights would prove to be his enemies by supporting the Duke of Brittany. Behind this plan was Charles's fixed intention to replace the Duke of Brittany with a governor who would rule the province until his own heirs were old enough to take control in his place.

The 5 August 1392 was a day of near-overwhelming heat. Always of a nervous disposition, King Charles was not feeling well; he was having giddy turns and running a temperature. It was noted that he just picked at a few morsels for breakfast, instead of wolfing chunks of cooked meat and washing them down with wine and ale like most of his companions. Once astride his horse, which he sat easily and well, as he headed his army he was conspicuous in a black velvet jerkin, which he wore over his armour, and a scarlet hood.

Froissart continues to give a first-hand description by a man who witnessed what then occurred:

> I have been told that as he was riding into the forest of Le Mans … there suddenly emerged, from between two trees a man wearing neither hat nor shoes, and clad in a smock of homespun cloth; he was quite obviously deranged and taking in his hands the reins of the king's horse he stopped him in his path and said: 'Ride no further, king, turn back for you are betrayed.'

These words badly affected the king's already weak mind and made his feverish state much worse, for he was seriously shaken by the incident.[1]

The man was still mumbling when the sergeant-at-arms leapt forward and struck the idiot's hands such a blow that he dropped the reins and staggered backwards. No one quite knew what happened next but, as other riders pushed forward, the man slipped away into the trees, never to be seen again.

Although clearly much shaken, the king pulled himself together to resume the march through the forest. The temperature was rising as the sun climbed into the heavens, but in the woods the heat was less noticeable thanks to the shade of the trees. Then, coming out into the open, it struck with all its force.

Now they were riding into a plain where the sand in the soil had turned to dust. The army was formed into companies, the king almost on his own to avoid the worst of the dirt thrown up by the horse's hooves. The heat was by then suffocating, the sand boiling to the touch. So also was the armour in which most of the soldiers were encased. Soon both men and horses were gasping for breath and dripping with sweat.

The king, who, his doctors protested, should never have gone out in the first place, was probably the worst affected, thanks to the fact that the velvet jerkin over his armour was black, a colour which draws heat. Behind him rode one of his pages wearing a fine Montauban helmet of steel, glittering in the rays of the sun. Then followed another page, proudly bearing a tall scarlet lance with silken pennants of the king's colours, this being one of twelve such weapons specially forged in Toulouse with points of shining steel which had been given by the Lord de La Rivière, one of the courtiers, to the king.

The columns moved on across the plain, both men and horses tormented by heat, dust and flies. Some began to doze in their saddles when suddenly they jerked awake at the sound of a loud clang. The boy carrying the banner had fallen asleep, or else his horse had stumbled, sending the steel tip of his lance into the steel helmet of the page ahead. Immediately there was panic. The horses, already fractious, stampeded in all directions. The king, the strange man's words still spinning through his mind, thinking doom had come upon him and that a great force was attacking, jerked his sword from its scabbard and turned on the pages, whom, failing to recognise them, he took to be his enemies. Thinking himself in the midst of a battle, he raised his sword and, shouting 'Forward! Advance on these traitors', laid about him in all directions.

Petrified, the pages fled, spurring their horses to safety beyond his deadly reach. Missing them, he made for his brother, Louis, Duke of Orléans, totally unaware of who he was. Orléans, glimpsing this wild apparition charging towards him, flashing sword above its head, eyes rolling red with both dust and madness, swung his horse round and fled, his brother chasing behind, screaming in mad pursuit.

Fortunately, hearing the pages' shouting and seeing the horses bolting, the Duke of Burgundy realised instantly what was happening. Swinging round in his saddle, he shouted to those within hearing: 'Holla there, disaster has befallen us! My lord the king is out of his mind! For God's sake follow after and capture him!' And then 'Fly, nephew of Orléans, fly! Or the king will kill you.'

'I can tell you the Duke of Orléans was not at all happy,' wrote Froissart:

And he fled as fast as his horse could carry him. Knights and squires began shouting and following the direction he had gone. Those who were riding on the right and left wings of the party thought a wolf or a hare had started, until they found out that the king was out of his mind.

However Louis of Orléans got away, by turning and counter-turning and with help from the others.

All the knights, squires and men-at-arms then formed a wide hedge around the king, and waited for him to exhaust himself: the more he charged about the weaker he became. When he came upon anyone, be it knight or squire, that person let himself fall under the blow. I never heard that anyone was killed in this sorry affair, but the king felled several of them, for no one offered resistance. [Other accounts claim that four men were killed]. Finally when he was worn out and his horse was exhausted and both were running with sweat from their exertions, a knight of Normandy, one Guillaume Martel, who was the king's chamberlain and of whom he was very fond, came up and gripped him from behind, holding him tight with his sword arm inactive. The other knights came near and removed his sword, lifted him down from his horse and laid him on the ground and then took off his doublet to cool him. When his brother and three uncles came to see him he did not recognise them or show them any sign of friendship. His eyes rolled horribly in their sockets and he spoke to no one.[2]

Stunned by what had happened, nobody knew what to do. Then two of King Charles's uncles, the dukes of Burgundy and Berry, decided after a brief exchange of words that the expedition into Brittany must be immediately postponed and that the only sensible, in fact the only feasible, thing to do was to return to Le Mans. With that they ordered men to use anything they could find – probably saddlecloths – as fans to cool the king down before laying him in a litter to carry back to the town.

Once there the doctors, who were immediately summoned, shook their heads in bewilderment as to what could have caused the attack of what is now believed to have been paranoid schizophrenia. Inevitably, both witchcraft and poison ran through people's minds. Rumour became rampant, focusing on the king's brother and uncles, who, as his nearest relations, were potential heirs to the throne in the event of his death.

Again it was Philip, Duke of Burgundy, who, though the youngest of the uncles, took command. Summoning the doctors, who explained to him that the king had been suffering from a kind of 'malady', as they put it, for some time. Burgundy then exonerated them of the blame laid upon them for allowing him to ride out on a day of such heat. He himself had seen Charles's determination and was one of those who had tried to dissuade him from embarking on such an expedition, but his advice had been ignored. Once Charles's mind was set on something, he was hell bent on carrying it out.

He then questioned them carefully about what Charles had taken, both in food and drink, before setting out that fateful morning. On the doctors' reply that 'it was so little that it was not worth mentioning', he merely sat and mused. Burgundy sent for his nephew's chief butler, Robert de Tanques, a squire from Picardy, who said that the last person to give him both food and drink had been Sir Helion de Lignac, who swore that both he and de Tanques had tasted the wine in front of the king. There was still some of the same wine in bottles, which both Burgundy and his brother the Duke of Berry could try. It was Berry who said that 'the only poison and sorcery the king has suffered is that of bad advice … let us hold such matters over for another occasion.'[3]

From Le Mans, King Charles was sent to Creil, where, under the care of Master Guillaume de Harselly, then one of the leading doctors in France, renowned for both his wisdom and his parsimony, Charles gradually recovered. Froissart says that he returned to Paris in September but does not give the year. He does mention, however, that during his absence the Duchess of Burgundy, by all accounts a terrifying woman, had been installed in the Hôtel Saint-Pol in Paris, presumably to act as helper and guardian to the young Queen Isabeau and her family.

Isabella, now 3 years old, appeared to be a healthy child, as was Joan, her younger sister, born in 1391. Marie, the fourth daughter, born in 1393, must be the baby to whom Froissart refers when he writes that the queen gave birth to another child, whom he thought was a daughter, at about this time.[4]

King Charles continued to suffer from bouts of frantic delusions, at increasingly frequent intervals. Sometimes he thought he was made of glass. At others, he ran until he collapsed in exhaustion. So confused did he become when afflicted by the disease – at the time thought to be caused by magic – that he did not know his wife, saying 'who is that woman, she gets in my view' before ordering her to be taken from his room.

The only person the king could bear to have near him during his attacks of madness was his sister-in-law, Valentina Visconti, wife of his brother

Louis, now Duke of Orléans. Her gentle presence soothed him. Needless to say, this caused friction with Isabeau, who did her best to ruin Valentina's name, seething with jealousy that any other woman should have influence over her husband.

Isabeau did not hesitate to ensure her increased authority. Knowing that her liaison with her brother-in-law, Louis of Orléans, was a source of widespread scandal, she connived to circulate the rumour that Valentina was in an adulterous relationship with King Charles.

Meanwhile, the Duke and Duchess of Burgundy were greatly alarmed that Valentina's influence over the king might strengthen that of her husband and enable him to win the power and the privileges they were scheming to win for themselves.

For a time, Isabeau moved to the Hôtel Babette, giving her enemies a chance to claim that she had abandoned her husband. The gap of two years between the births of Marie in 1393 and Michelle in 1395, suggests that it was then that the royal couple lived apart. Nonetheless, in his more lucid moments, Charles recognised her capability and his own incapacity, and allowed Isabeau to have a seat on the regency council, giving her far greater power than was usual for a queen. As guardian of their children, she had control of their son, the dauphin Louis, an arrangement which was to last until he reached the age of 13.

When the king did return to lucidity, the doctors advised strongly against his being burdened with too many affairs of state. Instead, they said he should have entertainment, anything to lift his mind from the depression which had been such a significant feature of his illness.

3

Le Bal des Sauvages

Diversions were hard to invent. Yet, on the doctors' orders, the king had to be entertained.

An opportunity came in January 1393, when a marriage was celebrated between a young knight of Vermandois and one of the queen's ladies-in-waiting, both members of the royal household. King Charles, delighted, declared that the wedding festivities must be held in his own palace of Saint-Pol. The many guests invited included the highest in the land, amongst them the king's brother the Duke of Orléans, his uncles the dukes of Berry and Normandy and their wives.

In the evening, the king hosted a supper for the assembled party, over which the queen was to preside. Everyone tried to be merry, encouraged by the sight of the king enjoying every minute, clearly himself once more. It was one of his distant relatives, a Norman knight called Hugonin de Guisay, who thought up an entertainment, in the form of a masked ball. But this would be a ball with a difference. Gone were the masks and dominoes. Instead, the guests would be savages, something never thought of before.

The preparations alone were hilarious. Six tight-fitting linen suits were made and then hidden in a room, where they were painted with tar on to which strips of flax were stuck to look like hair. Hugonin de Guisay supervised as the king, laughing with pleasure, was fitted into one of them. The Count of Joigny, a particularly handsome young man, was stuffed into another. Count Charles of Poitiers, son of the Count of Valentinois, into a third. Yvain, the bastard of Foix, wore the fourth; the son of the Lord of Nantouillet, the fifth; and the last one de Guisay put on himself. All were carefully sewn up so that they looked remarkably like savages, sprouting hair from the top of their heads to the soles of their feet.

The king, looking down at what he could see of himself and then at his companions, laughed aloud in joy, thrilled at taking part in such a game. Only Yvain de Foix foresaw possible danger, and begged Charles to give orders that no torch should be brought near them, the suits, covered in tar, being obviously inflammable. 'By God, Yvain, that's a sound warning,' said the king, suddenly aware of the potential danger and instructing the servants that no one should follow after them. He then called in a sergeant-at-arms who was standing at the door and told him, 'Go into the hall where the ladies are assembled and tell them it is the king's order that all the torches should be placed to one side and that no one is to come close to the six savages who are about to enter.' The sergeant did as he was told. The torchbearers were withdrawn to one of the walls and given the king's orders that no one was to go near the dancers until the savages had left the hall.

All should have been safe … but the Duke of Orléans arrived late with some companions, four knights and six torchbearers, all of them – no doubt having been drinking – out to have some fun. With his eyes on the prettiest women, Orléans plunged into the dancing with great energy, totally unaware (or so he claimed afterwards) of what the high point of the evening's entertainment was to be.

His brother, the king, came in first, gesticulating and grimacing like a primitive man, as he led the five others, for some reason tied together, in the dance. No one recognised any of them, so clever was their disguise. The king, totally delighted at such a wonderful ploy, was unable to resist the temptation of showing himself off to the ladies. Passing the queen, he stood in front of the Duchess of Berry, his youngest aunt, who tried to find out who he was by pestering him to give his name, telling him that he would not escape her until she knew who he was. The dancing had now stopped and while this interchange was taking place, Charles of Orléans, bored with the inactivity, impulsive as a young man of 21, seized a torch that his servant was carrying and held it close to one of the savages, peering into his half-covered face, to try to make out who it was.

Within seconds the flax was on fire. The tar holding it to the linen began to melt and the men in the tight-fitting suits, sewn on to their bodies, screamed as they felt themselves burn. Petrified, no one dared go near them until some knights, braver than others, tried to help them, tearing at their flaming, sizzling clothes. But they were sewn on so tightly that their hands were badly burned.

No one who heard it could ever forget the screaming. The little Princess Isabella, even if up in her nursery, must have heard it piercing the very stones of the building.

In the great hall the burning figures, writhing, yelling and sobbing in their torture, finally fell to the floor. Of the six 'savages', only two remained alive. One was Isabella's father, the king, who dived under the wide skirts of his young aunt the Duchess of Berry. As he struggled to escape from her petticoats, she told him he must go at once to his wife who believed he was dead. On seeing him, Isabeau fainted and had to be carried from the room.

The other survivor was Nantouillet, who had remembered that there was a large tub of water in the buttery used for the washing up. His suit alight, he had dashed into the room, scattering the terrified servants, and plunged into the tub, sizzling and badly burned, but alive.

Not so fortunate were the rest, of whom two died on the spot. The bastard of Foix and the Count of Joigny were carried to their lodgings and, after two days of excruciating agony, were mercifully released by death.

4

A Journey of Diplomacy

England 1395

In 1395, Sir John Froissart, the canon Treasurer of Chimay, decided to make a return visit to England, the country which, as a young man, he had become familiar with and grown to love. Born in Valenciennes in Hainault around 1335, he was nearly 60, considered old in those days. From his poem 'L'espinette amoureuse' ('The Thorn Bush of Love'), thought to be largely autobiographical, he seems to have been educated in a mixed school, probably a religious house, where he enjoyed giving the girls presents and fighting with the boys. He also says that he liked *ballades* and *rondeaux* rather than lessons and must, even at a young age, have been interested in all that was happening in what was then known of the world.

The supposition that he had a religious education seems borne out by his being in minor orders by the age of 23. That he was also a writer is evident from his journey to London in 1326, when he took with him a manuscript describing the Battle of Poitiers and the events of subsequent years as a gift for Philippa of Hainault, King Edward III's queen.

His present achieved its objective. Under her protection, he remained with the court for six years. He must have told her of his intention of writing a history of the times, for he was granted permission to travel to Scotland, where he met King David II, the grandson of Robert the Bruce. In England, he stayed at Berkeley Castle, where he heard at first hand the grim story of the death by torture with (supposedly) a red-hot poker of the king's father, Edward II.

Returning to London, he had related his travels to Queen Philippa, who loved having a native of her homeland in the court, where French was the language of the nobility. King John of France, taken prisoner by Edward the Prince of Wales (dubbed the Black Prince because of the colour of his armour), and some of his fellow captives were also about the court on parole.

Froissart had loved every minute of the time he spent in England, where he wrote of the embassy of Chaucer and claimed to have met Petrarch. Back in France, he went with the Black Prince to Aquitaine and was actually in Bordeaux when Richard II was born there. Later, in Italy, he was present at the wedding of King Edward's son, the Duke of Clarence, in 1386–9. Then, tragically for him, Queen Philippa died.

The king's mistress, Alice Perrers, who had seduced him to the great grief of his wife before her death, had no time for Froissart. Described by Thomas Walsingham as 'a shameless woman and wanton harlot ... of base kindred ... being neither beautiful nor fair, she knew how to cover these defects with her flattering tongue,' she may have feared he would malign her should he be allowed to remain. Ostracised from England, he went back to Hainault to find a new patron to support his literary works.

In 1395 he wrote:

For my own part I had prepared a collection of all the treatises on love and morals that with God's grace I had written over a period of thirty-four years: when these had been copied in a fair hand and illuminated, my desire to go and see King Richard of England was redoubled. Having provided myself with horses and other equipment, I crossed the sea from Calais and arrived at Dover on the twelfth day of July.

He was initially disappointed. In Dover itself he found that he knew no one and that even the inns he had once frequented had disappeared. Having stayed for a day to rest both himself and his horses, he rode on to Canterbury to see the splendid new tomb of the Black Prince, the Prince of Wales. There he was told that the king was just back from Ireland, where he had been for nine months. King Richard was due to arrive on a pilgrimage to the shrine of St Thomas of Canterbury.

While waiting patiently to see him, Froissart allowed his mind to wander back to the time, now twenty-eight years ago, when, on the night of Epiphany, 6 January 1367,[1] he had sat with the other courtiers huddled over a fire which did little to heat the room, in the abbey of Bordeaux. Through the night they had crouched there, waiting for news, while Joan, the Princess of Wales, lay in labour in a room above. At last, at three o'clock in the morning on that freezing night, they had heard the thin wail of a newborn baby, before one of the princess's ladies came in to say that the princess had been safely delivered of, what appeared to be, a healthy boy.

Froissart had then attended the christening of the red-haired child, which had taken place three days later in the great cathedral of Bordeaux. Gathered round the font were kings, princes and knights, most of them with only a few words of English. Known as Richard of Bordeaux, after the place of his birth, none could have guessed that they were watching the baptism of a child who, within the space of a decade, would be King of England. Subsequently, Froissart had seen Richard grow up, at first by the side of his older brother Edward of Angoulême, until that boy died suddenly when Richard was only 4.

Richard had been largely brought up by his mother, while his father, Edward, waged war in Spain. While he waited to see Richard at Canterbury, Froissart dwelt on his memories of the beauty of Joan's face and form. How could anyone forget her? Joan the Fair Maid of Kent.

Joan's attraction to the chronicler was increased rather than detracted by the scandals of her early life. She was the daughter of Edmund Woodstock, the 1st Earl of Kent, a son of King Edward I and his second wife the Princess Margaret of France. Following her father's execution by Queen Isabella and her lover Roger Mortimer after Edward II's death, she had largely been brought up at court by Edward III and his queen, Philippa of Hainault. Promiscuous, even as a child, Joan had secretly married Thomas Holland before being forced into a marriage with William Montacute, Earl of Salisbury, in whose house her former husband had held the post of seneschal. This second marriage had been annulled in 1349, when Joan had been ordered to return to her first husband by no less an authority than the Pope. In around 1373, Thomas had been created Lord Holland before becoming the Earl of Kent on the death of Joan's brother.

After Holland died in 1360, Joan had made another secret marriage to Edward Prince of Wales, the man who had loved her since their childhood together at court. Again the Pope was appealed to and this time, despite their degree of consanguinity, had allowed the Archbishop of Canterbury to marry them at Windsor Castle in 1361. In the following year, when Prince Edward was invested as the Prince of Aquitaine, he and Joan had moved to Bordeaux, the main city of the principality, and would live there for the next nine years, during which time both their sons were born.

Edward the Black Prince had held Aquitaine through the conquest of his father, Edward III. The Treaty of Brétigny (later ratified as the Treaty of Calais) signed on 25 May 1360 between King John II, then a prisoner in English hands, and the victorious English king, had given Edward all of Aquitaine. Naturally this was much resented by King John's son and successor, King Charles V, who, in revenge, had supported Henry of Trastamara, usurper of the throne of Castile, against the rightful claimant King Pedro of Spain. The Black Prince, seeing that it was to his advantage, had agreed to support Pedro and for this reason had sent, not only his own army, but mercenaries employed by his younger brother John of Gaunt, over the Pass of Roncesvalles into Spain. The English and French armies had met on 3 April 1367, at Nájera, mid-way between Burgos and Pamplona where the two sons of Edward III had won an overwhelming victory over the French.

Nájera, the greatest of the Black Prince's victories, was also his last. Wracked with recurrent dysentery, he had returned to England a dying man. He was, though, a national hero. When his wife, the beautiful Joan had landed near Plymouth in 1371 with her 4-year-old son, who had inherited much of her good looks, they had been cheered all the way back to London to be met with a tremendous welcome as they arrived.

The Black Prince's death by dysentery on 8 June 1376 had been swiftly followed by that of his father Edward III, King of England for over fifty years. On 25 June 1376, the last act of the Commons, what was known as the Good Parliament, had been to insist that Richard be brought to it in order 'that they might see and honour him as the heir-apparent'.[2] Less than a year later, on Midsummer's Day 1377, Richard had succeeded his grandfather as King of England at the age of only 10.

How eagerly had Froissart then waited for news from across the Channel, 'the Narrow Sea', as then they called it, for news of what was taking place in England, with its king no more than a boy.

It was difficult to learn anything, for news of the old king's death and his grandson's succession was kept as long as possible from the French, who might otherwise have seized the chance to invade. Already the ships of France and Castile were patrolling the Channel, almost totally unopposed. French soldiers had landed on the Isle of Wight and overrun it. South coast ports were raided, the prior of Lewes was taken prisoner, while even nearer to London, Gravesend was sacked and burned. The trouble did not end there. In the north, the Scots took advantage of the confusion elsewhere and conducted raids across the border, pillaging all they could find. England seemed leaderless to the extent that Froissart had written in his memoirs that she 'was losing all her great captains one by one'.[3]

In fact, what then happened was, that immediately following the young king's coronation, a Great Council had been summoned to appoint a regency of eight men. It was headed by the Duke of Gaunt's chancellor, the Bishop of Salisbury, and Edmund, Earl of March, who, married to Philippa, daughter of Gaunt's elder brother Lionel, Duke of Clarence, was the father of Roger Mortimer, Earl of March, the heir presumptive to the throne.

From travellers, mostly merchants connected with the wool trade who reached Paris, Froissart now remembered hearing the dark rumours of the great unrest in England, which the Council of Regency appeared unable to control. All classes of people were affected, from the highest to the low. Many of the aristocracy who had made fortunes by raising their men to fight the French and winning wealth from both ransoms and plunder, disliked the government for ending this lucrative form of income, while the soldiers, finding themselves unpaid, were highly resentful of their lords. Disaffected parsons, railing at the wealth of the higher churchmen, while they themselves were poorly paid, disturbed the smooth running of the Church. Foremost amongst those who protested against what they saw as the heresy of the English Church, was John Wycliffe, a professor of theology at Oxford, one of the earliest opponents of papal authority over the clergy Froissart had heard rumours of a coming civil war. A poll tax imposed in 1371, demanding a shilling from every adult in the land, was proving to be more than people could stand. Froissart had therefore been unsurprised when word reached Paris in May that the men of Essex had risen against the government and a dangerous conflict had begun. How perilous the situation had been was only later revealed. The rebellion had spread to Kent and soon the whole of the south of England was in a state of turmoil, as the insurgents converged upon London in a terrifying threatening force.

The rebels had been led by a man from Maidstone called Wat Tyler, another was named Jack Straw and there was also a parson, John Ball, originally from York. Describing one of Ball's sermons, presumably relayed to him by word of mouth, Froissart wrote how he incited his followers to rebel against the men who exploited them:

> What have we deserved, or why should we be kept thus in servage? We be all come from one father and one mother, Adam and Eve; whereby can they say or shew that they be greater Lords than we be, saving by that they cause us to win and labour for that they dispend? They are clothed in velvet and camlet furred with grise, and we be vestured with poor cloth ... they dwell in their houses, and we have pain and travail, rain and wind in the fields, and by that cometh of our labours they keep and maintain their estates; we be called their bondsmen, and without we do them readily their service, we be beaten; and we have no sovereign to whom we may complain ... Let us go to the King, he is young, and shew him what servage we be in ... and when the King seeth us, we shall have some remedy, either by fairness or otherwise.[4]

Richard had been at Windsor Castle when he was told that the rising had begun. Both he and his mother had then been hastily removed to the Tower of London, from whence he had had himself rowed down the River Thames to confront Wat Tyler, who was demanding to speak to him. Approaching, he and those with him had seen the protesters to be hostile, shouting words that were incomprehensible and putting arrows to their bows. Alarmed, Richard's companions had told the oarsmen to turn round and row the king back to the Tower.

Thought to be impregnable, the Tower of London soon was under siege. The Alderman of London, Walter Sybyle, sympathised with the rebels and raised the drawbridge, allowing the insurgents to swarm into London to burn many buildings in the city, including John of Gaunt's Savoy Palace. From the Tower, Richard could see the smoke and flames, as part of his capital was destroyed.

On the morning of Friday 14 June, he rode out of the Tower. With only a few armed men beside him he again went to meet Wat Tyler, this time in the fields of Mile End. On his approach, a spokesman had come forward with a petition demanding that what was described as villeinage should be abolished and that all feudal dues and services should be commuted for a rent of 4d per acre and that a general amnesty and pardon be declared. Surprisingly, the king agreed to their demands. No less than thirty clerks were promptly employed to write documents granting pardon and freedom bearing the king's seal, to every village, manor and shire. In addition, Richard's banner had been presented to every shire in warranty of his word.

It had seemed that everything was settled, but on returning to London, Richard had been met with the news that the Tower had fallen to the rebels. Thankfully his mother, Princess Joan, fainting with terror, had been taken to the royal office at the Wardrobe in Carter Lane. Young Henry Lancaster, Earl of Derby and son of John of Gaunt had escaped but the Archbishop of Canterbury Simon Sudbury, Chancellor of the Realm, and Sir John Hayes, the Treasurer, had been dragged to immediate execution on Tower Hill.

No one could guess better than Froissart at the grief and overwhelming anger at such bestial cruelty which had then inflamed Richard's sensitive mind. Having first consoled his mother, he rode out by Ludgate and Fleet Street, fury forcing his spurs. Knowing what lay before them, he and his escort of knights were wearing corselets of steel. A meeting with Wat Tyler was arranged to take place at Smithfield, a market just beyond the New Gate of the city. Tyler very cockily rode over on a pony to where Richard the king, a boy of 14 but well grown for his age, sat erect astride his big horse.

'Brother', began Tyler, the familiarity of his address shocking to those within hearing, so Froissart had been told, 'be of good cheer, for you now have 40,000 men at your back, and we shall all be good friends.'

Richard regarded him coldly before demanding to know why his followers refused to disperse. Tyler then became truculent, and replied that they would only do so when all their demands had been met. 'What demands?'

Richard had asked. Whereupon, Tyler, rudely rinsing his mouth out in front of the king while saying he was quenching a great thirst, had announced that he knew no law but the law of Winchester, no lordship but the king's disestablishment of the Church, the recognition of only one bishop, no serfage, no villeinage, and freedom and equality for all.

It was apparently at this point, or so Froissart was informed, that one of Richard's escort, infuriated by Tyler's rudeness to his sovereign, insulted Tyler to his face, bawling over the heads of those around him that he was the greatest thief in Kent. Tyler, mad with rage, had ordered his men to kill him for his insolence, whereupon the king had told a Major Walworth to arrest Tyler for contempt. Tyler lunged at Walworth with his dagger, but heard the point of it ring against the steel of his breastplate, as, in the same moment, Walworth struck him with his sword.

Wounded, Tyler had hauled at his pony's mouth to pull it away, but lost his balance as it swung round. Falling from the saddle, his foot had caught in the stirrup, so that the terrified animal had dragged him across the marketplace, leaving a trail of blood. His men, all 40,000 of them as Tyler had claimed, had stood silent, horrified as their leader vanished in a scrimmage of men blocking him from their view.

It was then that Richard had ridden forward alone, erect in the saddle, even as Tyler's men drew their bows. 'Let me be your leader,' he had yelled at them, his voice clear above the noise. Dumbfounded, bewildered, they followed him to the meadow known as Clerkenwell Fields, from where they then disbanded, muttering amongst themselves in amazement at the courage of the boy who, to the great majority of them, seemed so fit to be their king.

That had been fourteen years ago. Now Richard, for whom Froissart waited, was a man of 28.

Soon there assembled a band of lords and ladies and their daughters, none of whom Froissart knew. Nonetheless he introduced himself to Sir Thomas Percy, High Steward of England, who suggested that he should accompany the royal party to Leeds Castle in Kent. There, in the great fortress, which had been built in the reign of Henry I on an island in the River Len, and been a royal residence for over a century, Froissart waited by the door of the great hall of the castle, eager to catch sight of Richard, now in his late twenties, whom he had last seen when only a little boy.

Straining his eyes against the distance, Froissart saw him approach at the head of a large retinue and his breath caught in his throat. He found Edmund, Duke of York, whom he had met in the house of King Edward and Queen Philippa many years before. York immediately recognised him and took him to his nephew, the king, who, after reading his letters of introduction, told Froissart that if he had been welcome in his grandfather's house he was equally so in his.

He had recognised him immediately – he was so like his father, the Black Prince. He remembered how old Archbishop Sudbury had described him (he who had placed the crown on Richard's head, before, as Chancellor of England, he had been so cruelly killed by rioting peasants). Sudbury had called him 'the very image of his father and fair to look upon'.

Now, as he watched Richard swing from the saddle and a groom run forward to hold his horse, Froissart saw before him a man, 6ft tall and changed but still instantly recognisable as the red-haired boy with the eyes of his mother, the beautiful Joan, whom he had often seen close to, following her train in the royal court in Bordeaux.

Froissart had brought a book to give King Richard but, taking the advice of Sir Thomas Percy, did not present it to him immediately for Richard was embroiled in sending a private embassy to King Charles of France regarding his projected marriage with Isabella, the king's eldest daughter, who was just 6 years old.

'On the next day,' continues the chronicler, 'the king and his council, together with Duke Edmund,' left for the royal palace of Eltham, halfway between London and Dartford. With them went Froissart, who took the opportunity, as they rode together, to ask Sir John de Grelly, captain of the garrison at Bouteville, about the king's intention to remarry. Richard's first wife, Anne of Bohemia, had been the eldest daughter of Charles IV, Holy Roman Emperor, the most powerful man in Europe. Richard had been devoted to her, and was so traumatised when she died of the plague at the Palace of Sheen, that he had had the building pulled down. Nor would he enter any of the rooms in the Palace of Westminster she had used. But, greatly as he mourned her, Anne had left no children, and Richard needed an heir.

'Now according to my information', Sir John Grelly told Froissart as they rode together, knee to knee:

the King of England is very keen to marry again, and has cast around everywhere but without success. If the Duke of Burgundy or the Count of Hainault had had marriageable daughters he would gladly have accepted such a match, but they have none that are not already married or betrothed. Some have suggested to him that the King of Navarre has sisters and daughters, but he is not interested. His uncle, the Duke of Gloucester, has a daughter old enough to be married and would be very glad to see her marry the king, but the king objects that she is too closely related, being his first cousin. It is the daughter of the King of France that appeals to King Richard, but all his countrymen are amazed that he wishes to marry his enemy's daughter; his popularity has decreased, but he does not mind, for he has always made it clear that if there is to be a war he would rather it was not against France, and he is known to support the view that there ought now to be a lasting peace between himself and the King of France and all their allies. The war between them, he says, has lasted too long, too many valiant men on both sides have lost their lives, too many evil deeds have been perpetrated, and too many Christian folk have been destroyed, to the great weakening of Christendom.

To break the king of this notion, which is so disagreeable to the English people, they have told him that the French princess is too young, and that in five or six years she will still be too young. To which he replies that God willing she will grow older each year, and that he would prefer she were too young than too old. He adds that if he marries her young he can bring her up according to his own desires, and educate her in the manners of the English, and that he is still young enough himself to wait until she reaches the age to be a wife. No one can get this project out of his head. You will see something of this before you leave us, for the king is now riding towards London to bring about a settlement in this matter.[5]

5

The French Bride

France 1395–96

Having landed at Calais, the English Embassy, led by the Earl of Rutland, the Earl Marshal and others, with no less than 600 horses, rode through Amiens on their way to Paris. Arriving there, they found the King of France in the palace of the Louvre, the fortress built by King Philip II on the right bank of the Seine, which had been converted into a royal residence by the present king's father, Charles V. Queen Isabeau and their children remained in the palace, they regarded as their family home, the Hôtel Saint-Pol. Elsewhere in the city were lodged the king's uncles, the dukes of Burgundy and Berry and his brother Orléans, summoned as part of the king's council to debate the proposals offered by the English lords.

Most were against the idea of marrying Princess Isabella to the English king before a secure peace was signed. The Chancellor of France, however, Sir Renaud de Corbie, considered this chance of a truce with England not to be missed. Much in agreement was the Duke of Burgundy, who, married to the heiress of Flanders, saw it as a heaven-sent way to increase the wool trade between that country and England. Thanks to their influence, the other councillors agreed to allow the English delegation to visit the queen and her children in the Hôtel Saint-Pol.

Isabella at once made a great impression by the dignity of her behaviour. In her long dress of heavy, bejewelled material reaching down to her little slippered feet, she stood erect before them. Kneeling before her, the Earl Marshal said, 'Madame, if it please God you shall be queen and mistress of England,' to which, without prompting, in her clear childish voice she replied, 'If it pleases God and my lord and father that I should be Queen of England, I shall gladly accept my lot, for they tell me I should then be a great lady.'[1] She then told the Earl Marshal to rise before leading him by the hand to her mother who, ambitious woman that she was, like everyone else in the room, was delighted with her daughter's little speech. The King of France hosted the English ambassadors in Paris for three weeks at the rate of 200 gold crowns a day for their own keep and that of their horses, and they frequently dined with the king and his brothers. During this stay, they were several times assured that a favourable answer to their request for the princess's hand was on its way. There were two main reasons for the delay. One, as they expected, was her age; the other that she was already betrothed to the elder son of the Duke of Brittany, an arrangement that would have to be cancelled before any new contract could be made. With no alternative but to be satisfied, the delegation returned to England, landing at Sandwich in October 1395.

> King Richard had sent frequent messages to keep the King of France aware of this matter, and the councillors of France were not hostile to this, because they were still hoping to put an end to the war. Negotiations continued so favourably, and the two kings wrote each other such conciliatory letters, that an advanced stage had now been reached. The King of England had given his word that he would exert the necessary influence over the English to ensure that there would be peace.[2]

As a result of all this arbitration, in December 1395, Richard signed a treaty for peace to last for twenty-five years, before, the following January, promising that the children of his wife (Isabella) would not inherit the French throne. The truce was extended to twenty-eight years and sealed on the day of the marriage contract.

Richard was perfectly satisfied with what the embassy had achieved so far. In France, the majority of the councillors were not. It was useless for the princess to marry the King of England unless a lasting peace was achieved, so ran the general opinion. But King Charles, his uncle Philip of

Burgundy, and the Chancellor still believed that an agreement of lasting peace could be achieved.

King Charles, at that time enjoying a period of sanity, corresponded with his counterpart in England throughout the winter months, until in February 1396, the Earl of Rutland (son of the Duke of York) led a still larger delegation back to Paris. This time there were so many men in the embassy – no less than 500 in all – that they took up all of the houses in a street called the Croix du Tiroir, on the corner of the rue St Honoré and the rue de l'Arbre-Sec, in those days, like Tyburn, a place of execution.

'They stayed more than three weeks in Paris,' writes Froissart:

where they were lavishly entertained by the king and queen, who paid all their expenses. Negotiations proceeded so well that the marriage they had come to arrange was, in fact agreed, and the Earl Marshal, by virtue of the powers he had received from the King of England, declared that Isabelle, eldest daughter of King Charles of France, was betrothed and espoused to the King of England and that she should henceforth be known as Queen of England. I am told it was a joy to see her, young as she was, for she knew how to act the queen.

When all this was concluded and the contract signed and sealed, on 9 March 1396, the ambassadors from England took leave of the King and Queen of France and of their daughter the Queen of England, and of all the lords. From Paris they went to Calais and so to England, to be most warmly received by the king and the Duke of Lancaster (John of Gaunt) and by those who favoured the king's policy.

But however glad some might be in England at this marriage, the Duke of Gloucester was not at all pleased, for he realised, that because of this alliance, there would again be peace between France and England, and this he did not want unless it be a peace which would be to England's honour ... He often made occasion to discuss this with his brother the Duke of York, because he considered his brother weak of mind and will and easily influenced. To the Duke of Lancaster, however, he scarcely dared to broach the matter, because he was a thorough supporter of the king's policy and was, moreover, delighted with the marriage, largely because of his own daughters, the Queens of Castile and Portugal.[3]

The terms of the marriage contract decreed that England would support French designs in Europe, and France would help Richard 'against any of his subjects' should the need arise. England would also oppose the Pope in Rome and assist in the election of a new pope to replace him, thus bringing an end to the Western Schism which had seen two popes, one in Avignon and one in Rome.

On 12 March 1396, three days after the completion of the treaty, Isabella and Richard were married by proxy. Richard then came twice to Calais before the final celebrations took place in October. While Richard, with his uncles John of Gaunt and Gloucester held court at Guînes, the French were likewise established at Ardres. All chroniclers of the day write of the magnificence displayed. 'Richard, on the first day, wore a long gown of red velvet, a headdress given to him by the King of France studded with precious stones, and on his breast the hart of his own livery.' His lords attending him were also in long velvet robes but wore the white 'bend' of the livery of his first wife, Queen Anne. On the second day the king wore 'a motley gown of white and red velvet'.

That Richard treasured Anne's memory is further shown by the gift of a necklace made of pearls and precious stones she had given him, which he now presented to his little bride. Isabella's own apparel on her wedding day, overlooked by the chroniclers, was no doubt as dazzling as her mother could contrive. Nothing less than a dress of rich material, oversewn with jewels, to show the importance of England's new queen.

To mark the peace sealed by the marriage both kings shared in the building of a chapel to 'Our Lady of Peace' in the place where their tents had stood. The climax of the whole occasion was then reached when the small princess was handed over to the care of a group of English ladies. Isabella was now Queen of England, not quite 7 years old.[4]

On 23 November, the young new queen made her formal entry into her new husband's capital, London. No expense had been spared to make her welcome, reputedly the then enormous sum of £2 million being spent. Then, at the beginning of January, as her coronation took place in Westminster Abbey, Richard watched with what amounted to fatherly pride as she was crowned.

Froissart himself, having stayed to watch the celebrations, then went back to Hainault, apparently reluctantly. As Canon of Lille and Chimay and Treasurer of the Abbey of Chimay, he must have had business to attend to after an absence of three months. His arrival in England to find that no one remembered him, had been made up for by King Richard's showing him 'warm hospitality because in my younger days I had been a clerk in the royal household and of terms of friendship with his grandfather King Edward III, of blessed memory, and of his wife the Lady Philippa of Hainault, Queen of England'.

Looking back on those days, he had been astonished, perhaps even a little shocked, to find how court life had changed. Richard lived in pomp and power hitherto unseen. 'Never did any King of England keep such state, spending as much as 100,000 florins a year to maintain his household.' Sir John Froissart's parting present from Richard was in keeping with the style to which, in the course of a season, he had grown pleasantly accustomed. 'When I took leave of him at Windsor he made me a present through one of his knights called Sir John Golofre, of a silver-gilt goblet weighing over a pound and containing a 100 gold nobles, which I have since valued the more and shall continue to treasure.'[5] Such was the impression made by Richard's kindness and generosity that, long after his death, the old Canon of Lille and Chimay would continue to pray for him.

6

A Poet is Born

France 1394–1404

On 24 November 1394, at ten o'clock in the evening at the Hôtel Saint-Pol, Valentina, wife of Louis of Orléans, gave birth to a boy. He was not her first child. A previous son, called Louis after his father, had died when a few months old. Mercifully, this infant seemed strong. King Charles, after whom he was named, became his godfather and was actually sane enough to hold him at the font.

During the first two years of his life, the tension around the infant Charles increased as his mother's circumstances grew increasingly difficult. As the doctor's efforts to control the king's illness became ever more futile, it was rumoured that Valentina's soothing influence on him was sorcery.

Isabeau did not hesitate to use her authority. Knowing that her liaison with her brother-in-law, Louis of Orléans was a source of widespread scandal, she connived to circulate the rumour that Valentina was in an adulterous relationship with her husband King Charles. Playing the outraged wife, Isabeau had the gentle and beautiful duchess summarily removed, not only from court but from Paris.

Deeply hurt by the accusations against her, Valentina nonetheless left the city in great state, her head held high. It was given out that she was going to visit one of her husband's castles, Asnières, in the county of

Beaumont, which she had never seen. With her went her little son, tod-dling on unsteady feet at 17 months old.

Much preparation was made for the journey, it being March and the weather still cold. Little Charles was given a long surcoat of green damask, trimmed at neck and wrists with the soft fur of squirrels' bellies, a tunic of fine vermilion cloth similarly furred, two caps of the same, two pairs of woollen hoses and two little doublets of Reims linen. His father ordered the king's shoemaker to make no less than eighteen pairs of leather shoes for the boy, a typical extravagance of Duke Louis, always profligate in expenditure, especially considering that the child's feet were going to grow.

But his spending did not end there. Every month during the summer, more clothes arrived from Paris. As the weather grew warmer, satin and damask took the place of wool for tunics, hose and caps. Vermilion, known as 'English green', or, for some reason, black, were the favourite colours and most of the tiny garments were embroidered with Orléans's emblems of genista (broom) flowers, trees or climbing wolves. Charles was not yet 2 when a long cloak of vermilion cloth was made for him, trimmed and lined with 162 skins of fur, and with a crossbow embroidered on the left side.[1]

This would seem a ridiculous amount of clothing for a small child, but as Enid McLeod explains, in her erudite biography of Charles, in the Middle Ages children always wore replicas of the styles of their elders, so that it would be expected that so young a boy should be a small copy of his father, dressed in similar, magnificent clothes.

Even in the country, they lived in constant dread of the plague and other fatal illnesses so common at the time. In July 1396, when Charles and his mother had only been at Asnières for about four months, there was a panic because the boy appeared to be ill. Two doctors, an apothecary, a clerk and three valets, one of them leading a spare horse for the baggage, were all sent by the duke, riding flat out in the summer heat over the rough coun-try roads, to visit the duchess and 'our very dear and beloved son Charles', who were indisposed.[2] The whole party stayed eight days. Charles's illness cannot have been serious for it is not mentioned again, but his mother's indisposition was obviously connected to the fact that later that month she gave birth to another boy. He was called Philip and, surprisingly, because of the known rivalry between the two families, his godfather was Philip, Duke of Burgundy. The little boys, less than two years apart, are known to have been the firmest of friends in childhood. Philip, later to become the Count of Vertus, always remained loyal to his older brother during the many vicissitudes that, in later life, he would have to endure.

Meanwhile, as children, Charles and Philip, and John (born in 1399 or 1400 and later to be known as the Count of Angoulême), lived in the country estates of their father, moving from one to another as was customary at the time. They spent many months at Villers-Cotterêts in what is now the Aisne in Picardy, exploring the beautiful forest beyond the castle walls. Then, after 1400, when King Charles gave his brother Château-Thierry, they spent much time there.

But their favourite home of all was Châteauneuf, in the entrancing Loire Valley, which their father, Duke Louis, had restored after its ruination by the English. They also loved the castle of Montils, close by, where Valentina added four rooms, each with its own fireplace, between the walls of the great hall and the fortress, in an attempt to make it less austere.

Valentina does not seem to have spent much time at Blois, which Charles loved so greatly. It would later become the home he dreamed about within prison walls. The castle of Châteauneuf stood on raised ground overlooking the sloping roofs of the little town to the River Loire and its ancient bridge. Described by Antonio Astesan, an Italian friend of Charles, as 'so vast that it could house several thousand men and horses', it was one of the greatest citadels in France.[3]

Wherever they lived, it was in splendour with a host of servants, both male and female, to serve them in every way. Yet it was not in the castle that Charles found the inspiration for the verses he was starting to write at the age of 10. He loved both the beauty and the sounds of the country, the ripple of water over stones, the unseen wind moving through trees, the chirping of crickets, the songs of birds. Most strikingly, the influence of his mother emerges through his poetry, the gentle, kind Valentina, who was mostly the only parent that he ever saw. That he inherited her character emerges from later descriptions, as well as from his verses.

Charles was only 4 when he abandoned the nursery for the schoolroom. His tutor, Nicolas Garbet, was a master of arts and bachelor of theology. Both Charles and Philip could read before they were 5 years old, as is shown by the fact that their mother ordered a Parisian craftsman to illumine in gold, azure and vermilion, and bind in Cordovan leather two little books for Monsieur of Angoulême, as Charles was known as a child, and Monsieur Philip of Orléans. Two years later, she bought them a psalter.

From Garbet they received the education that was common to the sons of noblemen at the time, learning to speak and write Latin. Also they studied both the classical and contemporary writers. Charles was later to claim that he knew the seven liberal arts: grammar, logic, rhetoric, arithmetic, geometry, music and astronomy. He also learnt at an early age to write in a beautiful hand, of which his signature, which changed little during his lifetime, is proof. A miniature at the top of the first leaf of Sallust's *Jugurtha*, one of the books they studied, shows a man wearing a crown instructing three little boys, wearing long surcoats and with wreaths on their heads, an image which is taken to be Garbet, instructing Charles, Philip and John.

Charles was still a boy when he started collecting books, which would become a life-long passion, eventually including the works of Ovid, Horace, Lucan, Cicero and Virgil. In doing so, he was following the example of his grandfather, Charles V, founder of the Bibliothèque nationale of Paris, later lodged in the Louvre. Amongst his favourites was *Le Roman de la Rose*, the poem begun by Guillaume de Lorris around 1230 and completed some forty to fifty years later in a different style by Jean de Meun. The work, constructed on the concept of courtly love as found in the poetry of the troubadours, is clearly reflected in one of the earliest poems that Charles wrote.

The first known poem attributed to Charles is called *Le Livre contre tout péché*. Describing the seven deadly sins, it shows the influence of Nicolas Garbet. The last stanza contains the statement that this little book was written when he was 10 years old:

Je, nommé: d'Orléans
Fiz quand j'eus accompli. X. ans.

Charles had been only 7 or 8 when their father, whose visits were always a cause of excitement, brought home with him a little boy called John. He turned out to be their half-brother, son of their father's mistress, Mariette d'Enghien, the wife of one of his own officers, a man named Albert of Cany. Louis now asked his wife Valentina to take the child into her household and, kind-hearted as she was, she did not refuse.

Valentina and her three sons became extremely fond of the boy, who would grow up to become the Count of Dunois, but would be better known as the Bastard of Orléans, famous as a military commander, supporter of Joan of Arc, and of his half-brother Charles, whom he served most loyally throughout his later tribulations.

7

The Little Queen

England 1396–1401

The Hôtel Saint-Pol had been a large house, but compared to Windsor Castle it was small. Isabella felt that the castle must go on forever as Richard, her husband, led her from one room to another, each seeming grander and larger than the one before.

Richard explained to Isabella, bewildered as she was both by its magnificence and its size, that the castle, originally founded 200 years before by his Norman ancestors, following their conquest of England, had been rebuilt by his grandfather, Edward III. Richard himself had not lived there as a boy. Born, as recorded by Froissart, on 12 January 1367 in the abbey of Bordeaux, during his father, the Black Prince's war in France, he had lived with his mother, Princess Joan, in Bordeaux and Cognac until he was 4 years old. Then, when the Fair Maid of Kent brought him back to England, they had lived in her manor of Berkhamsted where, in 1376, his father died of the dysentery he had caught while campaigning.

During his married life with Anne, Richard had lived mostly in her favourite manor of Sheen, or in the Palace of Westminster from where he had good reason to be absent because of the scale of reconstruction work. He had famously let loose his love of architecture in the hall, built as the seat of government, whose magnificent hammer-beam roof would be both the largest and finest in Europe.

With the loss of Anne still raw in his mind, Richard told Isabella that Windsor was to be their home. Here he believed it might be possible, if not to forget, then at least to expunge some of the vibrant memories of the woman he had so greatly loved and to find tranquillity of a kind. Richard certainly treated Isabella with great kindness and affection, as if, so people noticed, she were the child he and Anne had never had. The marriage by law could not be consummated until she reached the age of 12, but meanwhile Isabella had a happy childhood, mostly at Windsor Castle, where the king gave her many presents and spent as much time with her as he could.

As a child of 8 she probably did not have to go to mass every morning as did many devout Christians at that time. Her nurse would have warmed her clothes by the fire and dressed her before she had breakfast, usually of saps, hot bread and milk, food suitable for a child.

Then she would have lessons. Madame de Courcy, the woman specially chosen by her parents to look after and protect her when leaving France, whose role can be described as that of a nursery governess, probably supervised. But she must have had tutors, most likely priests in her husband's household. Isabella is known to have spoken and written in both her own first language of French and Latin, which suggests that she was intelligent, as had already been shown by her address of Richard's envoys in France.

Dinner was early, usually about twelve for the benefit of those forbidden to eat before mass. It is likely that Isabella sat beside Richard when he was living in the castle. The mind's eye conjures up the picture of a small upright figure, a tiny golden crown on her curls, dwarfed by the tall robed figure of her husband, as they sit at the top of the table, eating and drinking carefully as she had been taught.

There were usually several courses, largely of various kinds of fowls and meat, but entirely of fish if it was Lent. Also, probably more enticing to a little girl, there were syllabubs and marvellous delicacies of marzipan and pastry concocted by specially trained pastry cooks. Isabella must have shown Richard her doll's house, brought from France, with its miniature silver furnishings. Maybe on fine days they rode together, he astride a courser, she riding side-saddle on a quiet pony, to look at the deer grazing below the great oak trees of Windsor Park.

When King Richard was away from Windsor Castle, occupied with state business in Westminster and elsewhere, his little Queen Isabella was left with her governess. Chroniclers do not describe Madame de Courcy other than to say that she was extravagant and light fingered, as was subsequently revealed. According to the official French records, made at Calais where Richard and Isabella's marriage by proxy had taken place, Isabella's dowry included two exceptionally beautiful crowns, in addition to necklaces and brooches amongst other valuable jewels, and gold and silver vessels for her chamber.

The jewels, which disappeared in England, included those on two gold harts, which were Richard II's badge, a pearl vanished from one, a sapphire from the other. Also, most distressing to Richard, a diamond was discovered to be missing from a collar of fern, which had belonged to his former wife. The thief was never identified but Madame de Courcy, by that time renowned for her profligacy and taken to be the most likely culprit, was blamed and, as will be seen later, subsequently dismissed.

In 1397, Richard reached the peak of his power. Eighteen years had passed since he had become king on the death of his grandfather, Edward III. During his minority, he had been forced to submit to the dictates of the council several of whose members, headed by his uncle, Thomas Duke of Gloucester, had forcibly assumed power.

Naturally aggressive, it would seem from the moment of his birth, Thomas, as the youngest son of Edward III, bore the royal title of Duke of Gloucester, and had made his name fighting in France. Returning to England, he had become the leader of the Lords Apellant, a group of powerful nobles, eleven in all, who had included the earls of Arundel and Warwick, Gloucester's brother-in-law the Earl of Derby (later to become Henry IV) and Thomas Mowbray, Duke of Norfolk, Earl Marshal and the Earl of Nottingham. In November 1387, having first established a Commission to govern England for a year, they had led their own armies to defeat Richard's, commanded by Richard de Vere, the Marquis of Ireland, at Waltham Cross. Triumphant, they had then published 'an appeal of treason' against the king's closest advisers, thereby reducing Richard to a mere figurehead robbed of power.

Taking refuge in the Tower of London, the king had then been alone and without friends: his uncle, John of Gaunt, the one man Gloucester feared, was still fighting in Spain. Meanwhile the Appelants had secured the allegiance of London, where all the guilds except the victuallers had agreed to join their cause.

The Merciless Parliament, as it came to be known, assembled in the White Hall of the Palace of Westminster the following year. A clerk read out the French document containing the thirty-nine articles which made up the Appelants' case. As the king had withdrawn amidst uproar, twelve of the Lords had been appointed to investigate the truth of the charges. Subsequently, a sentence of impeachment had been imposed on Richard's confessor, the Bishop of Chichester and all the king's justices.

Then had come the trial of the four knights of the royal household, who included Richard's oldest friend and tutor Sir Simon Burley. This was the cruellest blow of all. Richard had pleaded desperately to save him. Queen Anne had gone down on her knees before Gloucester begging for his life, only to be told rudely that she would do better to pray for herself and her husband instead. It had been useless. The honoured man, who had been King Edward's companion in arms, had only been spared the traitor's hideous death on the gallows for execution by the axe. In spite of the position of lawyers and of moderate Lords, the chief Appelants had reduced the king to a cipher.

But John of Gaunt, Gloucester's elder brother, as loyal to his nephew Richard as Thomas of Gloucester was false, had then come back from Spain. At a meeting of the Great Council on 3 May 1389, acting on his advice, Richard had staged a well-rehearsed coup d'état. On entering the chamber at Westminster, to the astonishment of the Lords assembled, he had asked them to tell him his age. After some consultation they had replied that he had turned 20 (actually, he was 22), whereupon he told them that:

> Therefore I am of full age to govern myself, my household and my realm for it seems wrong to me that I should be treated with less consideration than the meanest of my subjects, for what heir in my realm, when he has passed his twentieth year and his parent is dead, is prevented from freely conducting his own affairs? Why therefore deny me what is conceded to others of lesser rank?[1]

Richard had turned the tables. There was no answer to his question other than to admit that he was right. From then on, with the weight of Gaunt behind him, he had contrived to subdue his enemies to the point where, by 1397, he held complete control. First, he had raised his own army, the soldiers rather endearingly calling him 'Dicon' – plainly he had the common touch though he quarrelled with his peers. With a force of archers and pikemen at his call, Richard had confidence enough to confront the private armies of the great lords. Secondly, he had built up a capable administrative government, enhanced by the loyal support of John of Gaunt. Third, he had carried out a successful show of force in Ireland, where a settlement showed good prospect of success, and lastly, and of enormous importance, he had obtained what promised to be a long period of truce, if not the end of the war with France, which had been a dreadful prolonged drain on the country's economy. Now, he could visualise the attainment of the full regality, which had been little more than a dream at the start of his reign.

It was at the Parliament of April 1397, two months after Isabella had arrived in England, that Richard quarrelled so fatally with his uncle, Thomas of Woodstock, as the Duke of Gloucester was commonly known.

Aware of Thomas's hostility towards him, it is hardly surprising that the atmosphere in the temporary hall, used to house Parliament during the rebuilding of Westminster Hall, was alive with fear and mistrust. Richard was taking no chances, making sure that 200 Cheshire archers of his bodyguard were ranged on either side of the meeting, bows at the ready. It was Richard's return of the fortress of Brest to the Duke of Brittany that fired off the confrontation. Gloucester, typically cantankerous, turned on him saying, 'Sire, you ought first to hazard your life in capturing a city from your enemies before you think of giving up any city which your ancestors have conquered.'

Richard was speechless in amazement. The return of Brest seemed only reasonable in view of the twenty-eight-year truce with France he had so recently made. He asked his uncle to repeat his accusation, before demanding to know whether he thought himself a merchant or a traitor.

This marked the beginning of what proved to be a deadly dispute. Gloucester stirred up the merchants of London, where he had much influence, telling them that they should be relieved of the taxation originally imposed to meet the cost of the wars, but which was now squandered on the king's entertainments.

He then approached his great-nephew, Roger Mortimer, Earl of March, grandson of Edward III's second son, Lionel Duke of Clarence, whom Gloucester would have liked to have seen on the throne in place of Richard. He tried to persuade Roger to join a band of conspirators that included the earls of Arundel and Warwick, with the idea of imprisoning both Richard and little Isabella in the Tower. Roger was horrified and, saying he needed time to think it over, departed hurriedly for Ireland, where he had extensive estates.

John of Gaunt, Duke of Lancaster, King Edward's third son, and thus elder brother of Thomas Woodstock of Gloucester, was always Richard's most loyal supporter. Rising to his feet in Parliament, he harangued the London merchants. In a long speech he pointed out to them that although Richard was accused of extravagance, most of the money he was supposed to have spent otherwise had gone to the defence of the English garrisons in France and guarding the roads and passes on the Scottish border and in Ireland. He then told them bluntly that they should be thankful to live in a peaceful land where they could pursue their commerce, and that furthermore they paid less tax than the merchants in France and Lombardy and other places where they traded their goods. The London merchants subsided and Thomas of Gloucester returned to his castle at Pleshey in Essex in high dudgeon.

But the danger was not over. Soon after, when the Count of Saint-Pol arrived from France on a goodwill mission to Richard and Isabella, he was told (presumably by John of Gaunt) of the peril threatening the king and begged him to take action before it was too late.

Rumours then ran wild through London that the count had come over to England to persuade Richard to give Calais back to the French. Subsequently, a delegation of London merchants took their fears to Thomas of Gloucester at Pleshey. Thomas seized the opportunity to stir up trouble against Richard again by telling them that it was all too likely that the stories were true: 'The French wouldn't mind if he took all their king's daughters, provided they became masters of Calais.'[2]

Thoroughly alarmed, the London merchants then asked for, and were granted, an audience with the king. Richard assured them that Saint-Pol's visit had been purely one of friendship and that the tales they had been told of a possible surrender of Calais were totally untrue.

Largely reassured, the merchants departed, but Richard, realising the duplicity of his uncle Thomas, became increasingly alarmed. His fear increased when he heard, from an apparently reliable source, of a plot to imprison himself and Isabella and give the authority to his three uncles, John of Gaunt of Lancaster, Edmund Langley of York, and Thomas Woodstock of Gloucester, together with the Earl of Arundel, to rule the country in his place. Once in power they would find an excuse to restart the Hundred Years War with France and send Isabella back to her father if she so chose.

Deeply shaken at finding treachery so close, Richard turned to Lancaster and York, the uncles he believed he could trust, to ask for their advice. They played down the danger of Thomas of Gloucester, calling him both unruly and rash, and promising that under no circumstances would they allow him to try to depose and imprison him or to resume the war with France. Aware, however, of the dispute that was developing between their younger brother and their nephew the king, Lancaster and York left London for their country estates, unwilling to become involved in what seemed to be an impending internecine war.

Gloucester, in great secrecy, then arranged a meeting at Arundel Castle, where he and a group of his confederates, who included Gaunt's eldest son, Henry Bolingbroke, Earl of Derby and the Earl of Nottingham (the Earl Marshal), swore an oath that they would not be satisfied until the king and his uncles of York and Lancaster were imprisoned for life. But Thomas Mowbray, Earl of Nottingham, betrayed them, taking the story to Richard, who was dining with some of his councillors in the London mansion of the Earl of Huntingdon. Froissart tells the story of what happened next.

Richard made an instant decision that Gloucester must be killed. Saying he was going deer hunting, he rode to a manor in Essex called Havering-atte-Bower with only a few of his retinue. The rest he had left guarding Isabella at Eltham Palace in the Royal Borough of Greenwich south-east of London. He reached Gloucester's castle at Pleshey at about five o'clock on an afternoon so warm and humid that the castle, a motte and bailey (a fortified tower surmounting an earthwork with an enclosed courtyard, protected by a moat and a wooden palisade), seemed to float in the heat haze above the houses of the village lying within the protection of its stone walls. Richard found no one on watch so he entered the castle unnoticed until someone caught sight of him and shouted out, 'The king is here!'

Gloucester had finished supper but he came out into the courtyard to greet the king with all the courtesy due, as did his wife and two daughters. Richard, at his uncle's invitation, went into the hall and from there into the chamber where a table was set for him laden with food. He ate only a little before saying, 'Uncle, have some of your horses saddled – not all but half a dozen – I want you to come to London with me. I have a meeting with the Londoners tomorrow at which my uncles of Lancaster and York will certainly be present, and I shall want your advice on how to deal with a request they are bringing to me. Tell your steward that the rest of your people must follow tomorrow and join you in London then.'

According to Froissart, the duke had no suspicions and readily agreed. Taking leave of his wife and daughters, he mounted his horse, taking with him only four squires and four servants. Thus they set out for London, riding so fast that they soon reached Stratford and the Thames. 'There, in a narrow place, the Earl Marshal [the Earl of Nottingham] was waiting in an ambush.' The king dug his spurs into his horse's sides and galloped on with Gloucester shouting behind him, knowing he was betrayed. The Earl Marshal then rode up to Gloucester and arrested him in the king's name.

Gloucester was then forced on to a barge lying moored on the River Thames. The Earl Marshal followed him on board and, taking advantage of the current and a calm sea, they reached Calais the next morning with the help of a following wind. The Duke of Gloucester was taken into the castle of Calais now terrified, guessing what lay ahead. He asked for a priest, who heard his confession before the altar, where he knelt for a long time.

'According to my information', writes Froissart:

just as the tables were laid for dinner in the castle of Calais and [Gloucester] was about to wash his hands, four men rushed out from a room and, twisting a towel round his neck, pulled so hard on the two ends that he staggered to the floor. There they finished strangling him, closed his eyes, and carried him now dead, to a bed on which they undressed his body. They placed him between two sheets, put a pillow under his head and covered him with fur mantles. Leaving the room, they went back into the hall, ready and primed with their story, and said this: that the Duke had had an apoplectic fit while he was washing his hands and had been carried to his bed with great difficulty. This version was given out in the castle and the town. Some believed it. Others not.[3]

Subsequently, the other main conspirators, the earls of Warwick and Arundel, were imprisoned in the Tower of London. Arundel was later executed and Warwick sent into exile on the Isle of Man, eventually to be freed. Richard rewarded Nottingham, the Earl Marshal with the dukedom of Norfolk, while Henry of Bolingbroke, son of Richard's most stalwart supporter, his uncle John of Gaunt, became Duke of Hereford.

8

The Fatal Challenge

Richard at that time was living in Eltham Palace, from whence he summoned all those who owed him homage. Having done so, he secured his own safety by ordering no less than 10,000 archers to stand guard in London, Kent and Sussex. Becoming obsessed with threats to his life, he was suspicious of almost anyone with a claim to the throne. Such was the extent of his terror that he is claimed to have commanded the Londoners not to harbour either John of Gaunt, most stalwart of his supporters, or his son Henry, the Earl of Derby (undoubtedly more suspect), to which the Londoners replied that they had nothing against either man. Also in London was Richard's other uncle, Edmund, Duke of York, whose son the Earl of Rutland was in Richard's great favour.

'With the Earl Marshal, the King loved him beyond reason'[1] wrote Froissart, although quite what he meant by that is difficult to say. Was he hinting at homosexuality? If so, there is no extant evidence. It is more likely that Richard, by now almost paranoid about treachery, showed excessive favour to the two men he thought he could trust. Rutland is said to have mediated with his father, Edmund of York, and his uncle John of Gaunt, over the death of their youngest brother Thomas of Gloucester, now publicly thought to have been ordered by Richard.

Certainly it was very much held against Richard that he took over of all of Gloucester's possessions, including his castle of Pleshey and his large acreage of land. However, in fairness, he was perfectly entitled to do so, the law in England being that the king had custody of the inheritance of all minors until their coming of age.

Subsequently, Thomas of Gloucester's son and heir, a boy called Humfrey who was about 10 years old, was forced to live in Richard's household. But this Humfrey was to die in 1399, after which the title would revert to the crown. His mother and two sisters, meanwhile, lived in Queen Isabella's household. The tension rose as, on the advice of his few closest and most trusted friends, Richard paid a company of archers to guard him and Isabella both day and night. Nonetheless, by the Christmas of 1397, his enemies were apparently subdued to the extent that Richard seemed established in the full strength of his power.

Yet it was to prove an illusion. Richard was accused of extravagance; the cost of rebuilding Westminster Palace and the huge expense of his wedding to Isabella were loudly decried. Nonetheless, it was the quarrel between the men he had just honoured, Nottingham, now the Duke of Norfolk and his first cousin Henry Derby, now Earl of Hereford, which proved to be a danger. Each accused the other of treachery until, in January 1398, the matter was referred to a Parliamentary Committee. Richard was then accused of acting as an absolute ruler for delegating a business of such contention, undermining the fundamental principle of representative government. The dispute dragged on until it was decided that it must be settled by a duel to take place in the lists at Coventry, where two of England's most famous knights would fight it out to the death. Wanting to be rid of both of them, Richard saw a way to do so by staging a spectacular contest.

The scene of pageantry surpassed everything hitherto seen or heard. The horses in particular were magnificent, great heavy beasts, strong enough to carry the weight of a knight in armour, their gleaming flanks and shoulders protected from the point of a badly aimed lance by thick, colourful, padded coats. The knights themselves wore jointed armour, of glistening burnished steel, their feet enclosed in the pointed shoes designed to come out of the stirrup in the event of a fall. As they reined up before the lists, steeds snorting and pawing the ground, there were cheers from the men and cries of joy from the women, who sat in the raised tiers of seats built for the spectators, their own appearance as colourful as that of the opponents in the lists below.

The women wore long, wide-skirted dresses of rich material embroidered with jewels, the trains so heavy that pages in the livery of their employers were needed to carry them, walking respectfully behind. Most spectacular of all were the high headdresses crowned with floating streamers, which were so in fashion at the time.

It is reasonable to think that Isabella, who is specifically described as presiding in great splendour with her ladies at another pageant, shortly afterwards, was present on this occasion. The small crowned figure would have been seated in a place of honour, from where, perhaps raised up on several cushions, she would have been able to identify the contestants by the banners carried by their squires, bearing their coats of arms.

It was a glorious and exciting occasion, even if the reason for it happening had not been clear to Isabella. Her eyes on her husband, who would give the signal to start the duel, she must have held her breath in excitement, as did most of the crowd. Then all eyes switched to the arena as bugles sounded the challenge for the contest to begin.

Hereford rode in first on a white charger 'banded with greene and blew velvet embroidered sumptuouslie with swans and antelops of goldsmiths woorke and armed at all points'. Next, King Richard entered to sit on the great dais, before Norfolk appeared, 'his horse being banded with crimson velvet embroidered richly with lions of silver and mulberie trees'.[2] It was a breathtaking sight. The trumpets sounded and the charge began. The combatants raced towards each other, lances ready to unhorse …

Then suddenly they stopped, reining their chargers back on to their haunches. The trumpets were changing tune. They were sounding a warning. Cheers changed to howls of disappointment and dismay: the king had dropped his staff. The duel was ended and both contestants were banished, Henry Bolingbroke, Duke of Hereford for ten years; Thomas Mowbray, Duke of Norfolk for life. Norfolk died the next year in Venice, on pilgrimage to Jerusalem, reputedly a broken man. Hereford, on the other hand, got no farther than Paris and the royal court of France. There he waited, planning and waiting for a suitable time to wreak his revenge.

Later, Richard would curse the day he spared Hereford execution. Had he not done so, he would have saved himself so much difficulty. But Henry of Hereford was John of Gaunt's eldest son and, although he acquiesced to his banishment, Richard could not condemn his cousin to the traitor's block.

Hereford was lucky that his father lived to save him, for John of Gaunt died on 3 February 1399. Gaunt's death meant the loss of Richard's, if not Henry's, greatest and most consistent supporter. Gaunt, the most influential man in England, despite the vagaries of his son, had been loyal to Richard to the very end of his life.

Richard was now in financial difficulty. A renewed expedition to Ireland would cost money, which had to be raised from somewhere. Aware of the unpopularity of taxation, he decided, or was persuaded, to claim the wealth of the two great landowners so recently sent into exile. Gaunt, had he lived, would most certainly have stopped the privation of his son, and in doing so would have prevented what proved to be Richard's greatest mistake.

The Parliamentary Committee, which had been established to end outstanding petitions and deal with the quarrel between Norfolk and Hereford, was resurrected and the king persuaded it to commit forgery by altering the Parliament Roll. The words 'to terminate petitions' now read 'to terminate petitions and all other matters and things moved in the presence of the king in accordance with what seems best to them'. Both Norfolk and Hereford had been granted by the terms of their exile the right to give power of attorney to those who would manage their estates. The Chancellor, on Richard's instruction, now announced that legal opinion dictated that this grant had been made 'inadvertently', as it could not apply to traitors such as Norfolk and Hereford had proven to be. A traitor could not inherit anything forfeited to the crown.

This meant that Henry of Hereford's huge estates, spread over England and including the towns of Leicester and Pontefract, over thirty castles, hundreds of manors, and most importantly the County Palatine of Lancaster, where, as Duke of Lancaster he would have had his own chancery and his own justices, and where the royal writ did not run, all of this huge inheritance was seized by the manipulation of adding a few words to the Parliament Roll. These few words gave Richard the right to forfeit the lands and privileges of the new Duke of Lancaster to the crown.[3]

Richard was either unaware of, or else chose to ignore, the strength of feeling against him generated by his manipulation of the law of England and his claim of the legal right to purloin the great wealth of his cousin's lands. Others of the great landowners felt threatened, convinced that they would be targeted in what they now saw as the king's avaricious search for wealth. It was not the populace Richard needed to beware of. It was the most powerful landowners in the country and behind them, the ever-increasing influence and wealth of the great merchants, not only of London but of other cities of the realm. His determination to rule in his own right, through ministers of his own choice, incited their fury.

Henry of Lancaster, as now he was known, with huge estates in the north of England, and thanks to Richard's banishment one of the leaders of the opposition against him, had reason to be convinced of the strength of his following – 40,000 people are said to have cheered him as he sailed for France. Henry bided his time.

The extent of Richard's unpopularity throughout the country can be seen in the reception given to his announcement, spread throughout his kingdom as far as Scotland, that a tournament was to be held at Windsor. Some forty knights and forty squires would challenge all comers. They were to be clothed in green with the device of a white falcon. The queen was to be there, accompanied by a large suite of ladies.

The feast was held. The queen came in full state. 'But', says the chronicler Froissart:

> very few lords attended, for at least two-thirds of the English knights and squires were strongly hostile to the king, not only because of the banishment of the Earl of Derby [Henry of Lancaster's former title] and the wrong done to his children, but also because of the murder of the Duke of Gloucester at Calais and the execution of the Earl of Arundel in London, so that none of the families of those nobles came to the feast. There was almost no one there.[4]

Though he was in Hainault, Froissart knew from the reports of merchants and envoys travelling back and forth to England that one of the main causes of Richard's unpopularity was the terms of his marriage contract with Isabella, which included English opposition to the pope in Rome. The quarrel within the Church, which became known as the Western or Papal Schism, meant that in 1399 there were two claimants to papal authority:

Pope Boniface IX in Rome and Antipope Benedict XIII in Avignon. As part of a pledge to support French power in Europe, Richard had agreed to give English allegiance to Benedict, much to the fury of some of the churchmen of his realm. A second bone of contention was that the French were committed to sending help to Richard to subdue any of his subjects should the need arise.

Apparently it was in admiration of the actions of the French King Charles against rebellious subjects that Richard had decided to rid himself of the men he most feared. This was the prime reason for ordering the murder of his uncle Thomas of Gloucester in Calais; the imprisonment of both Richard Beauchamp, Earl of Warwick and Thomas, Earl of Arundel, the main instigators of the plot against him; and the exile for life of Arundel's brother, the Archbishop of Canterbury.

Then, fatally, believing himself free of his enemies, Richard had put his trust in others whom he believed to be incorruptible: Henry Bolingbroke, John of Gaunt's son, now Earl of Hereford, and Thomas Mowbray, Duke of Norfolk. It was the duel between Henry Bolingbroke and the Duke of Norfolk – so famously stopped by Richard almost as their lances clashed – and the exile and forfeiture of both, that had ignited distrust of the king in the minds of other magnates, who saw themselves threatened by a despot who empowered himself to strip them of land and possessions, without respect of the law.

Their fear of this increased as Richard began claiming large sums of money for pardons of even trivial offences. Claiming to be impoverished, he was seen to be spending ever more lavishly on court life and entertainments, the tournament at Windsor being just one example of his reckless extravagance. The king was now ruling without a Parliament over subjects who saw themselves becoming powerless against a tyrant who believed himself above the law.

Isabella, who had probably looked forward to the tournament as an opportunity to show off a new robe and her jewels, must have been hugely disappointed and shocked by the insult to her husband, and the sight of the tiers of empty seats. She must also have sensed the hostility to Richard this evinced even to her inexperienced mind. Bewildered and perhaps frightened, unable to understand the reasons for such an affront to the kind, gentle man she knew her husband to be, one can imagine her clutching her small hands in fury against these unseen enemies whose hatred was now so rudely exposed.

Froissart then claims that it was on the occasion of this shunned celebration that Richard announced his intention to make another expedition to Ireland, remarking rather facetiously that it was 'to find use for his time and his men'.[5]

Word of this must have reached France, where Henry of Lancaster had been warmly welcomed by King Charles VI, who was planning to make a match for him with the widowed daughter of the Duke of Berry. Henry had other ideas. Not only had he already fallen in love with the wife of the Duke of Brittany, in whose household he had lived for some time, but on word of Richard's departure for Ireland he saw his chance of retribution for his banishment and loss of land.

Richard made his second expedition to Ireland in the month of May 1399. News had reached him that his cousin Roger Mortimer, Earl of March, had been killed fighting the King of Leinster at the Battle of Kellistown (or Kells) in Carlow. The grandson of Lionel, Duke of Clarence, second son of Edward III, Roger had held precedence over the descendants of Edward's third son, John of Gaunt, and had thus been Richard's heir. Much distressed on being told of his death, Richard immediately named Roger Mortimer's young son Edmund as heir presumptive to the throne. He then began planning a second Irish expedition, which he himself would lead, both to avenge Mortimer's death and to reassert his authority over Art MacMurrough the King of Leinster, who had broken the oath of fealty sworn on his submission to Richard four years earlier, in 1395.

It was time to say goodbye. His last act before leaving for Bristol, Richard went to Windsor Castle to say farewell to Isabella, his child queen. It was here that, Professor Hutchison says, he made a thorough investigation of the misdoings of Lady de Courcy, whose untoward extravagance was now blatantly revealed. Having dismissed her, he appointed the widow of Roger Mortimer to be Isabella's guardian.

Those who were there as witnesses were moved by the sadness of the scene as Richard said goodbye to the girl of whom he had become so extremely fond in the three short years of their marriage. All those about the court saw how he had grown to love her, taking pride in her appearance – she was growing to be a pretty girl – and in her intelligence, proven by her grasp of the English language, which she had found so difficult at first. She for her part adored him, the man who brought her so many presents and who talked with her and played with her in a way so unlike that strange man who was her real father, whom she now felt she had never really known. Sobbing, she clung to Richard, begging him not to go to this unknown country peopled, she had been told, by warlocks and witches. He promised it would be but for a short time. He assured her that he would soon be back. But nine long months went by without a sign of his return.

9

Lancaster's Revenge

Isabella begged God in her prayers to keep Richard safe. When told in whispers by the frightened women who looked after her that he was dead, she cried wretchedly for the husband who had been more like a father to her in the brief times they had spent together during the last three years.

Although, as already described, in the *Chronique de la Traison et Mort de Richard II* (English Historical Society, London 1846) Richard had dismissed Lady de Courcy on his last visit to Windsor, the other French chronicler Froissart gives a different version of what took place. According to him, Isabella had been moved to the great moated fortress of Leeds Castle in Kent, to ensure her safety during Richard's absence in Ireland. It was here that a delegation of what Froissart describes as 'prominent citizens' went to Lady de Courcy, who had not been dismissed, and said:

Lady, get ready and have all your things packed. You must clear out of here.

And make quite certain not to show the Queen any displeasure when you leave. Say that your husband and your daughters have sent for you. If we see you do anything else, your life will answer for it. You must ask no questions, that's all you need to know. You will be taken to Dover and given a boat to take you across to Boulogne.

Very frightened by these threats and knowing how hard and relentless the English were, the Lady de Courcy had answered: 'I swear I will do everything you say.' She was soon ready. She was provided with horses and hackneys for herself and her attendants. All of them went; not a single Frenchman or Frenchwoman stayed behind. They set out on the road and were escorted to Dover, where they were well and generously paid, each according to his station. At the first tide they boarded a ship and sailed across to Boulogne.

The young queen's household was so broken up that neither man, woman nor child was left to her. They were all thrown out, those of French nationality and many of English nationality who favoured King Richard. A new court was formed with other ladies and maids-of-honour, household officers and servants, and all of them were warned in advance never to speak of King Richard if they valued their lives, not even among themselves.[1]

Later, in the interests of still greater security, Isabella is said to have been transferred to Porchester Castle with its gateway to the sea. Charles of Orléans, imprisoned at Dover, so vividly describes his longing for France in one of his most famous poems (see Appendix 2). Isabella's longing can have been no less intense.

From the windows of the great tower of Porchester Castle, standing on tiptoe, she must have been able to see the waves of the English Channel crashing against the outward defences. Beyond the water lay France, such a short distance. Boats sailed back and forth the whole time. If Richard did not return, would she be allowed to go home? The hours passed slowly, days and nights seeming to lengthen as she waited, hearing only the sounds of the sea and the screaming gulls, praying for word of what was happening in the great world outside. Stone walls surrounded her, iron bars across the windows imprisoned her, shutting out all that she so desperately longed to know.

Isabella was too young to be told immediately. Only later would she discover the true horror of all that had occurred. Richard's second campaign in Ireland had got off to a propitious start. With a fair wind behind them, his ships had taken only two days to cross the Irish Sea. According to a French esquire named Creton, who was there, Richard took many people with him, including several high-ranking churchmen, and the staff of the royal wardrobe. Four young hostages went along as a precaution against trouble in England during Richard's absence: Henry Beaufort, Bishop of Lincoln, son of John of Gaunt and his third wife Catherine Swynford was held in security for his elder brother the Earl of Dorset; others were the sons of the dead Duke of Gloucester and Earl of Arundel; but most important of all was the exiled Lancaster's own son, another Henry, who, unbeknown to anyone at the time, was later to become Henry V. Missing from the party was the Earl of Northumberland. Scandalised by what he considered to be Richard's duplicity in his treatment of Lancaster, he had refused to join the summons to mobilise in South Wales, using the excuse of ill health.

Having left England in May, Richard was already on his way to Ireland when the annexation of Henry Bolingbroke, Duke of Lancaster's huge estates became known. Landing at Waterford, the English army had waited for six days for the arrival of the Earl of Rutland (son of Richard's uncle, the Duke of York), then much in favour with Richard who had just made him Duke of Albermarle. Impatient at the delay, refusing to stay longer at Waterford, Richard had then marched to Kilkenny, where, as he waited for Albermarle to join him, he had knighted the son of the man he knew to be his enemy, Henry of Lancaster.

Creton then gives a vivid first-hand description of the suffering of Richard's army as it struggled through the Wicklow Mountains, harassed by the caterans of the King of Leinster who, thanks to their local knowledge, swept down from hidden places to kill indiscriminately while skilfully avoiding pitched battles. Watching Richard, Creton was impressed by the way he led his men. Once again he was Dicon, sharing their hardships and the hunger exacerbated by a lack of supplies. Because of the shortage of food available in the country, Richard pushed on over the hills to Dublin with his main army, leaving Thomas Despenser (given Gloucester's earldom) to meet with MacMurrough, who had offered to try to make terms.

Thomas's escort included Creton, who described how they met in a wild glen of the Black Mountains where MacMurrough sat astride a beautiful thoroughbred horse without saddle or even a saddlecloth, facing the deputation armed only with a spear. Nothing would induce the Irish king to negotiate. Defiant, he swore to fight the invaders of his country, even at the cost of his life.

Despenser could only ride on to Dublin to report the failure of his mission to Richard, who swore that he would take MacMurrough dead or alive.

The army had now been saved from starvation by the arrival of Albermarle with 100 barges laden with supplies. The king was planning a new attack on the Irish leader who taunted him when, on 10 July, Sir William Bagot arrived from England bringing terrible news.

He told how Henry of Lancaster, informed of what was happening in Ireland, had taken advantage of Richard's prolonged absence from England, returning from France to raise a rebellion against him, claiming the justification of the king's theft of his lands.

The story told by Froissart that Thomas Arundel, deprived of the see of Canterbury and sent into exile after his brother's execution in 1397, had joined Henry of Lancaster in Paris, offering him the crown on behalf of the people of London, cannot be substantiated. However, it is possible that Arundel returned secretly to England to confer with Henry's supporters before returning with their assurances that they would willingly acclaim Henry as king should he supplant Richard. Equally unsubstantiated is the legend that Henry first landed at Plymouth, from where, while living in hiding, he sent a rider to the Lord Mayor of London, who despatched a deputation of 100 leading citizens from Guildford to swear loyalty to Henry and pledge him both money and arms.

It is known, however, that Henry sailed up the east coast of England and landed at Ravenspur, on the estuary of the Humber, on 4 July. At Pontefract, back on what had been his family's land, he raised his standard, and men came to join the son of the great hero John of Gaunt.

On word of this, the king's only surviving uncle, Edmund, Duke of York, then acting as Richard's regent in his absence, raised an army at St Albans to confront those from the north, but was heavily defeated near Bristol on 27 July. Many of his men deserted, joining the winning force and York himself, a weak man, as his brother Gloucester had known, then turned his coat to join his nephew, the triumphant Henry of Lancaster. Most of the great barons of England followed his example, abandoning their sworn fealty to their sovereign to adhere to what was proving to be an undefeatable, irresistible force.

Hearing of what was happening from Sir William Bagot, of the danger that faced him in England, Richard returned with all possible speed, but it was two weeks before he landed at Milford Haven in Pembrokeshire on 25 July. From there he rode to Conwy, a distance of some 160 miles, a journey that took every ounce of his strength wearing the armour that always hurt his back. Believing he would find an army waiting, he reached Conwy to discover what he least expected, that the loyal Earl of Salisbury had been deserted by most of his men. Realising then that Henry of Lancaster had outwitted him, to the point where he could no longer hope to defeat him in an open battle, Richard sent the earls of Exeter and Surrey to him, promising to return Henry's estates and to find out what else he wanted to end the rebellion he had raised.

Meanwhile, the former Archbishop of Canterbury, Thomas Arundel, and the Earl of Northumberland had been sent by Henry to take Richard prisoner by any possible means. Richard's position was now desperate, as he himself well knew. He had lost two armies. His only hope lay in finding refuge in one of the strong Welsh castles from which he could escape to France by sea.

Henry's delegates went in search of him at Conwy Castle, where spies had told them he would be. With them went 400 lancers and 1,000 archers, of which only a few reached Conwy, the rest remaining hidden in the mountains somewhere between Conwy and Rhuddlan, so historians say. Richard must have been warned of their coming for on their arrival they found him in council, to which Northumberland put forward what appeared to be reasonable terms. Richard could remain as king, on condition that he declared a free parliament, restored Henry's estates and, most important of all, surrendered to his free mercy.

The king's council at Conwy had very little alternative but to accept Northumberland's conditions in the knowledge that, made under duress, this decision could be revoked afterwards. Northumberland, having achieved what he wanted, then swore over the Host that Henry had no treasonable intent. Thus assured of his safety, at the instigation of Northumberland and Archbishop Arundel, Richard moved to Flint Castle . in Wales, one of the fortresses built to hold a garrison by Edward I.

The legend goes that Henry himself rode up with 200 men. Dismounting at the gate, he found it locked, as he expected, and banged on it, demanding to be let in. A voice from inside asked who wished to enter, whereupon Henry shouted at the top of his voice, 'I am Henry of Lancaster. I have come to take back my inheritance of the Duchy of Lancaster from the king. Go and tell him so from me.' After some hesitation, the king instructed the messenger to tell Henry that he could enter the castle but with no more than eleven men.

'When the king saw him, he changed colour,'[2] so Froissart says. Henry then asked Richard if he had breakfasted and, when Richard said no, told him he must eat something for he had a long journey in front of him.

'What journey'? asked Richard, to which Henry told him bluntly that he had to go to London. Richard then called for a table to be laid, and did attempt to eat, but on rising and looking from the window, he saw hundreds of armed soldiers below. Henry said they were men from London who had come to take him to the Tower. He then led Richard from the keep to the courtyard, where horses were being saddled for the journey.

The two were talking together as they waited, when Richard's own greyhound, Math, a magnificent animal that followed him everywhere when he went riding and would obey no one else, was let off its lead. As usual it rushed up to Richard to stand on its hind legs and put its massive paws on his shoulders to lick his face. Then the dog turned to Henry and did exactly the same to him. Richard said sadly, 'Cousin, it is an excellent omen for you and a bad one for me.' 'What do you mean?' asked Henry. 'I mean', Richard replied, 'that the dog is hailing and honouring you today as the King of England, which you will be, while I shall be deposed. The dog knows it by instinct. So keep him with you for he will stay with you and leave me.' Henry stroked the greyhound, which henceforth ignored Richard to the utter astonishment of a great many people who witnessed the scene. Thus runs the legend, touching in its poignancy, of a sad and desperate man deserted by those he thought loyal to him, even down to his dog.[3]

Riding then to Chester with only a small escort, trusting to Henry's word, Richard had left the coastal track and was entering into one of the wild valleys leading up from the sea, when flashes of steel caught his eye. Then he heard men shouting and the pounding or horses' hoofs as Henry's main army bore down on him, and he knew he had been betrayed. Northumberland had committed the greatest sin of the chivalric code, breaking his word.

Made prisoner, guarded as a thief or a murderer, Richard was taken through St Albans to London, to be lodged forthwith in the Tower. Henry then rode in triumph into London, where 'the bells of the churches and monasteries rang so merrily that you could not even hear God thundering', as the French chronicler of *de la Traison et Mort de Richard II* wrote. How bitter must Richard have felt as he heard them from his cell in the Tower.

10

My God! A Wonderful Land is This!

Froissart tells a horrendous story of the four household knights of Richard's inner council who were blamed for advising him to execute Gloucester, Arundel and Sir Thomas Corbet, which cannot be substantiated.

According to the chronicler, the mayor and the officers appointed to kill them assembled in the Guildhall before going to the Tower. The four wretched knights were taken into the courtyard, each to be tied behind two horses, in full view of all the men in the Tower, including the king. From there they were dragged on their buttocks through the streets of London to Cheapside, where their heads were cut off on a fishmonger's slab and put up on four pikes at the entrance to London Bridge, while their corpses were hauled to the London gibbet for display.

Such grizzly tales of medieval savagery are not uncommon, so there may be truth in the tale. Froissart, plainly biased in favour of the Lancastrians, also describes Richard as shaking with terror and going pale with fright, descriptions not found elsewhere.[1]

The official record of Richard's abdication is recorded in the Rolls of Parliament. On the day before Parliament was to assemble, the Duke of Northumberland led a delegation to interview the king in the Tower. Having first suggested that, as agreed at Conwy, he should abdicate, they gave him the details of the agreement he would be asked to sign.

Demanding time to read them, Richard also requested an interview with Henry, to which they agreed.

The official record, written in Latin, reads that 'Richard cheerfully signed away his crown, gave his signet to Henry and asked that the Archbishop of York and the Bishop of Hereford should be his proxies at the forthcoming meeting of Parliament.'

The chronicler Froissart, however, tells a very different tale. Henry, on getting Richard's message, had himself rowed down the Thames although the light was failing, it being late in the day. Reaching the Tower, he entered by a postern gate and went to the king, who 'received him courteously and very humbly, in the manner of one who feels his life is in great danger'. Richard then said, after some preamble, that 'I therefore resign to you, of my own free will, the heritage and the crown of England, and beg you to accept my abdication and this gift in love'.

Lancaster accepted graciously before, turning on Richard, he accused him of being illegitimate, saying that rumour had spread in England and elsewhere that Richard was never the son of the Prince of Wales. His mother, Joan Woodstock, he claimed, had ensnared the Black Prince, 'having won him in marriage by subtle cunning', while she, afraid that he might divorce her, got herself pregnant, 'so that you were born and another before you … it is commonly said, here and elsewhere, that you were the son of a clerk or canon, for when you were conceived and born in Bordeaux there were plenty of handsome young priests in the prince's household'.[2]

Richard then had to endure a monologue lasting a full two hours, in which all the evils and abuses of which he was accused were flung at him by his cousin whom, at the end of it, he could only beg that his life might be spared. To Richard's intense relief, Henry then departed to his own house, rowed by the light of torches, in what was by then pitch darkness, this time against the current, up the Thames.

Richard had acquiesced to his cousin in the hopes of saving his life, but the next day, that appointed for the Parliament, his famous temper sprang out of control. Again the French chronicler of *la Traison* gives what sounds like the true version of what actually happened. Henry appeared at the Tower with a large group of nobles and churchmen. Amongst them were his uncle, the Duke of York and the latter's son, the Earl of Rutland, recently demoted by Henry from the dukedom of Albermarle, as had

Thomas Despenser been of the earldom of Gloucester. It was the sight of Rutland, to whom he had shown great favours, only recently making him Duke of Albermarle, that finally made Richard lose his temper, calling him a traitor to his face. Greatly offended, Rutland threw down his bonnet in a challenge and Richard, in his fury, kicked it away.

Henry told Rutland to be silent, explaining to Richard that he was still king, but that 'the council of the realm have ordered that you should be kept in confinement until the day of the meeting of Parliament'. Richard then asked that he might be allowed to see his young wife and when Henry told him that the Council would not permit it, he completely lost control, cursing them all and finally flinging down his bonnet in challenge to a combat of arms.

As the others in the room shrank back in horror, afraid that Richard had gone mad, Henry begged him 'to be quiet until the meeting of Parliament'. Richard calmed down but when he asked to be given a fair trial, Henry only prevaricated. 'My lord, be not afraid, nothing unreasonable shall be done to you,' came his evasive reply.

Against this, the official story states that, wearing his royal robes, carrying his sceptre and wearing his crown, Richard stood alone as he addressed the assembled conclave: 'I have been King of England, Duke of Aquitaine, and Lord of Ireland for some twenty-two years, and the heritage of this realm, this sceptre and this crown I now freely and fully resign to my cousin Henry, Duke of Lancaster.'[3] Then, having handed his sceptre to Henry, who immediately passed it on to the Archbishop of Canterbury, he took off his crown and held it out to Henry, saying 'Fair cousin, Henry of Lancaster, I give and deliver to you this crown with which I was crowned King of England, and with all the rights belonging to it.'[4] Having taken the crown, Henry immediately gave it over to the Archbishop of Canterbury, in the knowledge that it was he who would set it on his head in the Parliament later on the same day.

Which of the versions of this story is correct? Now, after over 600 years, it is impossible to know what really occurred on that fateful day of 30 September 1399. If the chronicler Adam of Usk is anything to go by, Richard was far from happy at the thought of abdication. At a dinner at which Adam was present, just a week before, surrounded by men he knew were spying on him, Richard had burst out in misery: 'My God! A wonderful land is this, and a fickle; which has exiled, slain, destroyed, or ruined so many Kings, rulers and great men, and is ever tainted and toileth with strife and variance and envy.'[5]

Adam of Usk, the Welsh priest who had risen to prominence as a lawyer and parliamentarian under the patronage of the Earl of March, though a Lancastrian supporter, claimed to have 'departed thence much moved at heart' on hearing this.[6]

Parliament met on 30 September in Richard's great hall at Westminster, the rebuilding now complete. Supposedly summoned by Richard, the assembly gathered before an empty throne. The charter of abdication bearing his signature was read out in Latin and Richard was indicted by the three estates, church, nobility and commoners, on a list of charges; it was decreed that on breaking his coronation oath, he had forfeited his right to the throne.

On 28 October 1399, King Richard II, forced into the clothes of a forester, was taken from the Tower to Leeds Castle in Kent. From there, for greater security, he was moved to Henry of Lancaster's own castle of Pontefract in West Yorkshire, heartland of his great estates.

According to Froissart, Henry did not want Richard killed. But he was urged by his closest advisers to get rid of him on the grounds that there would be no peace with France if Richard were known to be alive. The King of France was bound to attempt to rescue him and restore him to the throne for the sake of his daughter, Queen Isabella. Henry replied that he was aware of this, but he had given his promise of protection to Richard, which could only be broken if Richard were found to be behaving treacherously against him. Afterwards he went out to see his falconers and, standing with a bird on his wrist, feeding it, was absorbed in silent thought for a very long time.

What happened in the cold dark dungeon of Henry of Lancaster's Pontefract Castle remains a mystery. The Lancastrians insisted that Richard had starved himself to death. Adam of Usk claimed that he died heartbroken, fettered and tormented by Sir Thomas Swinford with food.

But rumours persisted. A more horrific version of his death is found in a note attached to the fourth book of Froissart's chronicle. Written by a 'commentator' who reproaches the author for passing over the truth concerning Richard's death, the note tells how Sir Piers Exton visited Richard in the Tower of London with four followers. In a fight that ensued, Richard showed extraordinary courage and killed the four men but was then killed himself by Sir Piers.

This seems unlikely in view of the fact that all contemporary accounts say that Richard died in Pontefract Castle, not the Tower of London. However, the anonymous scribe then adds that 'some believed that Richard had allowed himself to die of starvation'.

It is hardly surprising that, due to the turmoil caused by King Richard's dethronement, his child wife was forgotten by historians in their scramble to record the events of the struggle for autocratic rule in England. Grand households at that time were peripatetic, moving from one large house to another, both to collect their rents in money and produce and to allow the building left behind to be cleaned.

As we have seen, according to Froissart, as her husband was being taken prisoner to the Tower, Isabella was living at Leeds Castle in Kent with her largely French entourage. This may be true, but it could also be a confusion with Lady de Courcy's dismissal, which other sources say Richard had ordered before leaving for Ireland. Froissart's account of a delegation of 'prominent citizens' from London arriving to tell Lady de Courcy that she must pack up and leave immediately, pretending her husband and daughter had sent for her so as not to upset the queen, seems the most likely. From time immemorial it has been the custom in royal households for the staff of a deceased king or queen to be entirely changed. It is said that Catherine Swynford, John of Gaunt's third wife and mother of the illustrious Beauforts, whom their half-brother Henry IV would shortly legitimise, if not one of her household, was Isabella's companion for some time.

Immediately following Richard's death, on the orders of the new king, Isabella was sent to the Bishop of Salisbury's palace at Sonning, near Reading on the Thames. Here she was held, virtually a prisoner, in the care of Joan de Geneville, 2nd Baroness Geneville, who supervised the running of her small household in the rooms allotted to her in the main buildings of the vast ecclesiastical complex. Tradesmen and others travelled frequently on the great River Thames, then one of the main routes across England. Those living in the palace must have heard from them of how King Richard's supporters had staged a coup against King Henry.

The conspirators were to gather at Kingston upon Thames, only 4 miles from Sonning, but the Duke of Rutland lost his nerve and confessed the plot, both to his father, the Duke of York, and to the king himself. Henry of Lancaster had escaped from Windsor to the safety of London almost as the men who had sworn to capture him took the castle. Warned of retaliation, the insurgents had left Windsor, riding hard for the West Country with Henry's army on their tail. Two of the instigators of the plot to capture the usurper, as they believed Henry to be, the Earl of Kent, and Richard's most loyal Lord Salisbury, were captured and beheaded in Cirencester while most of the others were imprisoned pending similar deaths.

There was still no news of Richard. Isabella waited, watching from the windows of the bishop's palace, begging servants for news, praying every morning and evening that Richard would keep his promise and come back to her soon. The long winter nights grew shorter. Outside, the snow melted, leaving the grass bare; inside, the long passages of the castle became less agonisingly cold. How long and how bitterly Isabella must have wept for Richard, listening for his footsteps coming up the stairs in that great castle, to swing her into his arms and kiss her as he had done so many times before.

Her nurse, or one of her ladies, must have told how his body was taken from Pontefract Castle to London, laid on a litter covered with a black cloth and drawn by four black horses led by men in black. Behind came four knights, also in full mourning, a hypocritical gesture in keeping with the entire performance. Leaving the Tower, they went through the streets of London to Cheapside, then the main thoroughfare of the capital. There they halted for two hours while citizens, said to be over 20,000 in number, flocked to take a last glimpse of the king who had ruled them for twenty-two years. All they could see was his face. The rest of his body was concealed, perhaps for good reason.

The public display ended, the corpse was borne from the city. The knights mounted the horses waiting for them outside the walls to escort the litter to the village of King's Langley in Hertfordshire, where Richard was buried, without royal ceremony, in the Dominican priory. Isabella herself was never to know that sixteen years later, the then king, Henry V, would allow her husband's body to be brought to London to lie in the magnificent tomb Richard had designed for himself and his first queen, Anne of Bohemia.

As Richard's body was carried to his burial, no one it seems gave a thought to his widow, the little girl held in the bishop's palace at Sonning. Would she, one wonders, have liked to have seen Richard's face, to have kissed the cold cheek in a last goodbye? Perhaps it is fortunate that no one thought of it, or if they did, that they considered the sight of his body too much for her, being as yet only 10 years old. Told of these happenings, Isabella did at last come to believe that Richard was really dead. But then her hopes of his survival were renewed as, insidiously, but persistently, the rumours began.

They came with the tradesmen from nearby Windsor and with couriers riding back and forth to London with messages from the governor of the castle to the court. This was nothing new. There was always speculation in such a fortress, particularly in uncertain times, the inmates waiting anxiously for news of what was happening elsewhere. Now it was probably from Baroness Grenville, speaking quietly, waiting until the servants had left them as they sat alone before the fire, that she heard the stories in circulation. Richard had escaped from Pontefract, some said to Scotland, others thought elsewhere. Isabella's breath caught in her throat as she heard the rumours. Richard would keep his promise. She had always known that he would …

But the days went by and the spring came bringing warmer weather so that, watched over by Lady Geneville, she could go down the spiral stair of the tower into the garden outside. Always she listened for hoof beats, the clamour of men arriving and Richard's voice calling for her as he came striding in to find her, the first thing he always did the moment he arrived. But it never happened. Richard never came.

At last, several months later, she was told the truth. The escape to Scotland was a myth, put about by a mysterious Scotsman called John MacDonald, Lord of the Isles. Seeking an alliance with Richard, he had actually sailed from his island, somewhere called Islay, on the west coast of that far away land, to find him at Westminster on the bank of the Thames. There they had reached an agreement, strange in the circumstances, between two men so unalike. Richard so courteous and elegant, John a rough warrior of the Hebridean seas, who stared in surprise as Richard and his courtiers used strips of linen they called handkerchiefs, while he, like most other people, was happy to use his sleeve to wipe his nose!

Somehow word had reached Islay of the shocking news that Richard had been usurped and taken prisoner by John of Gaunt's son, his cousin Henry of Lancaster, now calling himself king. Determined to cause a diversion, which might be construed as an attempt to frighten the man who had betrayed his king, John of the Isles found a red-headed scullion in his kitchen at Finlaggan Castle, on the island in the loch of that name, before noising it around that this was Richard, to whom he was giving sanctuary in his impregnable fortress. Few believed him. No one who knew Richard was ever allowed to see the Mammet of Islay, the impostor, as the scullion was soon proved to be. But for a while the story, unlikely as it was, gave hope to the little girl who waited so hopefully at Sonning, refusing to believe the possibility that she would never see her husband again.

Only much later was Isabella forced to accept the truth, that Richard had died in the dungeon of Pontefract Castle. The horror of it appalled her. Like most of those who had loved Richard, she could not bear to think that the man who, despite what others said of him, had been so gentle and kind to her, who had taught her to love pictures and the beauty and skill of architecture, the man who had overseen the rebuilding of the Palace of Westminster, one of the greatest buildings in the world, had been killed.

Her mind was full of what had happened to him, helpless in that dungeon, deprived of all human dignity and substance, waiting for the release of death. Did he, she must have wondered, think of her in his agony, the girl he had married to make peace with France, to end the destruction of a long, continuous war, but whom he had grown to love as she loved him? Or was it always of Anne that he thought, the wife who had never borne him children but whom he had so adored that he pulled down the manor house where she had lived, unable to enter it without her?

After Richard's death, Isabella stayed on for some time at Sonning with her own household despite the demands of her father, in one of his saner periods, that she be sent home. Otherwise, all that is known of her is that she had to receive a delegation sent by Henry IV, who came with a proposal that she should marry his eldest son, Henry of Monmouth, who was also heir to the throne. Had she accepted, Isabella might have been Queen of England for a second time. But, understandably, the idea so greatly offended her that she sent back a refusal regardless of any reprisals that might ensue.

One can only picture the scene. The delegates arriving, enrobed and bowing respectfully before the young widow wearing the black of mourning she is known to have refused to discard. Expecting a demure girl who would humbly accept their proposal, they drew back as the small virago stamped her foot in tearful fury telling them that never would she even consider marrying the son of the man who had murdered her lawful husband, her beloved Richard, and moreover had stolen his throne.

Humiliated by their failure, the ambassadors returned to Henry, who nonetheless accepted Isabella's refusal. Small and alone, she had defied the most powerful king in Europe, who, respectful of her courage, did not attempt to make her change her mind.

11

The Only Chance of Safety

Scotland 1390–1406

K ing Richard was not the only one to die of starvation, if that was indeed the cause of his death, in those days of bestial cruelty amongst even the highest born, as was soon to be shown.

The old king stood on the drawbridge across the moat surrounding Rothesay Castle on the Scottish Isle of Bute, to watch them ride away. His body bent, his mind confused, he prayed for his younger son's safety with all the strength of his soul.

It was January. Below him the water, still for lack of a breeze, was skimmed with ice. King Robert of Scotland, crippled since a young man by a kick of Douglas of Dalkeith's vicious horse, felt the freezing damp in his bones. It was not the pain which bothered him though, but fear, a near uncontrollable terror of what, in the event of his death, or even before it, would happen to his surviving son.

Robert III, known originally as John, Earl of Carrick, had succeeded his father Robert II in 1390. On doing so he had changed his name to Robert (John being thought unlucky, on account of the previous monarch of that name, John Balliol, believed to have betrayed his country to England's

Edward I). However, fortune did not favour Robert, dogged as he was by disaster throughout most of his life.

By far his greatest happiness had come from his determination to marry the woman he loved. Annabella, daughter of Sir John Drummond of Stobhall in Perthshire, had been so beautiful that he had married her in defiance of the protocol which demanded a high-born princess. The daughter of a mere knight, Annabella had not been considered of high enough rank to be Queen of Scotland.

Robert and Annabella had had seven children, three sons and four daughters, all except the youngest born before the start of his reign. Of the sons, David, the eldest, had been born in 1378; the second, Robert, had died while still a boy; while the youngest, James, born in the royal lodging attached to the monastery of Dunfermline in July 1394, was very much the afterthought. The name James, not hereditary in the Stewarts, had been given to him because Saint James's day falls on the 25th of that month. As a child, he was hardly aware of the catastrophic events that were overtaking his family as his father lost his grip on power.

Due to his incapacity to travel far, thanks to his crippled leg, Robert III was unable to govern effectively and had handed over the administration of his country to his brother. At a time when the ability to administer a kingdom depended largely on mobility, King Robert had been deemed unfit to rule on his accession, thanks to his physical disablement. His sons being too young, his brother, Robert Earl of Fife, in charge in the last years of their father's reign, had been deputed to hold the seat of power. Robert had trusted him, fatally, as soon became clear. The Earl of Fife saw the chance offered by his brother's weakness to usurp him and take the kingdom for himself.

Robert III had been a peaceful man, remarked on for his humanity in the common violence of the times. Two of his first acts, on succeeding his father Robert II, had been to renew the truce with England and to ratify the Scottish alliance with France, by then in existence for nearly 100 years. When the negotiations with England, conducted by John of Gaunt, Duke of Lancaster, had become difficult because the Scots could produce no one of equal rank, King Robert had bestowed dukedoms on both his brother, and his son. Thus Robert, Earl of Fife, had become Duke of Albany, and David, King Robert's eldes son, Duke of Rothesay.[1]

David, Duke of Rothesay, by then a young man of 20, as heir apparent to the throne had much resented his Uncle Albany's authority. However, subsequently David had won his way, when the council-general, meeting in Perth in 1399, had decreed that the Duke of Rothesay be made the king's lieutenant. A council of twenty 'wyse men' would assist him, by whose advice he should rule in the absence of the council-general.

But David Rothesay had refused to listen to advice.

The trouble had begun over his proposed marriage to Euphemia Lindsay, daughter of Sir William Lindsay, she being thought too low-born for the future king. The Earl of March had offered a large bribe to King Robert to affiance his daughter, Elizabeth, to David. The Earl of Douglas had then offered an even larger one on behalf of his daughter, Marjorie, whereupon March, furious at being outbid, announced that he was going to give his allegiance to the English king, Richard II.

When David's mother, Queen Annabella, died, in the autumn of 1401, his behaviour without her restraint had become totally outrageous. While she lived, David, headstrong, foolish and encouraged by the bad company he kept, had shown respect for his mother who held some influence over him.

His councillors despaired of him, complaining to his father that he was totally out of their control and King Robert, bewildered and lost without the support of his wife, had turned to his brother to help him, believing that Albany had his best interests at heart.

How disastrously he was mistaken became clear only too soon. Concerned solely with his own advancement, Albany had no filial love. The old king, totally ignorant of the animosity towards his eldest son, had even sent a letter to his brother, advising David's temporary imprisonment as a way of curbing his irresponsible actions. Amazingly, the man chosen to deliver this instruction, was none other than Sir William Lindsay, whose daughter David had jilted, and who, for that reason alone, must have relished the chance of retribution. This proof that King Robert was by then no longer of sound mind was soon further shown by the dreadful events that were to come.

David had been on his way to St Andrews, with only a few armed men, to take possession of the castle during the vacant diocese. Ambushed, he was arrested by men who were sent by his Uncle Albany and the latter's brother-in-law, the Earl of Douglas. Overpowered and helpless, David was taken in a horse-drawn wagon to Falkland Palace, where he died.

Albany and Douglas had put it about that David had succumbed to dysentery. But soon rumours were spreading that he had starved, that 'emprisoned within the castle of Fflalkland that by duress of samyn hee eate his awne handes and died in grete distress and myserie, the whiche was against goddes lawe and manes lawe and pittie to any prince whatsoever he be'.[2]

It was for this reason that King Robert, old and increasingly bewildered, but aware that he had been deceived and realising at last the duplicity of his brother, had decided to take the enormous risk of sending James, his only surviving son, to France. It was the last desperate decision of a disillusioned, distracted man. The dangers of the journey to France were manifold, but to stay in Scotland, and stand between his uncle and the throne, would, his father knew, result in certain death for James.

Now, the farewells over, tearful for both father and son, King Robert saw James depart. Aged 12, he rode a palfrey, being now too tall for a pony, while his escort of knights and grooms rode larger horses. All of them, James included, wore steel corselets, daggers in their belts and swords in scabbards at their sides. At their head rode Sir David Fleming, the king's faithful counsellor, one of the few men he could trust. Behind Fleming, the young James glanced back once more at the bent figure of his father, leaning heavily on the stick he had used since his leg was broken, watching him ride away.

Though greatly saddened at leaving his widowed father in their family home of Rothesay Castle, James was nonetheless excited by the adventure that lay ahead. He had been on the sea before but only once, when they went to Rothesay Castle following David's death. This time, as the horses were led on to the flat-bottomed barge that would carry them to the mainland, he saw that the sea was calm.

Landing in Ayrshire, they rode on through the Lowlands of Scotland, bypassing Edinburgh and into what is now East Lothian. It was February and the nights were too cold for sleeping out, the ground hard with frost. Stopping only at houses and hostelries where Sir David knew his reputation would guarantee their safety, they rode on through the flat lands bordered by the North Sea, where some of the local nobles joined the escort guarding the young prince. In North Berwick, below the conical shape of the Law, Sir David hired a boat in which men rowed them out to that other famous feature of the east coast, the Bass Rock.

Here he said farewell to James, who must have felt some sadness as the now familiar figure of the stalwart man who had guided and protected him for so many days was taken back to the shore. James was to spend a month on that rock jutting out of the North Sea, living in the bare stone building that was kept as a prison by the Douglasses of Tantallon Castle, that sinister red stone fortress that loomed above the cliffs across the strip of water dividing the Bass from the mainland.

It was on the Bass that Henry, Earl of Orkney, Sir Archibald Edmonstone and Sir William Giffard, the prince's escort to France joined him. They rowed out from North Berwick bringing disastrous news. Sir David Fleming was dead. Returning through East Lothian, he had been set upon by Douglas of Balveny, Alexander Seton of Gordon and William St Clair of Herdmanston, and had been killed in a fierce struggle.

In constant fear of discovery by the sharp-eyed sentries on the battlements of Tantallon Castle looming above the cliffs just a short stretch of water away, James was forced to remain hidden in Sir Robert Lauder's cramped and primitive castle. He would never forget the smell of the straw, wet with sea air, on which he had to sleep, and the fleas seeking blood from a warm body. His small room had only a crack for a window and the smoke from the fire of sea coal stung his eyes and made it hard to breathe. The food was mostly young gannets taken from their nests in the summer by men let down the rock on ropes. Salted, they were kept in tubs. The smell and the taste made him retch.

He had to stay hidden, however much he longed for fresh air and exercise to loosen his limbs. Only a castle servant, taking a bucket of offal to throw into the sea, or pretending to fish with a line, could reach a vantage point with a clear view over the Firth to watch for approaching ships. One after another, they sailed past, heading out into the North Sea. But at last, after a month of waiting, a vessel put about to head towards the Bass Rock.

She was the *Maryenknyght* of Danzig, her master one Henry Bereholt, sailing from Leith with a cargo of wool and hides. She came in close to the sheltered side of the Bass when the light was fading and James and his escort went aboard. The sentries on Tantallon, keen eyed as they were, could only have picked out dim, unrecognisable figures, if they saw anything at all.

Freedom! The ice-cold spume stinging his face, the juddering of the boat against the waves as she left the lee of the Bass made James shout for joy. Seeing the land disappear, he felt like a bird escaping from its cage. Out past the Isle of May they went, into the pitching waves of the North Sea. But off Flamborough Head in the East Riding of Yorkshire, the ship was seized by a pirates from Great Yarmouth and Cley in Norfolk, a powerful gang of cut-throats led by one Hugh atte Fen.

James and most of the passengers were taken to Henry IV at Westminster, who gave atte Fen and his crew the ship's cargo as a reward. Henry, always short of money and knowing what his ransom might fetch, was delighted to have the young Prince James in his hands. Told that he had been heading for France, he exclaimed, 'If the Scots were grateful, they would have sent this youth to be taught by me, for I too know the French language.'

In Scotland, at Rothesay Castle, old King Robert collapsed on hearing of his son's capture, possibly suffering a stroke. Refusing to eat thereafter, he died on 4 April 1406, Palm Sunday. At least he was spared the knowledge that his brother and regent, the Duke of Albany, would refuse to pay his nephew's ransom so that James would remain a prisoner in England for eighteen years.

James was already held in the White Tower, the part of the Tower of London reserved for political prisoners, when he learned that his father had died of grief and despair hearing of his capture. He would also learn before long that his uncle was claiming that Scotland was too poor to pay his ransom, and would do nothing to set him free.

12

City of Anarchy

France 1401–06

After much diplomatic argument, Isabella did return to France eventually in 1401.

On her arrival, the people jostled in the streets to see her, as she was taken in procession into Paris. Expecting a queen, whose beauty had been rumoured, they were much disappointed at the sight of a teenager in widow's weeds. Beneath the black veil, they could only catch glimpses of a girl of 17, taller and slimmer than her mother, but lacking the vitality of Isabeau's dark eyes and erect figure, now so familiar to the Parisians since her own famous entry to the city sixteen years ago. Also, something was missing. Those watching turned to each other to ask, Where are her fabulous jewels? They were known to have gone with her, as part of the promised trousseau, when she went to England as a bride.

The jewellery withheld by King Henry, was to prove a long-lasting cause of controversy in Anglo-French relations. Most of the items listed in the marriage contract were quite quickly returned, but the splendid presents sent to Isabella and Richard by her parents and great-uncles, the dukes of Burgundy and Berry, were kept in England by Henry and his successors, who claimed they belonged to the English crown.

Isabella came home to France to find it on the verge of civil war. Since the disastrous expedition into Brittany, on which her father had been seized by madness, his uncle, Philip of Burgundy (son of John II, who had died a prisoner in England) had held control over the government of the country. King Charles's brother, Louis, Duke of Orléans, had become increasingly resentful of the power of their uncle, particularly as far as finances were concerned. Renowned for extravagance, Louis was unpopular with the majority of the people of Paris, who saw the sober Philip of Burgundy as the most suitable ruler of the two. Rivalry between these magnates continued until just after Isabella's return, when her father yielded to Louis's insistence that, as his brother, he took precedence over Burgundy, who was only an uncle. Charles then appointed Louis as regent.

Louis of Orléans was already the official tax collector. Once in the seat of power, in agreement with Queen Isabeau, he raised the level of taxation. In 1401, he went further, using his own men to collect the royal revenue. Burgundy, whose income came largely from that source, believed himself defrauded and retaliated by threatening Paris with an army, said to number 600 men and sixty knights. Queen Isabeau proved her powers of diplomacy by contriving to mediate between Burgundy and Orléans to prevent their jealousy developing into war. King Charles gratefully gave her complete control of the treasury.

Louis, so famously attractive to women, so immaculately dressed, jewels flashing from his clothes, such an excellent dancer and amusing in conversation, was anything but faithful to Valentina, who nonetheless forgave him, it would seem from the goodness of her heart. Queen Isabeau's concern over her husband to some extent belies the stories that were circulating of her illicit affair with his brother. She herself was to tell her youngest son Charles, born in 1403, that he was illegitimate, but nothing is known of his supposed paternity.

This gave the scandalmongers further material. Historians of her own time blackened Isabeau's reputation, accusing her of incest, moral corruption, treason, avarice and profligacy, to name but a few of the transgressions for which they blamed her. Her husband's mental illness being totally unexplained, the charge of witchcraft was added to the list. In 1397, after Louis of Orléans's wife, Valentina Visconti, was also accused of sorcery and forced to leave Paris, tales of Isabeau's supposed adultery with Louis gained strength, running wild throughout the city. King Charles was said to be neglected, while his wife and brother lived scandalously, exploiting the delights of the flesh. Moreover, they were extravagant, throwing away money, badly needed elsewhere, on court entertainment. Isabeau certainly spent much on her appearance, buying jewels and dresses so voluminous that doors had to be widened to let her through. She is pictured in elaborate headdresses, pointed like witches' hats, with veils flowing like pennants from their peaks.

It was not only on her own appearance that the queen spent money. An avid collector of art, she began the craze for pieces of ronde-bosse, a newly invented method of covering gold pieces in enamel. In 1404, Isabeau gave Charles a particularly beautiful example of this work, known as the *Little Golden Horse Shrine*. Made of solid gold, weighing 26lb (12kg), it is covered with rubies, sapphires and pearls. Charles is depicted kneeling on a platform before the Virgin Mary and the baby Jesus. John the Evangelist and John the Baptist stand beside them under a trellis covered with jewels, while beneath a squire holds the little golden horse. Fortunately, this exquisite work of art is now preserved for posterity in the convent church of Altötting, in Isabeau's homeland of Bavaria.

But quite apart from profligacy, it was Isabeau's influence, particularly as she was a woman, which caused jealousy and gave force to the scandal of her rumoured affair with Orléans, her brother-in-law. Isabella came back to Paris to find her mother pregnant with the child that would be a sixth daughter, whose paternity was a question on many tongues.

The child, a girl named Catherine, the tenth of the twelve recorded children of Charles VI and Isabeau of Bavaria, was born in the Hôtel Saint-Pol in Paris on 27 October 1401. Providentially, her birth coincided with one of her father's increasingly rare moments of lucidity. It was now nine years since his first attack of madness on that hot August day in 1392, when he had sent his pages galloping for their lives from the sword he wielded murderously, in a bout of uncontrollable dementia.

Isabella's return from England was a great joy to her father, who had used all the persistence of which he was intermittently capable to get her back. To her mother she was largely an encumbrance, a widowed queen of no great political importance, for whom another marriage would somehow have to be found. Writers of the day do not mention her, so it must be presumed that Isabella lived very quietly, overshadowed by the rest of her family, particularly her father, his state of mind unpredictable from day to day, and more especially her mother, volatile, embroiled both in politics and, supposedly, an outrageous liaison.

Isabella had in fact come home to find herself in an unenviable position. Now 13 years old, an age at which her marriage to Richard could have been consummated, she was handed back to her parents, for whom, at least for her mother, she was an unwanted child. Accustomed to having her own household and ladies-in-waiting, it must have been both demeaning and galling for her to have to accept the discipline dictated by her mother, in a house which was no longer her own.

Lonely and without any real vocation in life, as she seems to have been at that time, it is easy to picture her, a slim girl still wearing the black of mourning, moving quietly through the rooms and corridors of that rambling house close to the Seine. At times it was quiet, only the sound of the footsteps and subdued voices of the inmates breaking the silence. At others, during his fits of dementia, it echoed with the sound of her father howling like a wolf.

Isabella had come back to live in the palace or as it was usually called, the Hôtel Saint-Pol, where she had been born. Contemporary historians have described it, detailing the magnificence of that time. Thirty years before her birth, in 1361, her grandfather Charles V, obsessed with his health and convinced that the foul odours of the city were killing him, had begun construction on the ruins of an earlier building of his ancestor Louis IX, situated to the south-west of the Quartier de l'Arsenal in the fourth arrondissement of Paris.

Charles V had spared no expense in creating what was to become his main residence. For three years he had worked to improve the range of buildings, in grounds stretching from the Quai des Célestins to the Rue Saint-Antoine, and from the Rue Saint-Paul to the Rue du Petit-Musc. The stonework completed, he had begun to decorate the interior with panels and furniture of the finest and rarest woods. Paintings by the most famous artists of the time covered some of the wall space, while hangings embroidered with pearls descended from ceilings to floors. Gold ornaments and objects embossed with both silver and gold, glittered from the surfaces of windowsills and tables, placed to give the greatest effect.

Most notably the book collection of Charles V's father, John II, together with his own, leather bound and embossed with gold, were shown in cases or on top of tables, where there was space amongst the ornaments. These volumes, the foundation of the Royal Library, were later to find a home in the Bibliothèque nationale of Paris. Suites of rooms included one for the king's council and two chapels, one for King Charles himself, the other for his wife, Joanna of Bourbon, the grandmother whom Isabella had never known, because she had died early, eleven years before Isabella was born.

Isabella discovered that there had been changes in the family during her four years in England. Joan, next to her in age, had been married to John, Duke of Brittany, and Marie, two years younger, was already in the convent of which she was destined to become prioress. Charles, her eldest surviving brother, Dauphin of France, was 8, Louis, a year younger and John just 3. Thus Michelle, her as yet unmarried sister, together with the infant Catherine, and their brothers Charles, Louis and John, were living with their parents in the great sprawling palace at the time of Isabella's return.

But the house, on her arrival, was quiet with the sadness of death. The dauphin Charles, a boy of 8, was fatally ill of the 'wasting illness', probably tuberculosis, of which he shortly died. Louis succeeded him as dauphin and John, for whom his mother already had marital ambitions, remained the youngest son. Then, just a year later, a little prince, named Charles after his dead brother, was born in the palace of Saint-Pol.

Despite the magnificence of their surroundings, the children lived in an atmosphere imbued with fear, a feeling of dread, which Isabella, for all her years, must have shared with her younger siblings. Their mother, small and rotund, showed her temperament in her flashing black eyes. Forceful and demanding, with her husband, her children and her servants, even the palace dogs lived in terror of the harshness of her tongue.

Terrified as they were of their mother, her behaviour was at least predictable; that of their father was not. Gentle and loving at one moment, he would fly into sudden rages, sobbing, tearing at his hair, throwing himself in what seemed uncontrollable grief to roll back and forth on the floor. Then, at their mother's command, strong armed men wearing the royal family's livery, would lead him away to a room far from the public apartments of the palace, from where, if the children crept closer, they could sometimes hear his sobs and screams, or else shrieks of wild laughter, stranger and more frightening even than his piteous bouts of grief.

The king's increasing spells of madness left power in the hands of his wife. But Isabeau was not without opponents skilful as she in intrigue. The struggle for supremacy continued between her husband's brother, Louis, Duke of Orléans and his uncle Philip 'the Bold', Duke of Burgundy.

King Charles, in the period of sanity coinciding with his daughter's return, did attempt a revolt against English occupation by encouraging the barons of Aquitaine to rebel. An army led by his brother Louis took some of the border castles but failed to go farther into the interior. His uncle Philip, the most powerful man in France, who through his marriage to Margaret, Countess of Flanders, ruled that province as well as his own, attempted to besiege Calais, the English bridgehead into France. But the garrison, reinforced from across the Channel, held out against him, forcing him into retreat.

Meanwhile, across that barrier of water, Henry IV, intending to continue the war against France, was thwarted both by his own bad health and by a rebellion in Wales, where the local hero Owain Glyndŵr (or, as the English pronounce it, Owen Glendower) was joined by 'Harry Hotspur', the Earl of Northumberland, who had quarrelled with King Henry over the distribution of land. The rising culminated in the Battle of Shrewsbury, on 20 July 1403, in which Henry, the Prince of Wales was badly wounded and Hotspur was killed.

Preoccupied as he was, and much against his will, the English king, Henry of Bolingbroke – as he was called after the place of his birth – allowed the French to ratify the Truce of Leulinghem, made by the man whose throne he had taken, the peace-loving King Richard II, with King Charles VI in 1389.

It was while banished by Richard, after his disruption of his famous duel with Norfolk, that Henry had lived as a refugee with John, Duke of Brittany and his Spanish-born wife Joan, daughter of the King of Navarre. Henry was by then a widower, his wife Mary de Bohun having died in 1394, so the claim 'that a strong affection developed between him and Joan' can be taken to mean that they fell in love. When John of Brittany died in 1399, Joan, the mother of his eight children, ruled Brittany for her eldest son, until he reached his majority in 1401 and reigned in his own right.

Once relieved of her responsibilities, she married Henry, first by proxy in April 1402, then in a formal ceremony in England the following year.

It was not a popular arrangement on either side of the Channel. The French, resenting her liaison with the English king, believed he was planning to break the twenty-eight-year truce by launching another war. The English, for their part, resented yet another French queen, convinced that both she and the French members of her household were spies. Later they thought themselves justified when, following Henry's death, the French were again the enemy, Joan was accused of witchcraft, in collusion with her confessor, and imprisoned in Leeds Castle. Denied the income from her dowry, she was eventually freed to live in poverty and seclusion for the rest of her life.

13

The Madness of King Charles

It must be accepted that Isabella lived very quietly: her name is not mentioned in the gossip and scandal concerning her mother that had all of Paris talking at the time.

Queen Isabeau continued to prove herself adroit in playing between the factions, earning a reputation for being both deceitful and immoral. When she gave her allegiance to Orléans, the Burgundians once again accused her of an illicit relationship with her brother-in-law.

So what was she really like, this woman whose exploits have sullied her reputation for more than 600 years? Described as squat and dark, proof of her Bavarian descent, she spoke with a strong German accent despite her many years in France. Small she may have been but she made up for her lack of height with headdresses, high and conical with a veil floating from the top.

Isabeau's love of magnificence has been variously described. Court dresses at the time were made of rich materials, such as velvet, silk and taffeta, and reached down to the ground. She flaunted low bodices, provocative to the point of seduction. A puritanical priest, raving from his pulpit, claimed that the queen was a jezebel throwing moral standards to the winds.

In 1403, it was decided that the king, by then suffering ever-more frequent attacks of madness, should retire from private life. He was immured in the Hôtel Saint-Pol with his children, who were reputedly ignored by

Queen Isabeau to the extent that they were described as being 'in a piteous state, nearly starved and loathsome with dirt, having no change of clothes or even of linen'. Exaggerated as this may have been – fans of Isabeau claim that the story was put about to discredit her – it was also claimed that she neglected to pay the servants at Saint-Pol, so that only a few faithful retainers remained in the vast building, where dust lay on fine furniture and covered the unswept floors.

The children, in their own quarters, must have been bewildered and frightened, particularly when, from behind locked doors, the screams and moans of their mad father echoed along the corridors to reach their rooms.

It is easy to picture those children. John trying to hide in terror, and Catherine in her dirty white smock, her fair hair unwashed and unbrushed tumbling down to her waist, always running in front of Charles, her timid little brother, down the long passages, their footsteps echoing in the still air of the barely inhabited house. Presumably the old servants fed them, but how often and on what is hard to tell. Plainly, however, ill fed and neglected as they were, they all managed to survive.

Inevitably, one wonders why their eldest sister Isabella, if indeed she was living in the house, did not look after her siblings. It is possible that she did but her mother's enemies ignored it, intent on ruining her name.

Isabeau's ill treatment of her children may well have been exaggerated, or even invented, by her enemies, for it is known that when the bubonic plague struck Paris in 1404, she moved them away from the city, possibly to the fortified castle of Melun, some 25 miles south-east of Paris, which she is known to have occupied during other crises in her lifetime.

For Isabeau, who loved luxury and comfort, the living conditions in the fortress were far from ideal. The small rooms, with their bare walls and cracks of windows, were cold and damp. The stone steps of the spiral staircase were steep and hard to climb when encumbered with voluminous heavy skirts. The food, unless specially brought in from outside, was execrable, mostly lumps of meat stewed with a few vegetables in large cauldrons over the kitchen fires.

Yet for all its discomforts, Melun was secure, safer anyway than any of the royal palaces where people could come and go with nothing more than cursory supervision. Bare walls could not conceal an assassin as tapestries and hidden arbours could. No one could enter Melun without going through the guard room at the entrance where, unless so familiar as to be instantly recognisable, whoever came had to give proof of their identity and, under any suspicion whatever, to surrender their arms before being allowed to pass through the inner door into the castle.

Wherever Isabeau took her children in 1404, it is well that she did so. The plague struck the capital and Philip the Bold, Duke of Burgundy was one of the many who died of that most dreaded of all the diseases of the time.

Philip was succeeded by his son John. Married to Margaret of Bavaria, daughter of Albrecht of Bavaria, Count of Holland and Hainault, John the Fearless, as he was soon known, was the uncle of Jacqueline, only daughter and heiress of the Count of Bavaria, to whose lands, as a male heir, he would later lay claim. A ruthless man, he persisted in his father's attempts to purloin the royal treasury for the income he insisted he was due.

Not without reason was he dubbed 'Jean sans Peur', an epithet he had gained while fighting for the Holy Roman Emperor, King Sigismund of Hungary against the Ottoman Sultan Bayezid I in the Battle of Nicopolis, eight years before he succeeded to the dukedom and titles of his father. His portrait, with a big nose and wide, sensuous mouth, suggests the masterful character for which John the Fearless was renowned.

Meanwhile, the rumours that Isabeau and her brother-in-law Orléans were engaged in a relationship continued to spread throughout Paris and beyond. In 1405, an Augustinian friar named Jacques Legrand let forth a diatribe to the court, leaving no one in any doubt of how often the helpless king was being cuckolded by his brother and his wife. After deriding her fashions – the low necks and bare shoulders of the gowns that she and her ladies wore – he turned on Isabeau and, at great personal risk, told her that if she did not believe what was thought of her, she should go out into the streets in disguise and hear the opinion of the people.

John the Fearless, taking advantage of the tide of public opinion, which was turning against her, again accused Isabeau and Orléans of mismanagement of the treasury and demanded the restoration of the royal revenues, accredited to his late father. On getting no satisfaction, he raised an army, reputedly of 1,000 knights, with which he stormed into Paris to assert his financial claims.

Appalled by this unexpected development, Queen Isabeau and her brother-in-law fled to the fortified castle of Melun. Queen Isabeau told her brother, the Duke of Bavaria, to follow them with the children. Obedient to his sister, the duke set off for Melun, taking not only his nieces and nephews, but two of the children of the Duke of Burgundy, who had been staying with them at Saint-Pol. (The reason for their visit being that Philip, son of John the Fearless (grandson and namesake of Philip the Bold) was already betrothed to Catherine's elder sister Michelle.)

The party travelled slowly, due both to the age of the young children, who could not travel long distances in a day, and also because their coach could only rumble over the rutted roads. They had not gone far before the sound of galloping hooves behind them made the coachman lash the horses to go faster. Inside the coach, Isabella must have clasped her little brother and sister to her, telling them not to be afraid. But she herself was frightened. Bandits, armed and roaming the country, were a constant danger in the unsettled land. Preparing to face them, the men of the party seized their swords. But, as the riders grew nearer, they recognised the dark red livery of the Duke of Burgundy with some relief.

Nonetheless, they were armed and aggressive in their demands that, on the order of their master the Duke of Burgundy, the children must be surrendered to them to return to Paris. None of the party dared to protest, the power and vengeance of Jean sans Peur being so well known.

Isabella had been back in France nearly two years when her mother devised a way to increase her own influence by marrying her second son, known as Prince John of Touraine. The fact that John himself was 6 and his intended bride was only 22 months old did not deter her in the least.

Jacqueline of Bavaria, born on 16 August 1401, was the only daughter of William, Duke of Bavaria and his wife Margaret of Burgundy, a daughter of Philip the Bold. As her father's heiress, she was described from the moment of her birth as 'of Holland', and would inherit the provinces of Bavaria, Zeeland and Hainault, where she was born, in the castle of Le Quesnoy.

The betrothal was formally re-enacted in Compiègne on 29 June 1406, by which time Jacqueline was 5 and John 8. Isabella must have attended the ceremony and it is possible that Catherine, by then 4 years old, did too. The fact that Catherine was later to call Jacqueline her 'childhood friend' suggests that they had a mutual fondness for each other, being two little girls only a year apart in age. It would prove to be an acquaintance that would have a cataclysmic end.

Visits between the great houses of Western Europe, a way of improving diplomatic relations, were then commonplace, often lasting for several months due to the travel involved. It is thus most probable that Catherine and her siblings accompanied their parents on visits to the castle of Le Quesnoy where John grew up with Jacqueline under the tutelage of her father, the kindly Duke of Bavaria, who regarded him as a son.

Such expeditions were invariably undertaken in the summer, when the roads were less rutted and tall grass grew in the meadows, on which the coach horses could graze. Equally certain is the commotion which even short journeys would entail. Court clothes, particularly the women's voluminous dresses and elaborate headgear, took up so much room they had to be packed into the baggage wagons that followed the line of coaches and were usually pulled by mules. In the coaches themselves, the royal family took precedence, their friends and relations coming behind in other vehicles to which they were carefully designated in order of their rank. Behind them came most of the army of servants without which no high-born lady or gentleman could exist.

The journey from Paris to the county of Hainault, about 100 miles as the crow flies and considerably further by road, included crossing several rivers, the largest of them being the Somme. In places, streams without bridges were passable only over fords.

Even from a distance, the great tower of the castle of Le Quesnay drew the traveller's eye. It was famous for its legend of the beautiful Lucia, rescued from the devil by a knight with three lions on his shield. Behind the castle rose the mountain down whose side, runs a torrent plunging through boulders, the Laizon, where the devil vanished and returned to hell. The legend was told to the children, probably by Jacqueline's nurse, imbued like most Norman women with the folklore of the land. John of Touraine, Catherine's brother, was to grow up at Le Quesnay, more like a brother than a husband to Jacqueline. Her father saw to it that he learned the arts of chivalry in preparation for the time when, as his successor, he would be lord of the province, which Jacqueline would inherit on his death. None could then foresee the far greater responsibility with which, in the event of a then-unexpected tragedy, John would have to contend, hardly out of his childhood.

John's marriage completed, Isabeau still had the problem of Isabella on her hands. The widowed wife of the King of England was of no great bargaining value but her mother solved the problem by marrying her off to her first cousin Charles, eldest son of the man with whom she was colluding, Louis of Orléans.

It can hardly have been a love match: Charles was ordered to marry the daughter of the woman who had broken up his parents' marriage, forcing his mother to leave Paris. Isabella for her part was furious. Having been married to Richard, twenty years older than herself, she now found herself being forced into wedlock with a boy five years younger. Boldly confronting Isabeau, Isabella told her that she could never love anyone but Richard. She would rather die, or join Marie in her convent, than submit to what she was now being ordered to do without any form of consultation.

Isabeau, however, unlike Henry IV's envoys sent to ask her to marry his son, would not accept a refusal, and was oblivious to her daughter's tears of rage. Charles, for his part, was probably bewildered. Born in 1394, he was only 10 years old and used to obeying his beautiful mother Valentina. Isabella wept throughout her wedding. She had loved Richard so greatly that no one, certainly not this shy, book-loving boy, could ever take his place.

Yet, surprisingly, the marriage was successful. Without realising it, Isabeau had chosen a second husband for her daughter who, in some ways, resembled her first. Charles, like Richard, was aesthetically minded and, despite his youth, was already starting to write the poetry for which he would be famous in later years. Historians do not describe the marriage as anything but happy, although something as trivial as domestic friction was hardly considered important in view of the traumatic events then taking place in France. King Charles had regained his senses and taken control of the government.

Isabella, newly married in 1406, cannot have guessed at what lay ahead for the family of the good-looking, studious boy whose wife she had now become, the dreamer whose verses she tried to understand when he showed them to her, the writer whose fantasy world, which he largely inhabited, would soon be brutally destroyed.

Their uncle, the Duke of Berry, believed he had achieved reconciliation between John of Burgundy and his cousin Louis of Orléans. But he was disastrously misled. The French historian Enguerrand de Monstrelet, who continued to chronicle events in French history following the death of Froissart in Flanders in 1405, takes up the tale.

It was one of the coldest winters that Paris had ever known. The city lay frost-bound for weeks on end without any sign of a thaw, smoke from the fires curling upwards into a windless sky. A few days after Berry's attempt to settle the feud between Burgundy and Orléans, on Wednesday, 23 November 1407, the Feast of the former pope St Clement occurred. At about seven o'clock, on a dark evening, Louis, Duke of Orléans left the warmth of his fireside after dinner, and rode through the ice-bound streets to visit Queen Isabeau in a house she had just bought from Montagu, Grand Master of the king's house-hold, near the Porte Barbette. Isabeau was still recovering from the birth of a son, who died on the day he was born, and may well have been fathered by Orléans considering the incapacity of the king.

In a hotel nearby, eighteen men were gathered plotting to kill Orléans. From there they sent a man called Thomas de Courteheuse, one of the king's servants, to find him, claiming to come from the king with a message for his brother, asking him to come immediately to discuss some urgent business that concerned them both.

Orléans left the queen at once to remount his mule, the temperature now below freezing in the dark of the night. With him went two squires, riding the same horse and four or five footmen, who ran in front and behind carrying torches to light the way. The assassins waited at the Porte Babette, crouching in the shadow of a house, their weapons ready. They leapt on the duke as he neared the gate, pouncing with the ferocity of tigers on their prey. One of them shouted 'Kill him!' and severed his wrist with an axe, 'to let the devil out', making him drop the reins. He screamed that he was the Duke of Orléans, and one of the men answered, 'That's just what we wanted to know.'

The others swarmed in upon him, knocking him off his mule and smashing his head so viciously that his brains ran out on to the sparkling cobbles of the road. Turning him over, they slashed at him, blood running dark over the diamonds of the frost, until satisfied that he was dead.

A squire who had been the duke's page tried to save him by throwing himself over his body, but he too was slashed to pieces in the attackers' rage. Terrified by the noise, the horse carrying the two squires bolted, the front rider pulling uselessly at the reins. Seeing Orléans's mule following, they thought he had fallen off. Catching it, they led it back, but seeing him in the torchlight, lying dead and butchered in the street, they spurred the horse to gallop to the queen's house yelling 'Murder!' at the top of their voices.

The murderers, having set a house alight to draw attention from their crime, added to the cacophony by yelling 'Fire!' Then, throwing callops (spikes deadly to horse's feet) behind them to make sure they were not followed, they disappeared down the street.

News of the assassination was already being shouted through the city when the leader of the killers, a Norman called Raoulet d'Auquetonville, who had detested Orléans for dismissing him from his post of counsellor general, crept through the backdoor into the Hôtel d'Artois with one or two of his henchmen, to tell Duke John of Burgundy that the deed was done and request their reward.

Next morning, in the faint early light of a freezing dawn, Orléans's men found his severed hand and part of his brains still lying in the road, and swept them up to put them beside his body in the coffin.

The aristocracy of Paris, including Louis, Duke of Anjou and King of Sicily, then staying in Paris and, amazingly, Burgundy himself, rode to the church of Saint-Guillaume wherein lay the murdered man's corpse. Only the king and queen were absent. Isabeau, terrified, had moved into the Hôtel Saint-Pol to join her husband and their children. It was King Louis of Sicily who, with the dukes of Berry, Burgundy and Bourbon, held the ends of the shroud covering the coffin, weeping – crocodile tears in the case of Burgundy. From there, a torch-lit procession followed the dead duke to the church of the Célestins, where the funeral service was followed by his burial in the chapel, which he himself had built and endowed.

After the funeral, the king summoned the princes and all the members of the council, together with the Provost of Paris and other men of the law, to make a concerted effort to discover the perpetrators of the crime. The gates into the city were closed, with the exception of two, which were closely guarded so that anyone leaving could be identified.

Rumours about suspects surged through Paris. A knight called Sir Aubert de Canny, known to have loathed Orléans, who had abducted his wife and had a child by her, was first assumed to be guilty. But eventually, when told that a house-by-house search was being carried out on the king's orders, Burgundy confessed to King Louis of Sicily and his uncle the Duke of Berry that 'by the temptation of the devil', he had ordered d'Auquetonville to kill Orléans.

Burgundy, seemingly oblivious of the danger, attempted to join a meeting of the council at the house of his uncle the Duke of Berry who, at sight of him, said, 'Fair nephew, do not go into the council today – not everyone will be pleased to see you.' Thus warned, Burgundy quickly mounted his horse and galloped out through the Porte Saint-Denis with only six men. Stopping only to change horses, he reached his castle at Bapaume, from where, after a short sleep, he went on to his own land of Flanders, the men he had left behind in Paris shortly joining him, afraid of their enemies' vengeance.

They escaped only just in time. Six score men under Sir Clugnet de Brabant pursued them, galloping over the frozen roads, their horses shod with studded shoes to prevent them slipping on the ice. The men, fully armed and lusting for Burgundy's blood, failed to catch him before a courier caught up with them with an order from King Charles to turn back.

Meanwhile, the murderer Raoulet d'Auquetonville and his gang of ruffians also escaped, in disguise. By now it was common knowledge that Burgundy had ordered the killing. The Parisians, under the impression that it was the Duke of Orléans who had imposed their heavy subsidies and taxes, shrugged their shoulders and whispered amongst themselves that he had deserved his fate.

Valentina was at Château-Thierry, some 60 miles from Paris, with her four children and her daughter-in-law Isabella when her husband was murdered. It was the day of Charles's thirteenth birthday when the dreadful news was brought to them by a messenger riding hard from Paris, a journey which took six hours. With him came a servant bringing Doucet, Louis's favourite dog, probably in a bag strapped to the saddle unless it ran behind the horse's hoofs.

On hearing what had happened, Valentina was totally prostrated by grief, the more so because she could not even attend her husband's funeral, which had taken place that very morning, as soon as possible after his death. She herself had been faithful to Louis for the eighteen years of their marriage, loving him, extrovert that he was, despite his many affairs. The shock of his death was followed by a bitter, all-consuming hatred for John of Burgundy, the cousin who had so ruthlessly ordered his death out of jealousy and self-aggrandisement.

The effect on Charles was bemusement. Later he was to say, 'As for the death of the late lord my father (whom God pardon), I was then a young child and did not know how to suffer grief.' The whole thing became more bewildering as he looked back on the day of his marriage at Compiègne, just over a year ago, when John the Fearless had seized the chance to make a public protestation of his undying love and friendship for his father. Alive in his memory was an image of the two of them standing side by side, his father, gorgeous as a peacock, in his black damask doublet and surcoats of crimson and tawny velvet, embroidered with no less than 714 pearls.

But Charles had little time for dreaming. His mother, terrified for his safety, sent him off to Blois in the care of a man called Sauvage de Villiers, a faithful family friend. Together with his brother Philip, he sailed down the Loire, reaching Jargeau on 10 December, when the citizens of Orléans came to welcome their young lord with a present of twelve fat capons, twelve pheasants and twelve dozen partridges and larks, as well as two barrels of the red and white wine of the country. There the boys were under the protection of Pierre de Mornay, the Governor of Orléans, who had long been loyal to their father.

Knowing that the older boys were safe, Valentina kept her daughter-in-law Isabella and her youngest son John with her. By the beginning of December she was ready to leave for Paris, the city from which she had been banned fourteen years earlier. Nothing would stop her returning now. There, and only there, could she win vengeance against John of Burgundy, the obsession of overwhelming hatred always uppermost in her mind.

Her cortège entered the city on 10 December 1407. Valentina and Isabella and their ladies were all in deepest mourning and Valentina's litter, and the four white horses that pulled it, were all draped in black. Also in mourning, a great procession of Louis's esquires and the men of his household followed them through the frozen streets. The cold was intensifying at the start of one of the bitterest winters that France was ever to know.

Attended by many of her husband's friends, Valentina, with Isabella and John following, drove straight to the Hôtel Saint-Pol, where the king was waiting for them. In tears, he embraced Valentina, who herself was crying, as was Isabella as they knelt before him. Then, having listened to what she told him concerning her husband, his brother, Louis's death, he promised to do whatever the council advised.

14

The Fairest Thing in Mortal Eyes

Five days later, in the great hall of the Hôtel Saint-Pol, the council assembled in the presence of the king. The handsome Count of Alençon, a young man of 22, led in Valentina, accompanied by her daughter-in-law Isabella, the latter's youngest sister, Princess Catherine, and Valentina's own youngest son, John. Details of the murder were described by one of the king's own advocates, whereupon the Archbishop of Sens, Chancellor of the kingdom, promised in a vague statement that justice would be done.

But nothing happened. The king's cousin, the Duke of Berry and the Duke of Anjou undertook to visit Burgundy, who had the amazing effrontery to tell them that he had done nothing wrong and in fact should be thanked for having rid France of a criminal. He then announced that he intended to come to Paris shortly to make his defence in public. Berry and Anjou told him that the king forbade him to do so, but he merely repeated his purpose.

So back came the envoys, defeated, to a city where the temperature was dropping to unprecedented depths. The Seine froze so hard that people used it as a highway. Nicolas de Baye, the Clerk of the Parliament, recorded later that he had been unable to write because the ink froze on his pen and sometimes even in the ink-horn, despite having a brazier behind his chair. The thaw, when it came, was even more catastrophic. Huge blocks of ice floated downstream, destroying the bridges that had houses on them, and the river became such a torrent that no one dared cross.

On 4 January, Valentina did homage to the king on behalf of herself and her children for her late husband's lands. Charles had been over generous to his brother, giving him everything he had asked for and more. The royal coffers were almost empty so the council now seized on the opportunity to reclaim some of these gifts, arguing that Louis's constant demands had obtained him more apanages than his father, the late King Charles V, had ordained as proper.

The land and castle of Crécy-en-Brie had been given by Louis to his daughter-in-law Isabella on her marriage; this the council failed to claw back, thanks to the wording of the gift. However, they proceeded to reclaim Château-Thierry, despite it being specifically left to Valentina in Louis's will, thus robbing her of the revenue of the land. She had nonetheless to pay off her husband's many debts, and so, her income depleted, she had to sell many family jewels. One of these, a gold ring set with a magnificent ruby, bought by the Duke of Berry, was afterwards known as 'the ruby of Berry'.

Valentina then left Paris for Blois, where, still terrified of what Burgundy might do to her and her children, she paid for the defences of both the town and the castle to be strengthened, provisioning both for a siege, while calling up Louis's men-at-arms and archers and setting guards at every gate.

Hardly had Valentina left the capital when, at the end of February, John the Fearless arrived. He came with a huge army of followers, all of whom he housed in his vast palace the Hôtel d'Artois. Once again the council was summoned to a meeting in the great hall of Saint-Pol, to take place on 8 March.

The 11-year-old dauphin took charge of the proceedings, the king being too unwell to attend. One wonders how the boy survived the ordeal of listening to the four-hour diatribe poured out by Jean Petit, the clever lawyer and master of theology hired by Burgundy to conduct his defence. Louis of Orléans was presented as a man of insatiable ambition and intrigue who had plotted to kill the king by every possible means, including witchcraft, to gain the crown for himself. Burgundy, he claimed, should be thanked, not punished for ridding the world of 'the criminal of Orléans'.

Having announced his Catholic faith, Burgundy then proceeded to list the sins of the man whose death he had ordered, accusing him of defrauding the treasury, debauchery and, most significantly, 'his evil influence over the queen'. The streets of Paris were so infested with danger, with supporters of Burgundy and Orléans fighting and looting houses, that Isabeau ordered soldiers to patrol them before she herself left the city for Melun.

Amazingly, Burgundy was soon on friendly terms with King Charles and given a free pardon, before being publicly reconciled to the nobility of France. Nonetheless, the conflict between the houses of Orléans and Burgundy intensified to the point where it verged on civil war. The Duke of Burgundy won the support of the university and the burgesses of Paris led by Simon Caboche, a skinner in the guild of butchers.

Queen Isabeau, in her well-fortified castle of Melun, then suddenly found common cause with Valentina, the sister-in-law she had treated so badly in the past. She suggested to Valentina that she should return to Paris to again plead her cause. Isabeau herself then made a formal entrance into the city, with the little dauphin, on 26 August. Mounted on a white horse, and followed by several thousand men-at-arms, she made an impression on the Parisians, who cheered her as she rode to the Louvre. Very different was Valentina's entry two days later, when she arrived with her daughter-in-law Isabella in a black-draped cortège.

This time the conference assembled in the great hall of the Louvre. With Valentina were Charles and Isabella and her great supporter Guillaume Cousinot, the chancellor of the duchy of Orléans. Her case was put by Seris, the Benedictine Abbot of Saint-Fiacre. He too talked for four hours, denouncing the ridiculous accusations of John Petit with some force, before pleading with great emotion for justice to be done.

Cousinot then rose to his feet and asked for the vengeance against Burgundy that Valentina rightly deserved. Following this, the king, who had not been well enough to attend the meeting, recovered and revoked the pardon he had given Burgundy. He then sent ambassadors to Burgundy to say that he intended to bring proceedings against him.

Hopeful at last that something was going to happen, Valentina returned to Blois with Isabella and Charles, both of whom, before leaving, did homage to the king for their lands and the help he had promised to give them.

The envoys returned with the calamitous news that Burgundy, oblivious of the king's orders, was marching upon Paris. Heroic whatever her other failings, the queen appealed to the people of Paris to help her. But they refused. Frightened, but still undefeated, she took refuge in the well-defended castle of Tours, with the king and other members of the royal family. Proceeding down the river, the messengers halted at Orléans to find Valentina too ill to receive them. Exhausted, her gallant spirit failed at last and she died on 4 December 1408.

Charles, Duke of Orléans was 14 at the time of his mother's death, an age at which, by a decree of his grandfather Charles V, men of royal birth came of age. Immediately he found himself faced with the enormous responsibility of a great inheritance. His mother, his closest companion and guiding star throughout his life, was suddenly gone. The sense of her loss was compensated only by a newfound companionship with his wife.

Charles and Isabella had been married for three years. The union, which had begun so badly, surprisingly developed into love. First they had found compatibility in a shared enjoyment in hunting and hawking. Isabella, having learned to ride in England, had become a surprisingly good horse-woman, a striking figure riding side-saddle in a beautifully tailored habit, the skirt falling to her feet. Charles, to his surprise, found that she could control difficult horses as competently, if not better, than himself. She also proved to have a natural talent for falconry, holding the angry spitting hawks on her wrist without any show of fear.

Then had come mutual physical attraction. The marriage was consummated and Isabella was pregnant when, in late autumn, they bought horses and a side-saddle for her to use after her confinement. The doctors assured her of an easy birth. Her mother, after all, had borne twelve children without much difficulty. She came of good breeding stock.

Sadly they were proved mistaken. We do not know what went wrong. The science of obstetrics in those days was so basic that almost anything could have happened. All that is certain is that she gave birth to a daughter named Jane at Blois on 13 September 1409, and that she died afterwards, perhaps from a haemorrhage.

Charles was totally devastated. His own parents were dead and he was left with three younger brothers all under 12, his little sister Margaret, only 3, and a motherless baby when he himself was only just 15.

He would never forget Isabella. Even thirty-seven years later, when he had been remarried twice, he arranged that a mass should be celebrated on the anniversary of the death of 'the excellent and most generous lady' as he called her, to commemorate her in the abbey church of Saint-Laumer, where she was buried.

Isabella's memory lives on in the beautiful poem beginning 'Las! Mort qui t'a fait si hardie', which Hilaire Belloc identified as being addressed to her by Charles. Below is an English translation by James Kirkup:

To make my lady's obsequies
My love a minister wrought
And, in the chantry, service there
Was sung by doleful thought;
The tapers were of burning sighs,
That light and odour gave:
And sorrows painted o'er with tears,
Elumined her grave;
And round about in quaintest guise,
Was carved: 'Within this tomb there lies
The fairest thing in mortal eyes.'
Above her lieth spread a tomb
Of gold and sapphires blue:
The gold doth show her blessedness,
The sapphires mark her true;
For blessedness and truth in her
Were livelily portrayed,
When gracious God with both his hands
Her goodly sustance made
He framed her in such wondrous wise,
She was, to speak without disguise,
The fairest thing in mortal eyes.
No more, no more! My heart doth faint
When I the life recall
Of her who lived so free from taint,
So virtuous deemed by all,
That in herself was so complete

I think that she was ta'en
By God to deck his paradise,
And with his saints to reign,
Whom while on earth each one did prize
The fairest thing in mortal eyes.
But naught our tears avail, or cries;
All soon or late in death shall sleep;
Nor living wight long time may keep
The fairest thing in mortal eyes.

PART II

CATHERINE

1

Mortal Rivalry

France 1409–10

With all his immense responsibilities, Charles of Orléans had no time to grieve for his beloved Isabella. Less than a month after her death, another brutal act of Burgundy galvanised him into action. By then virtually a dictator, John the Fearless had banned Charles of Orléans and his allies from the council, thus giving himself a free hand.

The mental instability of the king and his vast generosity had led to much corruption. King Charles himself was by now reduced to poverty, while those of his court indulged in wild extravagance. Most widely blamed was Jean de Montagu, Grand Master of the household. Burgundy made him a scapegoat. On 7 October 1409, Pierre des Essarts, appointed Provost of Paris by Burgundy the previous year, arrested Montagu and imprisoned him in the Châtelet (a stronghold on the right bank of the Seine on the site of what is now the Place du Châtelet) on the main charge of collaborating with Charles of Orléans's dead father, Louis, to use evil influence on the king. Tortured into signing a confession, the wretched man was beheaded and his body hung on a gibbet as a grim warning of what traitors might expect.

Horrified at what had happened, Charles of Orléans immediately began to raise an army and to summon help from all his allies while keeping the queen informed. On 24 October, just a week after the unfortunate Montagu's death, Charles and his brothers signed a military agreement with the great Count Bernard of Armagnac, one of the king's strongest supporters. Charles VI had in fact made Armagnac his lieutenant general for Languedoc.

Count Bernard, with his legion of fierce fighters, was a man greatly to be feared. Another supporter was the Duke of Berry (whose first wife Jane had saved the king's life, as he dived under her skirts at the disastrous ball of the savages.) Finally, on 15 April at Gien-sur-Loire, the dukes of Berry, Brittany and Orléans and the counts of Alençon, Clermont and Armagnac signed an alliance against Burgundy.[1]

Another matter of even greater importance to Charles of Orléans was arranged at the same meeting, namely that he would marry Bonne, the 11-year-old third daughter of the Count of Armagnac and granddaughter of the Duke of Berry, who took a special delight in her betrothal. The dowry of 100,000 francs once arranged, the Lord of Armagnac agreed to clothe his daughter 'well and honourably according to her rank', and promised to send her a year and a day later, at his expense, to Riom, one of her grandfather's castles, to be handed over to Charles, who for his part swore to 'enjewel' her according to her rank.

Charles then returned to Blois, from where he sent Bonne the gift of an image of Our Lady in gold; to her mother he sent a Book of Hours, 'quite new', its covers of massive gold enamelled with figures and flowers, in a box of vermilion satin, enclosed in a case of gilded leather. Shortly afterwards, he agreed to the betrothal of his 8-month-old daughter Jane to the 6-year-old son of his new supporter, John, Count of Alençon.[2] Whether Bonne lived with him at Blois during her childhood, or remained in her parents' care, is unknown. The latter seems more likely, in view of the political struggle in which Charles was at that time embroiled.

The old Duke Louis of Bourbon died in 1410 to be succeeded by his son John, Count of Clermont, who rather naturally expected to follow his father as the Great Chamberlain of France. But before anyone knew what had happened, Burgundy had seized the position for his brother Philip, Count of Nevers.

The Duke of Berry, the king's only surviving uncle, now headed a deputation of the Orléanists, or Armagnacs, as they were more generally known, in sending a manifesto to the king assuring him of their loyalty and desire to restore him to his rightful position. A similar missive to the Parliament, describing both Charles VI's poverty and deprivation of power, shows how deplorable his situation had become. They then immediately began to raise an army by enlisting the men of their lands. But it was to prove expensive. Weaponry, provisions and armoury had to be purchased. The men had to be paid. Charles was forced to sell family treasures, including gems and a ship made of gold.

Then suddenly there was no need for war. The Duke of Burgundy offered terms. He would forego his annual pension from the royal treasury and serve the king loyally forthwith. He would withdraw his occupying soldiers to his own province provided his opponents did the same. Moreover, he would even allow his favourite, Pierre des Essarts, to be replaced as Provost of Paris by one chosen by the king. Lastly, the Duke of Berry would be reinstated to the royal council, specifically to influence the actions of the dauphin.

The second marriage of Charles of Orléans greatly increased the rivalry between himself and John, Duke of Burgundy, a master in double-dealing. Civil war between the two parties seemed imminent, but in March 1409, following the Peace of Chartres, after John of Burgundy and Charles, Duke of Orléans had made a public show of reconciliation in Chartres Cathedral, John the Fearless was formally reinstated to the royal council.

Queen Isabeau had by then switched her loyalty to the Burgundians. In August, she made a much-heralded and applauded entry into Paris with Louis, the 13-year-old dauphin. Then in December, in recognition of what was assumed to be his loyalty to the crown, she granted the *tutelle* or guardianship of Louis to Burgundy, by then so popular, thanks to his opposition to the taxes imposed by the Armagnacs, as to be virtually in control of Paris.

Once again royal marriages were arranged with the aim of preventing aggression. The participants were trained from birth in the knowledge that, unless they retired to a religious order for poor health or any other valid reason, such an arrangement was a foregone conclusion. In this instance, in 1409, the year Isabella died, her younger sister Michelle, fifth of their mother's daughters, married Burgundy's son Philip, and the dauphin, Louis, married Burgundy's daughter Margaret in a double wedding.

Despite this public rapprochement, in the autumn of 1410, an army of the Armagnacs marched into Paris to seize the dauphin before, in the following year, rivalry between the parties resulted in the long-expected civil war. Nonetheless, the Peace of Paris was signed on 2 November 1410. Significantly, it contained a clause to the effect that hostilities could not be resumed until Easter 1412.

England, 1400–12

As news of the turmoil in France crossed the Channel, the King of England, Henry IV and his son Prince Henry took opposing positions. Henry was the eldest of the king's four sons born by his first wife Blanche, daughter and heiress of Henry of Grosmont, Duke of Lancaster. Created a duchy by Edward III, for his third son John of Gaunt on his marriage, Lancaster comprised an enormous estate of 45,600 acres from the town of Manchester in the west, to the River Humber with its prosperous ports on the east coast.

One of Henry V's first acts, on becoming king, had been to declare that his Lancastrian inheritance held separately from the other possessions of the Crown should descend to his male heirs, stipulating that while they received the income, the capital must remain intact.

The wealth emanating from the duchy had been the main reason why Richard II, about to launch an extremely expensive campaign in Ireland and desperate for ready money to pay for all that it entailed, had banished Henry, then, before his father's death, Earl of Hereford, and forfeited his lands in perpetuity on the grounds of his alleged treachery.

Now, with the wealth of his property once more in his hands, King Henry saw good reason to take advantage of the great disturbance raging in France to renew the war against that country. Basically, the ambition of Henry IV, from the moment of his usurpation of King Richard, had been the continuation of the possession of Aquitaine, the province made English by the marriage of Eleanor, the greatest heiress in France, to Henry II, who became King of England in 1154. Shortly after his accession, in October 1399, Henry IV, or Henry of Bolingbroke, created his eldest son Henry of Monmouth (named after the Welsh castle in which he was born) Duke of Aquitaine.

The older Henry believed with passion that the French must be made to honour his grandfather's Treaty of Brétigny of 1360. The French king, John II, had been taken prisoner at the Battle of Poitiers and, his eldest son Charles (later Charles V) acting as regent, had agreed to the surrender of Aquitaine to the English, together with an exorbitant ransom, to secure his father's release. The greater part of the ransom had remained unpaid since King John had died in the English castle, to which he had returned voluntarily, after his younger son Louis had reneged on the deal, his honour thus unscathed.

The Black Prince had then ruled Aquitaine until illness had forced him to return to England, after which his brother, John of Gaunt, acting as his deputy, had been created Duke of Aquitaine. But, as already told, in 1389, Gaunt had been summoned back to England by his nephew Richard II, who had begged him to return 'with every possible haste' to assist and advise him in suppressing his rebellious subjects. By that time, the French armies, led by the national hero, Bertrand du Guesclin, had recaptured most of the English possessions, so that only Calais and a coastal strip of Gascony remained in English possession.

In England, although of less consequence, dissension raged between King Henry IV and his son Henry Prince of Wales. While both saw the difficulties in France as an opportunity for profitable intervention, the king favoured diplomacy in the cause of the Armagnacs, while his son supported the Burgundians. Often at odds, the one thing father and son agreed upon was that the marriage of Princess Catherine to Henry Prince of Wales had to be arranged in order to enforce both the re-establishment of the settlement of the English claim to Aquitaine and the final payment of King John's ransom.

The mediation of King Richard II, which resulted in the treaty agreed at his marriage to Princess Isabella, had seemed at the time to ensure a long and prosperous peace between France and England. While the French bought English wool from merchants including, most famously, Dick Whittington, now for the second time Mayor of London, the English did much business with French wine growers, particularly in Bordeaux.

But England's most important trading partner was Flanders, which had been part of the domains of Burgundy since the marriage of Philip the Bold to Margaret, Countess of Flanders. English wool sent to the Flemish weavers returned to England as finely woven cloth, a reciprocal commerce of much value to both countries concerned. This was the main reason why Henry, Prince of Wales insisted that good relations be maintained.

Prince Henry believed that a Burgundian alliance would open the gateway for an English invasion through the great port of Calais. His father was convinced that a league with the Armagnacs would secure the allegiance of Gascony, held by the English as vassals of the French king for 180 years from 1152 until, in May 1337, the Great Council of Paris, having decreed the arrangement no longer valid, had returned the province to King Philip VI.

From the start of his reign, Henry IV had been preoccupied with a rising of the Welsh, fighting for freedom under their national hero Owain Glendower. On 2 November 1401, the guerrilla commander, joined by a contingent from Scotland, led by the Earl of Douglas, raised his standard – a golden dragon on a white field – outside the walls of Caernarfon Castle as a full-scale revolution began.

The following August, when the garrison of the beleaguered castle appealed for help, King Henry led an army into Wales. In the spring of 1403, Henry Prince of Wales was given the command as his father's lieu-tenant on the Welsh Marches. Then in July of the same year, King Henry received a formal challenge from the Earl of Northumberland, head of the Percies, who accused him of breaking the promise he had made on his landing at Ravenspur, that he had come merely to claim his own lands, not to usurp King Richard.

Northumberland's son, Harry Hotspur, so famously portrayed by Shakespeare, marched down to Chester with the Scottish Earl of Douglas, but due to poor communication failed to join forces with Glendower. At the same time, the young Prince Henry led an army to meet his father, marching at great speed to Shrewsbury before Hotspur and Douglas could arrive. The battle there took place on 21 July 1403. The royal army had been divided into two divisions, the left commanded by the king, the right by his son the Prince of Wales. Prince Henry was wounded in the face by the first flight of arrows, as their enemies attacked from a hill, but fought on throughout the battle in which Harry Hotspur was killed and the Earl of Douglas taken prisoner.

Supported by Welsh families, including the Tudors in Anglesea, Owen Glendower defied their attack. In August 1405 he held a parliament at

Harlech, where he told the assembled members of a promise of aid from France. Shortly afterwards a French fleet came ashore at Milford Haven carrying 800 men-at-arms, 600 crossbowmen and 1,200 lightly armed troops who, together with Glendower's own army, penetrated as far as Worcestershire. But by the following spring the French army departed, disappointed by the lack of plunder.

On 5 April 1406, Prince Henry was reappointed to full-time supreme command as the Lieutenant of Wales. At the siege of Harlech in 1409, Owain's son Griffith, heavily defeated by Lord Grey of Codnor, was captured in the forest of Monkswood and taken to be held securely in the Tower of London.[1] Owain himself, never captured, remained hiding in the hills, but, his army dispersed, the probability of renewed rebellion no longer threatened the king.[2]

Henry IV was still both mentally and physically a strong man in 1406. But two years later he had the first of the epileptic fits from which he suffered at intervals for the remainder of his life.

The Duke of Burgundy had already tried to win the King of England to his cause by promising him support both in Flanders and Normandy should he invade those regions. Subsequently, during one of Henry IV's periods of incapacity, in September 1411, when the prince was president of the council, he contrived to persuade its members to sanction an expedition to help Burgundy in his war against the Armagnacs.

In command was Thomas Earl of Arundel, son of that Richard Fitzalan, Earl of Arundel, executed as a traitor by King Richard in 1397. In 1400, one of Henry IV's first actions on becoming king had been to restore by act of Parliament the titles and estates forfeited by his father. The small English army won Paris for Burgundy and forced the Armagnacs to retreat beyond the Loire. Lavishly rewarded by Burgundy, Arundel returned to England in triumph after this unexpected success.

King Henry, once recovered, immediately backed the Armagnacs, led by Louis, the young dauphin, who proved himself an inspiring commander at the age of only 15. But, instead of allowing her son to lead their men, his mother, Queen Isabeau, changed sides once again, giving her support to his cousin, Charles, Duke of Orléans, her former son-in-law. Infuriated, the dauphin also switched sides, giving his allegiance to John the Fearless of Burgundy in defiance of his devious mother.

2

A Challenge of War

France 1411–12

Despite the supposed rapprochement with Burgundy, Charles of Orléans and his brother Philip of Vertus, spent the following winter repairing and adding to the fortifications of their castles in preparation for war. Everything they could possibly dispose of, down to a birdcage with a goldfinch in it, was sold to pay for the repairs to the buildings and the wages of their soldiers, who were not dispersed.

Charles wrote again to the king, asking him to avenge his father's murder, for which he held Burgundy responsible. He received a mere conciliatory reply. A second letter, in which he graphically described his father's death, ended with a reminder of the broken promises made to their mother Valentina, and implored the king for vengeance on his father's murderer, whom he must recognise as 'a liar, evil, false, treacherous, cruel and disloyal'.[1]

Infuriated by the king's prevarication, Charles and his younger brothers resolved to wage war on their own. On 24 July 1411, they sent a herald to Burgundy to tell him of their intentions. Addressing him contemptuously as 'John, who call yourself Duke of Burgundy', they informed him:

We are writing to let you know, that from this time forth we are going to harm you with all our power, and against you and the disloyalty and treason you have committed we call on our God and all the honest men of this world.[2]

Burgundy showed his contempt for what he termed 'the Orléans children' by ignoring this missive for a month. When he eventually replied, he said that his conscience had forced him to kill Louis of Orléans, 'because of his foul treason':

And since you and your brothers are following in the footsteps of your perfidious father, and wish to attain the same ends as he, we have received your letter of defiance with the keenest joy. As for their contents, we declare that you have lied, like infamous impostors and detestable traitors.[3]

Plainly he had thrown down the gauntlet in a challenge of war.

Charles began selling more family treasures to pay for men, armour and horses, not only for himself but for some of his allies as well. Then, in the midst of all the preparations, he faced a family crisis caused by the threat of disease. In the hot weather of August, it was possible that the plague was making a return. Taking no chances, Charles ordered one of his officers to take his sister Margaret, his brother John and his own baby daughter Jane away from Blois to one of his other castles at Châteauneuf-sur-Loire. Then later, in September, his little brother John was escorted to yet another place of safety, perhaps to avoid the danger of kidnap rather than that of infection.

Shortly after this, the army of the allies began its march towards Paris. Charles himself commanded the main force, his new father-in-law, Count Bernard of Armagnac the advance guard and the Count of Alençon the rear. Burgundy, who had not taken the challenge of the 'Orléans children' seriously, now grew so thoroughly alarmed that he appealed to Henry IV, who promised to send a relief force under the Earl of Arundel's command.

On 4 October the allies reached the outskirts of Paris. Refused entry to the city, they encamped at Saint-Ouen before laying siege to Saint-Denis. A week later, on the 11th, the beleaguered fortress surrendered, after which they captured Saint-Cloud with its bridge across the River Seine. The Parisians were then at their mercy, cut off from all supplies carried by boat up the river. Charles for some reason missed the opportunity of quickly invading the city. Instead, at the end of October, Burgundy rode into Paris at the head of his army to the wild joy of the inhabitants who, headed by the guild of the butchers, were always his strongest supporters.

On 9 November Burgundy's French and English soldiers left Paris in darkness to reach Saint-Cloud in the early morning. At the same time, ships carrying pitch set fire to the wooden bridge. The allies, trapped between the Seine and Burgundy's advancing army, were totally defeated within the space of three hours. Told the dreadful news, Charles, still at Saint-Ouen, realised that he now had no alternative but to return to Orléans with what remained of his army. But, even as he withdrew, the sentence of excommunication was passed on him and his followers in Notre-Dame, so that no one would bury the dead, who were left for the birds and the wolves. 'The Duke of Orléans, seeking to avenge the death of his father, incurred great harm and loss of people,' wrote Monstrelet, summing up.[4]

Charles had indeed caused disastrous losses, both for his followers and himself. Many of his estates were forfeited to the king and the dauphin, robbing him of revenue and manpower. Left with only his land around the Loire, he was now in such desperate need of money that his old family doctor, Pierre de Vaulx, lent him six silver cups to use in any way he wished 'in the great need wherein he stands'.[5]

Depressed and desperate, Charles was driven into making what proved to be a fatal mistake. In January 1412, supported by his allies, he sent ambassadors to Henry IV of England asking for military support.

Delighted, King Henry saw his chance to win back some of the formerly English lands in France. A treaty of English assistance was signed on 25 January. Then, in the early spring, Henry sent his second son, Thomas of Lancaster, with an escort of soldiers, to lay down the terms to Charles of Orléans of what such help would entail. These were harsh indeed. Not only must Charles and his allies agree to the English king's claim to Aquitaine, but Charles must hold his regions of Angoulême and Périgord as Henry's vassal. Moreover, following his death, these lands would be Henry's inheritance.

Even more disastrously, Charles was told that he had to pay the wages of 1,000 men-at-arms and the 4,300 archers that he had asked for three months after they reached Blois. It having been decided that the English expedition should sail on 8 June, Charles, the dukes of Berry and Bourbon, and the Count of Alençon eventually signed the alliance on 18 May.

But while these negotiations were happening an unforeseen event occurred. The king recovered his senses and copies of the letters from Orléans and his uncle Berry to Henry IV somehow reached his hands. Furious, he decided to join forces with Burgundy to fight the Orléanist traitors, as he called them. Thus, already on 4 May 1412, the king and the dauphin began leading their army south, accompanied by John the Fearless with a strong force of his men.

They besieged the ancient city of Bourges in the first week of June, but it was saved by the dauphin, who as heir of the Duke of Berry, could not bear to see his future inheritance destroyed. Subsequently, on 21 June, on King Charles's orders, Berry declared the agreement with Henry IV to be null and void.

The Orléans brothers, Charles and Philip, then had no option but to obey their king's command. On 22 August, in what was termed the Peace of Auxerre, they had to sign documents to comply with Burgundy and renounce their treaty with King Henry IV. Charles was then promised that his estates would be returned to him, though compensation for such vandalism as the sale of lead piping at Coucy was not to be offered. The king did, however, immediately return Chauny, the town on the banks of the Oise, in Picardy, with permission to raise 60,000 gold florins in taxes imposed thereon.

But Charles was then plagued by a new problem. The English army, commanded by Thomas of Lancaster, recently created Clarence, had already landed in France. Marching slowly to Blois, his soldiers, as was their habit, engaged in random destruction on their way. Clarence was met with the news that he and his army were no longer wanted. Peace had been made between the opposing parties.

Clarence had no intention of returning home empty-handed. Insisting that the agreement signed the previous January be honoured, he demanded recompense for all that the expedition had involved. The total payment was finally settled at 210,000 gold écus, of which the major part was to go to Clarence for the payment and provisioning of his men.

But the money was simply not there. Clarence therefore demanded jewels – the Duke of Berry provided a magnificent gold cross set with precious stones. But even this was not enough. Hostages were needed to guarantee full payment of the debt. It then being the custom to send close relatives in this capacity, Charles had to decide between his brother Philip of Vertus, on whose support he so greatly relied, and his youngest brother John of Angoulême, who was only a boy of 12. The duty fell to John. Harsh as it may seem now, it was thought he would soon be redeemed. Also, he would go to England with six other men he knew well.

Charles did his best for John, buying a quiet black mare with a long tail for him to ride when he went to join Clarence. He also gave John and his companions money for the journey that lay ahead. For the boy, it was an adventure. He believed he would soon come home.

The council was soon to issue letters authorising Charles to raise 40,000 livres in taxes on his own lands in order to pay his brother's ransom. But the money did not appear, most of the parishes protesting that, because of the destruction of the English, who had killed so many of their men, they could not afford to maintain themselves let alone pay taxes.

In the winter of 1413, Charles found himself faced with near destitution. Despite their assurances, the councillors still refused to hand back his estates. Burgundy controlled the king. The government was beset by corruption.

3

The Cabochien Revolt

Paris

War raged on in Paris. Many of the common people, as disillusioned with Queen Isabeau as was her son, joined John the Fearless in what became known as the Cabochien Revolt. A group of tradesmen and men who belonged to the butchers and skinners guilds, united themselves under a skinner, Simon Lecoustellier, known as Caboche. Enraged by the corrupt methods of the government and the extravagance of the court, they attached themselves to the Duke of Burgundy. Anarchy was rampant. Houses were sacked and burnt. The streets, packed hard with horse dung, were soon streaked with running blood as men and women roamed them, breaking into wine cellars and shouting drunken curses besmirching the infidel queen.

Monstrelet, who was there in 1413, tells of how several young renegades, already in trouble for some sort of misdemeanour, went secretly to the Lord of L'Isle-Adam, the Governor of Paris, who was with the garrison at Pontoise. L'Isle-Adam said he could enlist a band of fighting men, who would meet outside the Porte Germain-des-Près on 29 May. The gate would then be opened to let them enter Paris.

Good as his word, the Lord of L'Isle-Adam gathered about 800 men, including some of the nobility, whom he led to Paris on the agreed day. One of the original conspirators, Pettinet de Clerc who, according to legend, had retrieved the keys from under his father the gatekeepers' pillow, unlocked the Porte Saint-Germain. The 800, headed by the Lord of L'Isle-Adam, surged into the city, all of them fully armed. The gate clanged behind them and Perrinet de Clerc hurled the keys over the wall.

It was now two o'clock in the morning and still dark. Monstrelet says 'they rode silently towards the Châtelet,' which suggests that they had muffled the hooves of their horses. Reaching the Châtelet, they joined up with another band of combatants, estimated at 400 strong, with whom they converged to attack the houses of the king's ministers. Dividing into two companies, they rode through the streets, yelling at the tops of their voices that all who wished for peace should join them in fighting. Little encouragement was needed: men and even women seized the chance to attack the ministers' houses while one band headed for the king's palace itself.

They broke into the dauphin's palace, where they arrested his uncle, his mother's brother the Duke of Bavaria and the Duke of Bar. Burgundy himself was with them and the dauphin bravely stood up to his father-in-law, telling him he should 'know for a certainty that the time will come when you will repent this, for matters will not always go according to your wish.' Burgundy, towering above him, replied contemptuously, 'My lord, you will be able to consider these things better when your anger has cooled.'[1]

In the Hôtel Saint-Pol they heard them coming, roaring and laughing in fiendish pleasure as they broke down windows and doors. Then came the sound of fists hammering, before the crashing of a broken door. There were screams of terror as the queen's ladies-in-waiting, said to be fifteen in all, were dragged out of the building, leaving only terrified servants behind.

Of the queen herself there is no mention. Was she hiding somewhere within the palace with her two youngest children, Catherine and Charles, crouching perhaps in an attic or cellar below ground? But Isabeau had never been cowed by anyone, at least in the public eye. Therefore it seems more likely, that as on previous occasions when trouble threatened, she had taken the precaution of holing herself up in the secure fortress of Melun.

Only one thing is certain: that wherever she and the children were, they had deserted the king. For it was he, brave in one of his saner moments, who came to meet the insurgents, some of whom must have broken into the house before seizing the unfortunate waiting women.

They persuaded him to get on his horse and ride with them through the streets of Paris with a brother of the King of Cyprus. They had hoped to capture the dauphin but found him gone. It turned out that only the day before, perhaps forewarned, he and his court had moved into the palace of the Louvre.

Fortunately the thieves were soon satisfied with their loot. Clasping armfuls of treasures, gold ornaments, mirrors and the lovely pearl-embroidered hangings, they staggered back into the street. But they had failed in their main object, the capture of the hated queen.

As one band of the insurgents was thus occupied in stripping the palace of Saint-Pol, the other was attacking the house of the Constable of France. Again they were to find themselves too late. Warned in advance, he had escaped in disguise and hidden in the house of a workman.

Tanguy du Châtel, Provost of Paris soon heard the uproar. He then rushed to the dauphin's house (the Louvre) and carried him in a blanket to the Bastille Saint-Antoine, together with several of his men who had come in from the streets.

Monstrelet then tells how looting and rioting convulsed the city for three whole days. The Burgundian lords and their followers, aided by the Parisian mob, raided the houses of the ministers and anyone to whom they thought they were connected. 'They robbed them of everything and took countless prisoners whom they shut up in the Palace [possibly Saint-Pol], the Louvre, the Châtelet and various other places.' Among them were the bishops of Senlis, Bayeaux and Coutances and many nobles.

All those attached to the Count of Armagnac were either robbed or imprisoned or else cruelly murdered. Though dismissed from his post as Provost of Paris on orders of the king, Tanguy du Châtel sent the dauphin to Montargis before summoning all his supporters to bring men-at-arms to join him in the Bastille Saint-Antoine. At the same time, the Lord of L'Isle-Adam issued a call to arms to all the Burgundian party, so that within a few days they were streaming into the city. But Tanguy du Châtel, with the Marshal de Rieux and the Lord of Barbasan then rode in through Porte-Saint Antoine at the head of 1,600 chosen men. Parading through the streets, banners flying, trumpets sounding, they reached the Hôtel de l'Ours, where they proclaimed the king, the dauphin and our constable, the Count of Armagnac.

The Parisians, hearing this, swarmed out to follow the Lord of L'Isle-Adam, the new provost, in a fierce battle with the Burgundians. Finally, overcome by sheer weight of numbers, the Marshal de Rieux and the Lord of Barbasan's men were forced to retreat to the Bastille, leaving three or four hundred of their best men lying dead on the ground.

The Burgundians, answering the summons, then arrived. Soon everyone in Paris was wearing the white badge, crossed with a saltire, Saint Anthony's Cross, to protect their lives. Tanguy du Châtel and his fellow commanders, having made terms with the Lord of L'Isle-Adam, eventually surrendered the Bastille. The Cabochien Revolt thus ended, having cost nearly 2,000 lives. Infuriated, Isabeau was quick to take her vengeance. Acting on her instructions, a force of Armagnacs, reputedly 60,000 strong, caused even more havoc in Paris before roaming in bands to make destruction throughout the region of Picardy.

The dauphin's words proved prophetic. The people of Paris were disgusted by the butchers and turned against them, blaming Burgundy for their atrocities. Encouraged as popular opinion swung towards them, Charles of Orléans, the Count of Alençon and others of their friends met to discuss the situation. Charles then sent a messenger to the king, protesting against the arrests and executions that had just been enacted, offering his support and that of his allies, and requesting the return of his lands. The king, influenced it would seem by the dauphin, then summoned Charles to join him at Vernon to discuss the matters in hand. Subsequently another treaty was drawn up, this time called the Peace of Pontoise. Immediately the prisoners taken by the Cabochiens were freed and on 1 August the terms of the 'Peace' were read before the king in council.

Paris echoed with jubilation, bells peeling from churches and towers. The Duke of Berry became the captain of the city and Tanguy du Châtel became Provost in place of Pierre des Essarts. Burgundy returned to Flanders but on 8 February 1314, he once more led an army towards Paris. Warned of Burgundy's advance, the dauphin immediately ordered all the Orléanist princes in Paris to attend him at the Hôtel de Ville. There he issued his orders. He himself would command the Bastille, the Duke of Berry the Temple, while Charles would hold the area of Saint-Martin-des-Champs near the Porte Saint-Martin.

The gates of the city were quickly closed. Burgundy, refused entrance, stormed up the heights of Montmartre, from where his archers shot in messages on the points of arrows, saying that he only wanted peace. No one believed him. Frustrated and humiliated, he withdrew.

Even as this was happening, a meeting of the learned men of France, under the leadership of the Bishop of Paris, was assembled to hear the verdict of the theologians who had examined the four-hour speech, made by John Petit before the council and the king in December 1407, to exonerate Burgundy for the murder of Louis of Orléans. The charges against Orléans were declared to be baseless. Petit's defence of his master was condemned and the parchment on which it was written publicly burned.

After six years of struggle, Charles had finally cleared his father's name.

Burgundy, however, saw this as provocation. In defiance, he garrisoned the royal towns of Compiègne and Soissons, of which Charles was the overlord. Predictably, on 2 March, the council declared war on Burgundy and, amazingly, the king himself took joint command with the dauphin of the forces gathered at Saint-Denis. Here they were joined by Charles of Orléans, whose own men-at-arms were now reinforced with Scottish archers led by John Stewart, Earl of Buchan, sent to France by Stewart's father, the regent Robert, Duke of Albany, in compliance with the Aulde Alliance between Scotland and France.

The campaign against Burgundy ended with the siege of Arras, where Burgundy was entrenched. Cannon balls could not dislodge him but in early September Burgundy offered a truce. The king and the dauphin accepted it, the latter much influenced by Burgundy's powerful sister, the Countess of Hainault, mother-in-law of his younger brother, John of Touraine.

Charles was furious at being forced to make peace with Burgundy and pardon him for killing his father. The king, his mind wandering, believed that Charles had agreed to forgive and forget all that Burgundy had done, but when the dauphin asked him to agree to the Peace of Arras, Charles bowed low and told him: 'My lord, I am not obliged to swear an oath, for I came only to serve my lord the king and you.' To this the dauphin replied by insisting, 'Fair cousin we beg you to swear to the peace,' to which Charles answered that he had not broken the peace and ought not to swear, begging him to be content.

But the dauphin persisted. He and Charles both lost their tempers until the Archbishop of Reims intervened, telling Charles 'to do as my Lord of

Aquitaine bids you'. Thus commanded, Charles reluctantly agreed to take the oath as demanded.[2]

Charles was to some extent mollified when, on their return to Paris on 5 January 1415, the eve of Epiphany, the king had the obsequies of his brother, Louis of Orléans, Charles's father, solemnly celebrated in Notre-Dame. Charles was there with his brother Philip and the dukes to whom they were related, all wearing the deepest black of mourning. They listened as Charles Gerson, chancellor of the university, gave an impassioned sermon praising Louis to the skies and condemning Burgundy for perjuring his soul. Other services followed so that Charles could feel that his father, if not avenged, was at least remembered with both honour and respect.

Despite their heated disagreement, Charles maintained a strong friendship with the dauphin. Both were young men longing to spread their wings and enjoy themselves, Charles being 19, the dauphin three years younger. Such was their love of fun that Charles engaged a tumbler and his three children to entertain them when, following the Peace of Arras, they stayed at his castle of Chauny on their way back to Paris.

It seems to have been the dauphin who persuaded Charles to abandon the black garments that he and his brother Philip had worn since their father's murder, to exchange them for those of more cheerful colours. The dauphin loved clothes – his critics accused him of extravagance but he was undoubtedly also a brave young man – and under his sway Charles indulged himself for the first time in what was one of the happiest periods of his life.

For their entry into Paris, after the expulsion of the Cabochiens, the dauphin had ordered violet cloaks and black and red headdresses for himself and his companions to wear. Then, the following September, Charles had procured a cloak of white satin trimmed with fur and no less than forty-one items of clothing embroidered with his device of a nettle and the words 'Le droit chemin' for his staff. Six surcoats, made for himself, were studded with jewels of small trembling leaves, made by a jeweller in Paris.

Most extravagant of all was a garment with sleeves embroidered with 960 pearls. Charles gave costly New Year presents, his favourite being his own knightly Order of the Camail as he called it, a continuation of the Order of the Porcupine founded by his father in 1393. The twenty-five members wore magnificent robes, the collars being ropes of twisted gold chains from which hung golden porcupines.

Yet despite his newfound love of pleasure, Charles was always haunted by the thought of his little brother John held prisoner in an English fortress. In December 1413 he had told some Florentine merchants in London to send 2,000 écus to John and to one of the other hostages. But then to his horror, he was told the following March that, in the charge of the Duke of Clarence, they were all suffering great want.

On word of this, Charles at once told his Treasurer General to give John 6,000 écus for himself, plus 5,000 for his servants and another 1,000 for the expenses of certain other individuals, to be taken from the revenues of Normandy. Following this, in June 1414, he sent another 2,000 to two of the other hostages through merchants in Lucca and Florence.

Despite these responsibilities, Charles still managed to enjoy the distractions of Paris, where he lived in one of the Orléans houses, either the Hôtel de Behaigne near the Louvre or the Séjour d'Orléans on the other side of the river. Foremost amongst his great friends were the Count of Alençon who, on 1 January 1415 was raised to the rank of duke, partly for his loyalty to the king during the recent rioting but also, as most people claimed, because he was the handsomest man in France! Another close companion was the young Duke of Bourbon, a charming character much addicted to hunting and the pursuit of women, but also a brave soldier in the field.

Charles himself could not resist beauty, as is proved by the *ballades* for which he is so famed. Unlike Bourbon, however, he proved constant to his true loves. Foremost of these was his wife Bonne, the 'young, gentle, matchless princess' to whom he poured out his devotion in a eulogy thought to have been written about this time. Unlike most men of his generation, he was not profligate. He had no illegitimate children, whereas his brother Philip had at least one love child, and others many more.

In the winter of 1415, while living for the most part in Paris, presumably with Bonne, by now 16, Charles kept in constant touch with his sister Margaret and his little daughter Jane, now 6 years old, at the main family home, the great castle of Blois. Told that the Duke of Anjou (the King of Sicily) was about to pay them a visit, he thoughtfully sent 'two antique, pointed diamonds' for them to give to their 'dear cousins'.

Little could they or he have known that this time of domestic happiness was soon so drastically to end.

4.

The Price of a Bride

Henry IV had already attempted to secure a marriage contract for his heir Henry with Catherine's eldest sister Isabella when she was still the child widow of Richard II. But this, as we have already seen, had failed when Isabella herself furiously refused to marry the son of the man she believed to have murdered her beloved Richard. Now the king envisaged Princess Catherine, not only as a bride for his son, but as a means of achieving his long-planned ambition of restoring the claims of Edward III and his successors to the kingdom of France. Queen Isabeau, thus seeing a chance to gain the English king's support to assert her own authority over her enemies, was perfectly willing to comply.

Whether Catherine knew of these plans is unknown. Hidden away in the convent to which she is believed to have been sent, probably to avoid the dangers of Paris, she was likely shielded from news of what was happening in the outside world. She may have been ignorant of the match that was planned for her, unless made aware of it by her sister Marie, who possibly guessed at their mother's intentions, if she was not actually informed of them. Catherine, 10, was tall for her age and showed promise of the striking looks for which she would afterwards be famed. The plans for her marriage were still undecided, due largely to exorbitant demands for her dowry and for recognition of England's claims to France, when King Henry died on 20 March 1413.

Inspired by the success of Lord Arundel's raid, Henry V ascended the throne of England determined to win back the lands won by his great-grandfather, Edward III. At the time of his second Parliament, held in Leicester, on 30 April 1414, he was negotiating with both parties in France. The Armagnacs, in control of the dauphin Louis, wanted a peace settlement but, far more importantly, the Burgundians, led by John the Fearless, offered an alliance in war. They did so in the now certain knowledge that the twenty-five-year truce signed by the peace-loving Richard II, as part of his marriage contract to Catherine's older sister, was about to be broken by the aggressive new king. During the Parliament held at Westminster, in November 1414, Henry was advised to exhaust the possibility of negotiation, but not to shrink from the necessity of war.[1]

Burgundy had no need to fear the pledges made at the Peace of Arras. He had no compunction in breaking his own word when, at the end of September 1414, the same month the agreement was signed, he renewed his secret treaty with Henry of England.

During the winter of 1414/15 following the Peace of Arras, the dauphin, despite his youth, began to take over the powers of government from his father. Although described by some as frivolous – he was certainly known to enjoy himself with his cousin Charles of Orléans and others – he was basically of sound mind. Monstrelet described him as 'the saviour of France'.

In April, seizing the chance of the court being at Melun, he went with a few companions to the Louvre, where they found large sums of money, which his mother the queen, long suspected of sending royal funds to her relations in Germany, had been hoarding. This done, he summoned the most important members of the university, together with the Provost of Paris, the Provost of the Merchants and many other dignitaries to a meeting at which they were told by the Chancellor, the Bishop of Chartres, how the royal treasury had been pillaged by men of high rank since the start of the king's incapacity. Specifically, he named the now dead dukes of Anjou, Burgundy and Orléans, and the present dukes of Burgundy and Berry. Louis's friend Charles of Orléans was not included in the charges.

Louis then announced that from now on he himself would manage the financial administration of the country, commanding the offending courtiers to return to their own lands. Burgundy, fuming with anger at his son-in-law, was then further insulted when Louis refused to pardon the Cabochiens, as agreed at the Peace of Arras the previous June. When Louis declined to listen to Burgundy's emissaries, they turned on him saying that if he refused to do as their lord asked, he would not feel himself bound to keep the peace. Furthermore, in the event of an attack by the English, neither Burgundy nor his vassals and subjects would fight for Louis.[2] From this it can be taken that Burgundy at least knew of King Henry's intentions of which Louis, like most of his compatriots, was at that time unaware.

It was now two months since Henry had sent a second embassy headed by the youngest of his step-uncles, Thomas Beaufort, Earl of Dorset, son of his grandfather's second marriage to Katherine Swynford, with a delegation of bishops and noblemen to dictate terms to the court of France. Amongst the great festivities, arranged to entertain them, was a tournament which lasted no less than three days. King Charles, at least temporarily himself, even took part, jousting with Charles of Orléans's great friend, the newly created Duke of Alençon, while Orléans himself 'fought very cordially' with Burgundy's brother the Duke of Brabant.[3]

The ambassadors went with instructions to claim the crown of France but, if this failed, as seemed most likely, they were to claim possession of Normandy, Anjou, Maine, Touraine and all the territories which had been ceded to Edward III by the Treaty of Brétigny in 1360. In addition, they were to demand possession of half of Provence and the castles and lands of Beaufort and Nugent as belonging to Henry through his Lancastrian birth right. Most insulting of all, they were to order payment of all the arrears of the ransom of King John of France, captured by Edward's son the Black Prince at Poitiers in 1356, amounting to 1,600,000 French crowns. Lastly, they were to ask for the hand of the Princess Catherine as a bride for King Henry V with a dowry of no less than 2 million crowns.

The French, under the auspices of King Charles's uncle, the Duke of Berry, were surprisingly conciliatory in their reply in view of the enormity of the demands. They offered the greater part of Aquitaine, which they thought reasonable repayment for the ransom of King John, now owing for sixty-nine years. However, should this claim be abandoned, King Charles declared himself willing to provide 600,000 gold crowns for his daughter's dowry, which, after some argument, he raised to 800,000 crowns, together with a magnificent trousseau for her marriage. Reasonable though these concessions seemed to be, they were immediately rejected, it seems on the instructions of the English king, his mind set upon war.

King Henry began his preparations on his ambassadors' return. Commissioners were sent into every town and county to enact the right of an English king to summon freemen to arms. The knights, who were the main strength of his army, obeyed his summons, riding in wearing corselets of steel. The full armour, together with the bascinet, a recent invention allowing freedom of head movement (replacing the old full helm moulded to the breastplate), which they would wear for battle, being transported by the esquires, and pages who formed their retinue or 'fiery tail'.

In addition, they brought their yeomen, farm hands and foresters, men who earned their living from the land. Richard II had been king when it was enacted that 'All servants and labourers should have bows and arrows, and practise shooting on Sundays and festivals, and not waste their time with such games as dice, quoits, football and suchlike play', a law endorsed by Henry IV.[4]

The English longbow men, so skilled that they could fire off six arrows a minute at a range of between 200 and 300 yards, had proved their worth at Crécy. The crossbow, used by the French, though also a deadly weapon, was slower and more unwieldy. The English foot soldiers also carried swords, battleaxes, pikes and billhooks. The company of foot soldiers raised by Henry for this expedition is estimated to have been 10,000 strong.

There were also countless horses, mostly of the heavy type, ancestors of the shires, strong enough to carry men in full armour often weighing as much as 84lb. Armaments included cannons and most importantly siege weapons, devised to throw both balls of metal and stone against walls and pots of burning oil to ignite wooden towers and palisades.

Henry, renowned even today as a brilliant administrator, detailed even the food and forage for horses that would be needed for such a campaign. Having told his royal commissioners to commandeer every ship that could carry twenty casks or more, he hired vessels from Holland to transport this enormous force across the English Channel.

It was now the beginning of July 1415, the French knew that plans for an invasion from England were under way. In desperation, aware that they were unprepared, they sent an embassy under the Archbishop of Bourges to try to stave off the impending attack and to find out, if it happened, where the landing was likely to take place.

The ambassadors arrived in London to discover that King Henry, having ridden through the city on 15 June, was already somewhere near the south coast. They finally found him, with his three brothers, in Winchester where, in the episcopal palace, the archbishop used all his eloquence to offer both land and money and more conducive terms for the forthcoming marriage of the Princess Catherine to Henry, on condition that he would abandon his planned invasion of France.

The archbishop's pleas were entirely in vain. Henry, through his confessor, Henry Chichele, Archbishop of Canterbury, demanded the territories that he wanted – Normandy, Aquitaine, Anjou, Touraine, Maine, Poitou, Ponthieu and others – as well as a financial settlement for his marriage to Princess Catherine. He then made sure that the envoy's return was delayed until it was too late for him to report on the numbers of men he was arming to lead to France.[5]

5

Invasion

The truce expired on 2 August 1415. The English soldiers of the garrison of Calais immediately began pillaging the surrounding country. Three days later, as his fleet of warships, provisioned and ready to sail, lay tugging at their anchors in Southampton Water, Henry despatched the Gloucester herald with a final ultimatum to King Charles of France. Couched in the most flattering terms, it read:

> To the very noble Prince Charles our cousin and adversary, of France – Henry, by the grace of God, King of England and of France. To give to each his due is, dear prince our cousin and adversary, a work of inspiration and wise counsel; in former days the noble kingdoms of France and England were united and now they are divided ... But alas! This ancient loyalty has perverted such fraternal aims, and Lot now persecutes Abraham for worldly reasons, the glory of brotherly love is departed, and the old sin of Dissension, mother of Wrath, has been raised from the dead. We, however, call to witness the wisdom of the Sovereign Judge, who is swayed by neither prayers nor by gifts, that we out of pure affection have done everything in our power to procure the means of peace. We shall therefore regain by the sword and by negotiation the just rights of our inheritance, with all our former rights.

Continuing to justify the coming war, Henry went on:

> Because of our alliance by marriage we recently were inclined to forgo
> the offer made to us of 50,000 gold crowns, because we desire peace more
> than wealth and wished to share the patrimony left to us by our vener-
> able ancestors with our dear cousin Catherine, your beloved daughter,
> rather than to pile up ill-gotten gains and so dishonour the crown of our
> realm, God forbid.
>
> Given under our privy seal in our castle of Southampton the fifth day
> of the month of August.[1]

On Sunday 11 August, in his magnificent ship *La Trinité Royale*, Henry V
led the fleet of 1,500 vessels from the Solent. Behind them, following from
the harbour, swam a flock of swans, an omen of good fortune, or so it
was believed.

Henry landed, not as expected at Calais, the nearest port across the
channel, but at Harfleur on the mouth of the River Seine, the reason for his
doing so being that the quickest route was up the river to Paris. Harfleur
surrendered on 22 September after a hard-fought siege in which many
were killed. Men did not only die in battle, a great number succumbed to
eating oysters found in contaminated mud flats at the river's mouth.

Charles of Orléans was at Blois, entertaining the Duke of Anjou and
his wife, Yolande of Aragon, with whom he developed a close friendship
due to their mutual love of books. Later Yolande would become famous
as the patroness of *Les Grandes heures de Rohan*, more commonly known
as the *Rohan Hours*, an illuminated manuscript book of hours, painted by
the anonymous artist the Rohan Master, which depicts the lamentations
of the mother of Jesus following his crucifixion, and is now a treasure
of the Bibliothèque nationale. She would also be instrumental, although
unbeknown to both of them at that time, in saving Charles's own precious
collection of books at Blois.

As with most aristocratic families in France, they were related, Yolande
being the great-granddaughter of King John II. Described by the Bishop
of Beauvais as 'the prettiest woman in the kingdom', she was also an intellectual and a strong enough character to defy no less a virago than Queen
Isabeau. Bourdigné, chronicler of the house of Anjou, called her 'the wisest

and most beautiful princess in Christendom', and her grandson, King Louis XI, would later aver that his grandmother had 'a man's heart in a woman's body'.

Great heiress as she was, Yolande had also been directly responsible for the marriage of Richard of England to Isabella. When Richard had opened negotiations for Yolande's hand in marriage, Charles VI, unwilling to let her leave France, had promptly offered his own daughter instead. Yolande's own marriage to Louis II, Duke of Anjou proved successful, producing a family of six children.

Presumably they came with her that summer to Blois, so that the great rambling building was filled with the sounds of children's laughter and the running of many feet. Also there was the boy to whom Yolande was a guardian, the French king's youngest son Charles, the Count of Ponthieu, a thin and painfully shy boy of 12 who, in Yolande's opinion, was shamefully neglected by his mother, as, in 1415, she so forcefully declared. Charles was only two years younger than Yolande's eldest daughter Marie, the girl he would eventually marry when, unknown by anyone at that time, he had just succeeded his father Charles VI, as King of France.

The long hot summer weather continued until September. At Blois, Charles entertained his visitors, hunting deer through the forests and flying hawks above the fields where partridges, chased by dogs from the stubble, rose into the sunlit air. It is probable that Yolande and her husband, Louis of Anjou, and their children were still at Blois when a messenger thundered up to the castle with the news that the English had invaded and that he bore a call to arms.

Charles wasted no time. First he bought himself a complete new set of steel armour and a bay horse, then two more horses for two of his pages.[2] He then sent out a summons to his archers and his men-at-arms to come from the surrounding country to join his army, and arranged with his treasurer, Pierre Renier, for them to be paid. Unsure of the outcome of the forthcoming campaign, Charles then settled all his debts and reimbursed his old doctor, Pierre de Vaulx, for those silver cups he had lent him when he was struggling to pay off the Duke of Clarence nearly four years before. Confident that he had left his affairs in order, he said farewell to his family, his young wife Bonne, his sister Margaret and most heartbreakingly- his little 6-year-old daughter Jane, to whom he had just given an ABC in parchment with gilded letters, perhaps as a parting present to console her before he rode away.

From Blois it was 250 miles to Rouen, where he found not only the king and the dauphin, but a great assemblage of nobles. Amongst them were his special friends, the dukes of Alençon and Bourbon, as well as his cousin the Duke of Berry, the counts of Eu, Vendôme and Richemont, and the Constable, Charles of Albret. Also there to welcome him was his old companion Pierre de Mornay, who had fought beside him against Burgundy, and whom he now made commander of his men-at-arms.

After his victory at Harfleur it was expected that, as advised by his council, Henry would return to England. But instead he pushed on, following the Seine through Normandy, the duchy he believed to be his own through hereditary right. The French thought that he was making for Rouen, capital of the province, to which he laid claim. Instead he turned north-east, heading for the port of Calais beyond the River Somme. Soon Henry learned from French prisoners that the ford of Blanchetaque, at the mouth of the river, crossed by Edward III after the Battle of Crécy, was strongly held by the enemy. Furthermore, in anticipation of the English advance, the French were patrolling the Somme. Warned of the danger ahead, Henry led his army up the left bank of the Somme to find a feasible crossing place.

As soon as word reached him of the location of Henry's army, Charles VI sent off an advanced guard of his own, specifically to prevent the English from crossing the Somme. Then the main army, commanded jointly by the dukes of Orléans and Bourbon, also set out in much the same direction, but taking a more southerly route, heading direct for Amiens, in the hopes of stopping Henry in his tracks. However, on reaching the town, on 17 October, they found themselves too late. The English had already been and gone, heading east along the river's southern bank. Thwarted, the French leaders then continued to Péronne, the town above the River Somme and its lakes, which, fortified since the ninth century, was a natural place of defence.

The English army, by this time, had passed the great bend of the Somme at Péronne and on 18 October, by now nearly 60 miles inland, they at last found a feasible ford in the river. Henry himself supervised the crossing of his army over low-lying swampy ground. It was during this manoeuvre that the king, with a clear insight of what was to come, ordered every one of the archers to cut a stave from the surrounding oak trees and sharpen it at both ends.

In the meantime, an argument had broken out amongst the French leaders. Albret, the Constable of France and Marshal de Boucicaut insisted that the English should be allowed to reach Calais unchallenged, while the joint commanders, Orléans and Bourbon, maintained that this was a heaven-sent chance to destroy the English army, tiny compared to their own, and get rid of their king forever.

On 20 October, the day after Henry's army had crossed the Somme, trumpets announced the arrival of more French heralds, this time sent by Charles of Orléans, John of Bourbon and Constable Albret to deliver a challenge to the English army on the field. This was common practice in medieval warfare: knights from either side fought a duel to prevent the inevitable loss of life that a full-scale conflict would involve.

But Henry was having none of it, replying simply that he would march on. They could find him wherever he happened to be.[3] He may have regretted this answer, or at least some of his soldiers must have done so, when, shortly afterwards, they saw traces on the muddy road of the large French army that had recently passed that way.

Unperturbed, at least outwardly, Henry pushed on north-west for Calais for another four days. By this time, his men-at-arms were wearing at least part of their armour in case of sudden attack, it being known that the French army, joined by a much larger force near Bapaume, was advancing only a short way ahead of them.

On 24 October, having crossed the small River Ternoise, the English, tired and dispirited, saw for the first time what they faced. Like a swarm of locusts, the massive French army blocked their way to Calais. It was probably this horrifying sight that prompted Sir Walter Hungerford to exclaim that he wished the king had 10,000 more archers under his command, to which Henry replied that 'since God would be there to protect his people, they would make do with what they had.'[4]

He then gave a strict order that the night was to be passed in total silence as his men slept in the orchards and fields round the village of Maisoncelle.

The English soldiers, many of them ill with dysentery, lay on sodden ground on a night of heavy rain. Their misery was worsened by the tantalising sounds of talk and laughter from the French forces gathered round their campfires. Men were throwing dice for their future prisoners, who would fetch large ransoms, some even for the English king, so great was their confidence of victory on the next day.

By this time, a force of about 50,000–60,000 men had assembled in answer to King Charles's call to arms. A great wave of patriotism had swept the country, bringing men from Picardy, Artois, Flanders and Hainault, the domains of Burgundy, who himself refused to obey his sovereign's call to arms, and forbade his son Philip of Charolais to do likewise, despite his desperate pleas. Had Burgundy, still in disgrace for his treacherous communication with King Henry, been allowed to command the French army, how different the outcome of the battle might have been.

Despite their lack of experience, the two young commanders of the huge French force had every reason to be confident of a forthcoming victory on the eve of this encounter. Charles of Orléans in particular was elated, buoyed up with excitement at the thought of leading his men to triumph in what promised to be the final defeat of the tyrant who had dared to invade French soil. Inspired by curiosity, unable to rest, he ordered his friend Arthur of Richemont to assemble about 2,000 of his knights and archers to accompany him, under cover of darkness, to the edge of the English camp. Arrows were loosed at them by sentries hearing their approach. The French briefly returned fire, but this being only a reconnaissance, Charles ordered his force to withdraw. Returning, he was knighted – by someone unspecified in the name of King Charles – an honour conferred even on great nobles for bravery in the field of war.

Very early the next morning, King Henry, fully armed except for his helmet, heard three Masses before putting on a spherical bascinet helmet encircled by a golden crown, an act of deliberate provocation to his enemies, who could thus pick him out from afar. He then mounted a small grey horse before giving orders for the army to take up position in the field. This was an area of recently ploughed land, hemmed in on one side by a wood wherein lay the village of Azincourt and on the other by another wood surrounding the village of Tramécourt. The field was narrower at the English end than on that occupied by the French army.

Henry had only about 6,000 men, an estimated 1,000 men-at-arms and 5,000 archers who dismounted to fight, their horses being led behind the lines. The archers were placed on the flanks of the infantry, stretched in a thin line across the field. Placing himself in the centre, conspicuous with his shining crown and banners of the Trinity, the Virgin and St George beside him, Henry made himself a target for the enemy as he had so carefully planned.

The French army had fewer archers and consisted largely of men-at-arms wearing heavy steel armour that reached below their knees. Their legs and arms were well covered, their heads encased in steel helmets.

Foremost, in the front line, stood the nobles. For three hours, between nine o'clock and noon, the two armies faced each other, waiting for the other to make a move across the churned up, slippery ground. In the end it was Henry who began the battle, shouting 'In the name of Almyghti God and Saynt George, avaunt banarer! And Saynte George, this day thyn help.'[5]

The English advanced slowly until the French came within range of their arrows. There, on command, the archers drove the stakes they had cut on the king's instruction into the ground to form a palisade. Then drawing their bows they fired with such great speed and accuracy that the sky darkened as though hidden by deadly rain.

The French cavalry charged, but their horses were impaled on the stakes. Those that were not threw their riders and headed back into the great mass of foot soldiers, causing great confusion as they advanced, rank upon rank. Eighteen of the French nobles, led by the Lord of Croy, had sworn that they would knock the crown off the English king's head or die in the attempt and easily picked out the English king. They nearly managed it.

Surging forward in the melee, one of them got close enough to crash his sword on to Henry's bascinet, holing it and breaking off part of the crown, before he himself was killed. Henry fought on in the midst of the scrimmage as if demented. His youngest brother, Humfrey, Duke of Gloucester, who fought 'like a lion', was wounded by the Duke of Alençon. Encumbered by his heavy armour, Humfrey lost his footing and fell helpless in the mud. His men would have left him for dead, but the king rushed forward with reinforcements and stood between his brother's legs keeping the enemy at bay till the wounded Humfrey had been carried to a place of safety.[6] Alençon himself – the handsomest man in France, beloved of so many fair ladies – then fell, immobilised in steel. Stretching out his hand towards Henry, he was giving his name and surrendering, when one of the guards sprang forward to kill him with a massive blow from a battleaxe.

The attack dissolved in confusion. The heavily armoured foot soldiers stumbled through the heavy soil as flight after flight of arrows continued to take their dreadful toll. Behind them, blocked by the piles of fallen bodies, the remainder of the French army broke ranks and fled.

Charles Duke of Orléans was probably one of the band of eighteen high-born Frenchmen following the Lord of Croy in what amounted to a suicidal attempt to kill Henry. In the press of bodies crushing him on all sides, he too slipped and fell to lie helpless under the weight of his new armour, until others crashed on top of him, trapping him beneath a pile of dead. Bruised and nearly suffocated, gasping with all his failing strength for breath, he was found and pulled out from below the pile of corpses by English soldiers, who, recognising him and guessing at the worth of his ransom, shouted with jubilation at thought of the prize money in store.

The casualties on the French side were horrendous, estimated at no less than 7,000 men. Amongst them, Albret the Constable and Jacques de Chatillon, Admiral of France, and two brothers of the Duke of Burgundy, the Duke of Brabant and the Count of Nevers, headed the list of fallen nobility, which touched nearly every aristocratic family in France. On the English side, the king's uncle, the Duke of York was killed, but the losses, estimated at only 400 to 500, were minor in comparison. Altogether, it is estimated that between 7,000 and 10,000 Frenchmen died at Agincourt that day, 700 or 800 of them nobles.[7]

On the evening of the battle, just a short way from the field of slaughter, Henry knighted several of his men at arms for their bravery. Amongst them, it is said, was a young Welshman, Owen Tudor, descended from one of the rebel lords whom Henry had subdued with such force just a few years before. In the moment of victory, if the story be true, Henry had singled out Tudor for honour, confirming his predominance over his Welsh subjects.

In Paris, an atmosphere of fear, verging upon panic, spread throughout the city. It was generally believed that the apparently invincible English army would abandon its advance upon Calais to march south-west to attack the capital. The relief was great when it was learned that King Henry had not changed direction, but was heading for Calais on his way to take ship back to England.

With him went his noble prisoners, to whom he showed great courtesy. Charles of Orléans, wracked with guilt and misery that his great friend John of Alençon, with whom, only recently, he had shared so much happiness, had died while he himself survived, was almost stunned with grief. What had happened seemed almost incomprehensible, as the details raced through his mind. He saw again the ring of torches burning round him, lighting the night, and felt the blade touching his shoulder in honour of his rash but successful sortie on the English camp. He heard his friends congratulating him, amongst them those who had tried to dissuade him from taking, what they had felt, to be a dangerous and unnecessary risk. Then once again, in that mad rush towards the banner marking out the English king, he felt his feet slipping as men pressed against his back. Stunned by the fall before regaining consciousness, he relived the horror of finding himself trapped, imprisoned in his armour, and unable to move as other men fell on top of him, pinning him helpless to the ground.

Told that this particularly valuable prisoner was refusing food and drink, Henry rode up to him to ask him why. Inventing an excuse for his abstinence, Charles replied that he was fasting, a falsehood the king instantly perceived. Wasting no time in false comfort at the sight of his obvious misery, the black hollows of sleeplessness plain beneath his eyes, Henry the soldier, hardened by years of fighting in which he had seen so many men die, did not attempt to find words of consolation for the abject young man who stood before him. Adrenalin, from his own triumph, still coursing through his veins, he nonetheless understood the reasons for the grief and responsibility for the deaths of so many, which Charles, inexperienced in battle, felt were his fault. Calling him cousin, he urged him to be of good cheer, telling him that God had given him the victory, not because he deserved it but to punish the French. He laid the guilt on the Almighty, hoping it might ease what he recognised as the almost unbearable weight of misery in Charles's mind.

Nothing that Henry or anyone else could say would help Charles escape what seemed like a blanket of sheer misery throttling the very processes of his mind. He rode on in deep depression, hardly able to comprehend that, in the space of only twenty-four hours, such unimagined disaster had taken place. Not only were so many friends and relations now dead, or badly wounded but, as it gradually became plain to him, France itself was denuded, damaged beyond comprehension, both King Charles and the dauphin being now at the mercy of John of Burgundy.

At Calais, while they waited for the ships to be prepared, Orléans gave money to his three pages for their journey home. They probably took with them the new steel armour he had ordered for the battle, he being forced to wear the damask robe that King Henry had ordered for each of his noble prisoners. He was, however, allowed to send for his secretary, Robert de Tuilières, to join him in Calais before taking him to London, since it was obvious that he would need clerical assistance in the administration of his duchy during his absence.[8]

Reaching London after a horrendous crossing lasting for four days, he entered the city on the eve of his twenty-first birthday, unaware that a quarter of a century would pass before he would see France again.

6

A Country Robbed of Rule

In Paris, the members of the French royal family, shocked and saddened by the death and imprisonment of so many of their friends and relations, were nonetheless thankful that they themselves had been spared. For Catherine it seemed that the whole of her future life had changed course. Under the present circumstances, her arranged marriage to King Henry must inevitably be annulled.

Perhaps she was grateful. The English monarch who had committed the dreadful atrocity of ordering the deaths of the French prisoners at Agincourt must be a monster, more heartless even than his soldiers who, if the stories brought back by survivors were true, had robbed the dead where they lay.

Catherine, at the age of 17, was confident that, in the event of the cancellation of her proposed marriage to the supposedly bestial King of England, she would soon be disposed of by her mother in betrothal to some other influential man. Becoming aware of her beauty, not only from the roving eyes of courtiers, and some of their lewd advances, but from the spoken admiration of her waiting women, she was also in no doubt as to her worth in furthering her mother's political ambitions. Confused and to some extent frightened by the uncertainty of all that was happening around her, she waited with apprehension for what the future might bring.

It seems likely that it was because of fears for her safety that Queen Isabeau had sent her youngest daughter to join her sister Marie in the comparative security of the religious order of Poissy, housed within stout stone walls. Marie, who may have been delicate, would eventually become a prioress, but a life of seclusion was not for Catherine. It did not suit her disposition, and she was now a prime bargaining chip in the eyes of her ambitious mother.

Life in a convent for a young girl, uncommitted to taking vows, can in many ways be likened to that in the boarding schools of later days. Although not remembered as intellectual – the scribes were too taken with her beauty to pay attention to her brain – Catherine must have received at least some education in accordance with the custom of the time. While the great mass of people were illiterate, churchmen and the sons and daughters of high-born people were at least taught to read and write. Catherine's now dead brother-in-law, Richard of England, had been both surprised and delighted to find that Isabella, young as she was when she married him, could understand and even write some Latin which, from the time of her engagement as the future Queen of England, she had been told that she must learn.

If Isabella had been so well educated, it is likely that Catherine, the possibility of a marriage to King Henry of England foremost in her mother's mind, had been likewise instructed in Latin, conceivably even a few words of Greek. It was not necessary to learn English, Anglo-Norman French being the language of the English court.

Taught by the nuns, Catherine learnt the finest embroidery stitches, a skill which, in the absence of books, other than religious tracts, killed many long hours in the convent. She may also have been shown how to make simple remedies from pounded down and distilled herbs, used to soothe the pain of the most common minor ailments, such as headaches, toothache and eye complaints, which the nuns in their charity administered, not only to each other, but to the poor.

As she followed their instructions, Catherine must have let her mind wander to her future prospects. Marriage to a man of similar standing was the only way of life open to women of high rank. None but those driven by religious conviction to enter a convent, or girls thought too physically weak to withstand the very grave risks of childbirth, could avoid marriage.

Catherine's older sister Marie, whether for reasons of health or a desire to serve God, chose to take a nun's vows, but Catherine, restless by nature and striking in looks, yearned for the outside world. Isolated as they were, confined by thick stone walls, Catherine and Marie heard only whisperings brought in by tradesmen, or by people afflicted by illness, devotedly nursed by the sisters, who knowingly risked infection from diseases, even the deadly plague, in their commitment to the sick.

With the uncertainty of her future ever present in her mind, Catherine could only hope, and perhaps pray, that her mother would find her a husband who would take her away from the life which she found so constricting, to a place where, whatever the circumstances, she might at least have some of the freedom for which she so deeply longed.

7

The Conqueror

Henry sailed back to England a hero. All over the country, church bells were ringing out in joyous acclamation of his triumph.

Meanwhile, in France, where his victory was barely recognised by chroniclers, the overpowering Bernard VII, Count of Armagnac was at once ordered to the royal presence at Rouen, where Charles VI made him Constable of France, replacing Charles of Albret, who was killed at the Battle of Agincourt. The country was in a perilous state. John the Fearless, Duke of Burgundy was intent on seizing the capital, and only 16 miles from Paris. Many of his supporters were ready to rise up in arms for him, so hated were the Armagnacs, followers of the new Constable.

On 18 December the situation worsened with tragedy as the dauphin Louis suddenly died, not yet 19 years old. He had been in poor health and of delicate appearance, but the reason for his death is unrecorded. It may well have been tuberculosis, so prevalent at the time. But for the people of his country, there could only have been one cause. The young prince was broken-hearted at the death of so many of his friends in the defeat of Agincourt.

The untimely death of Louis meant that the political power of the two parties contesting rule in France suddenly and dramatically changed. Although married to Margaret, daughter of John of Burgundy, Louis had become the figurehead of the Orléanist (Armagnac) camp, which, in 1415, held dominance in France. However, John, Duke of Touraine, who at the age of 17 succeeded his brother Louis as dauphin, was married to Jacqueline of Hainault, only daughter and heiress of Duke William II of Bavaria and Margaret of Burgundy, a sister of John, Duke of Burgundy.

It had been at Burgundy's instigation that Duke William had abducted Isabeau's younger children when she had called for them to join her and the Duke of Orléans at Melun. This time as Queen Isabeau tried to arrange a meeting with her daughter-in-law Jacqueline, plainly to win her to her side, she was thwarted by the girl's father Count William, who not only refused to countenance any form of reconciliation with the Burgundians, but banned John of Touraine from entering Paris.

Surprisingly, however, in that moment of crisis, John of Burgundy decided that an immediate attack on Paris would be too dangerous, and withdrew his army to his own country of Flanders.

In February 1416, the Count of Armagnac nearly succeeded in defeating a smaller English force under Thomas Beaufort, Earl of Dorset, at Valmont. Only after a desperate struggle did Dorset's soldiers manage to reach the safety of their garrison in Harfleur. Besieged there, the English defenders must have blessed the dissension between the rival parties in France when, in May, Armagnac returned with his army to Paris to ruthlessly put down a rising by supporters of the Duke of Burgundy.

But the respite was brief and it was not until 15 August 1416 that a fleet of English ships sailed from Southampton under the command of Henry's brother John, Duke of Bedford. Although wounded he defeated the larger and less manoeuvrable vessels of the combined French and Genoese fleet in the narrow estuary of the river, in what was called the Battle of the Seine.

That King Henry did not sail to fight in person in that contest was due to the fact that he was deep in negotiation with Sigismund, King of Hungary, the elected King of the Romans and Holy Roman Emperor since 1410.

Prior to reaching England, Sigismund had visited Paris to be lavishly entertained by the king and the dauphin and the dukes of Berry, Anjou and Armagnac. Aware of their distress that so many of their relations were kept prisoner in England, he promised them that he would try to negotiate a peace with King Henry. Arriving in London at the beginning of May 1416, he was lodged in the king's own Palace of Westminster and magnificently entertained. At a great banquet in Westminster Hall, Charles of Orléans sat on his right with the Duke of Bourbon (also a prisoner), and on the emperor's left was the Count of Hainault and, among other nobles, the Archbishop of Reims.

Yet despite the discussions that took place during the emperor's nearly four-month visit, no agreement regarding France was reached. This was largely due to Orléans's father-in-law, Count Bernard of Armagnac, who not only laid siege to Henry's newly conquered town of Harfleur, preventing him from provisioning the garrison, but dissuaded Charles VI and his council from accepting proposals for a three-year truce, suggested by the Count of Hainault, on the grounds that Henry could not be trusted.

Subsequently, on 15 August, the day of the Battle of the Seine, the English king signed the Treaty of Canterbury, a complete offensive and defensive alliance by which the Holy Roman Emperor, as his ally, warranted all his claims on France.

Sigismund and Henry sailed to Calais to meet the French ambassadors in an attempt to reconcile the warring parties. Henry wanted to conclude a treaty with Burgundy, but John the Fearless prevaricated, seeing the English king's continued aggression with the Armagnacs as potentially playing into his hand. Agreeing only to neutrality, he returned to Flanders. Sigismund went back to the Council of Constance, leaving Henry to renew his attempts to conquer France, assured of the Holy Roman Emperor's support.

In April 1417 tragedy again hit France when John of Touraine, dauphin for just a year following the death of his brother Louis, also died suddenly. Naturally there were rumours of poison, directed mainly at Queen Isabeau, his mother. Both her sons had been under the influence of Burgundy, with whom Isabeau was now in league.

Most outspoken was Yolande, Countess of Anjou, who had so recently stayed with Charles of Orléans in those halcyon days before his capture at Agincourt. The protectress of the new dauphin (another Charles, who had also been at Blois and had since married her daughter Marie – their romance apparently started there) Yolande defended him with all the ferocity of a tigress protecting her cub. Refusing Queen Isabeau's orders to return Charles to the French Court, she told her:

> We have not nurtured and cherished this one for you to make him die like his brothers or to go mad like his father, or to become English like you. I keep him for my own. Come and take him away, if you dare.[1]

Queen Isabeau, ever fractious, now quarrelled violently with Count Bernard of Armagnac who, in May 1417, imprisoned her, first at Blois and then at Tours. Having confiscated her jewels and money, he then dismantled her household and dismissed her ladies-in-waiting. While this was happening, her youngest daughter Catherine presumably remained in the convent at Poissy, her whereabouts being unrecorded elsewhere.

Given the circumstances, it is hardly surprising that the location of the queen's sixth daughter should have been of little consequence to the chroniclers of the time. Paris and indeed all of northern France was alive with frightened speculation about what was about to occur. It was now common knowledge that the King of England was gathering a flotilla of ships to transport an army even greater than before across the channel to invade France again.

Their arrival was expected in the spring of 1417, this being the time when, the winter over, most campaigns began. But Henry was so involved in raising money to equip his enormous army that it was not until 30 July that he set sail, once more from Southampton, with the largest army ever to leave England's shores. The soldiers alone, including nobles, knights, archers and artillerymen, were estimated to number 16,400 in all. In addition went another force, of smiths, carpenter, miners, servants, horses and a mass of every kind of equipment, from scaling ladders to guns.

Having disembarked at Touques, west of the mouth of the Seine, the great invasion of France began on 1 August 1417. Henry first advanced upon Caen, the most important fortress of lower Normandy, which he captured in just over two weeks. From there he advanced through Normandy, converging upon Rouen, capital of the province and one of the largest and most important cities in France. The town was defended by Burgundians for John of Burgundy, bitterly opposed to the Armagnacs, and was equally determined to defy the claims of King Henry of England to sovereignty of France.

Thus began the siege which, for the next six months, would bring such terrible suffering not only to the soldiers but to the people of the town.

8

A Princess Lovely to the Eye

Isabeau's imprisonment lasted a mere six months. Rescued by John of Burgundy, she went with him to Chartres, where he was planning an attack on Paris. Once free, and now openly allied to Burgundy, Isabeau proclaimed herself regent before, at Troyes in January 1418, delegating her authority to Burgundy, naming him Governor of France.

John the Fearless made his long-awaited entry into Paris on 29 May 1418, a date remembered for what became known as the Burgundian terror, the slaughter of the Armagnacs. On 12 June, Charles of Orléans's father-in-law, Count Bernard of Armagnac, was himself murdered. The dauphin, who refused his mother's invitation to ride with her into the city, fled before he could be captured to find safety with his Armagnac supporters at Melun. Thus, it was John the Fearless who rode into Paris with Isabeau, on 14 July, to be received by the pathetic mad King Charles.

Two weeks later, on 31 July 1418, English guns began to batter the walls of Rouen. Burgundian soldiers, ordered there by John the Fearless, defended the city. The siege was to last over six months, during which time, in the words of the historian C.L. Kingsford, Henry was involved in 'an astute diplomacy which kept the French divided while Rouen perished'.[1]

Negotiations had already begun the previous November, when an English delegation led by the Earl of Salisbury had met with the dauphin at Alençon on the border of Normandy. Already claiming the provinces of Aquitaine and Guienne, through heredity from Edward III, Henry had told his delegates to demand the surrender of Anjou, Maine, Touraine and Flanders, while emphasising his possession of his recent conquests in Normandy. Having done so, they were to suggest that their king's proposed marriage to the Princess Catherine would unite the English and the Armagnacs to defeat the Duke of Burgundy and restore the dauphin to his rightful place as heir to the French throne.

Henry was in fact playing a waiting game, to see which of the warring French parties most greatly favoured his cause. Within days he was in touch with the Duke of Burgundy, suggesting a meeting at the Pont de l'Arche at the beginning of the following month. The Burgundians, on this occasion, were led by the Bishop of Beauvais and Cardinal Orsini, who arrived with a portrait of Princess Catherine.

Henry was delighted with the picture, painted from life, of a pretty fair-haired girl. Nonetheless, he demanded 1 million gold crowns for her dowry, together with all the land, granted by King John the Good of France, in the Treaty of Brétigny in 1360.

Catherine, in the convent at Poissy, heard news – so terrible it could only be whispered – of what had occurred at Rouen. Believing that the Duke of Burgundy was coming to help them, the defenders of the town had held out against the English battering the walls with their guns. But Burgundy had betrayed them, believing that, in view of Henry's successes in his latest Normandy campaign, a liaison with the king would be more advantageous than defiance. Henry had built a new wooden bridge above Rouen, supported by chainbooms from bank to bank. Over and above this, he even had ships dragged overland, out of range of the besieged, to be anchored in midstream. Rouen was completely cut off, while ships bringing food and ammunition to the invading army from England could still come up the Seine.

Holed up within the town, people began to starve. They ate cats, rats, dogs and even mice in a desperate bid to survive. Then horror mounted as it was reported that of the estimated 12,000 refugees who had thronged into the town for safety, those unfit to fight had been thrown out through the gates. Henry had given orders that they must not be allowed through the English lines and, with the gates shut behind them, they were left in the fosse where most of them, including many children, died of cold and starvation in the worst winter weather.

Even the English pitied them. On Christmas Day, the king had offered them food. The Captain of Rouen, haughtily refusing such charity, had at least been persuaded to allow two priests to take some small sustenance and communion wine to the wretched survivors in the wide open ditch below the town's walls. But the suffering had all been useless. On 13 January 1419, the men of the beleaguered garrison of Rouen who, like the townspeople they protected, were dying of hunger, finally surrendered. Henry, now the conqueror of all Normandy, was in an even stronger position to dictate his terms.

Catherine knelt with the sisters of Poissy in supplication for the souls of the dying and the dead. But even as she did so, thoughts of what her own future might hold must have been foremost in her mind. King Henry had again expressed his wish to marry her and negotiations between him and her parents were, as she knew, already under way. She often discussed what the outcome of these consultations might be with her sister Marie. In particular, they speculated as to what Henry himself was like, this man they called the greatest soldier in Europe, who seemed able to conquer anything, be it city, church or village in Normandy, a province he claimed through his descent. Was he the ogre some thought him to be, ready to put old women and little children to the sword? Or was he, as others claimed, very much maligned? One thing above all else remained obvious, both the sisters agreed: Catherine would soon have to meet him, helpless as the sacrificial lamb. Their predictions were realised when a courier arrived at the convent with orders from her mother that she travel with an escort immediately to join her at Meulan, where she was to meet the English king.

Henry, on a much stronger footing now that Rouen, the capital city of Normandy, was in his hands, tried to arrange a meeting with the dauphin at Évreux in early spring. But because the dauphin Charles prevaricated, the parley never took place. Henry was unperturbed. By this time, John the Fearless was sending envoys to confer with him and, playing one party against the other, he seized on the chance to make fresh demands for the return of the other French provinces that had once been English.

Steadily advancing towards Paris, Henry had reached the town of Mantes by May. From there, his emissaries indicated to John of Burgundy that the King of England might be persuaded to modify his claims to the French kingdom were he to marry the Princess Catherine, as had been previously arranged.

The Burgundians having replied that this might be acceptable, negotiations were made for a conference to be held forthwith. On 7 May, at Vernon, Henry issued powers to two delegates, Sir Walter Hungerford and Sir Gilbert Umfraville, to negotiate a marriage between himself and the Princess Catherine. At the same time, Hungerford and Lord Fitzhugh, the king's chamberlain, were given full authority to negotiate the terms of a final peace between the two kingdoms. This time the English king demanded a written undertaking from the French involved in these very important discussions that, unlike at Évreux, they would in fact make an appearance.

The meeting, postponed from mid-May, took place at the end of the month. The site, carefully chosen, was a field called 'le champ de la chat' lying close to the western gate of the fortress town of Meulan, built on two small islands in the Seine, a mere 20 miles to the north-west of Paris. The ground was prepared with great care, measurements being taken by pacing them out, to decide what should be common space.

Finally, on 29 May 1419, assured that all was ready, King Henry left Mantes with his entourage of knights and courtiers to attend the conference. On the same day, Queen Isabeau arrived at the agreed destination with the Duke of Burgundy, King Charles being absent, convulsed by a fit of madness.

The two parties met within a beautifully decorated pavilion erected between the rows of tented camps, English on one side, French on the other. The first meeting, conducted in French, ended with a feast, before, two days later, the real business began. Henry, bored with the palaver, waited in increasing impatience for the preliminaries to be done. This was the moment he would meet the Princess Catherine, whose beauty in the portrait already presented to him remained so vivid in his mind.

He was not to be disappointed. The Burgundians, on behalf of Queen Isabeau, had surpassed themselves, spending no less than 3,000 florins on dressing her daughter in a robe of rich material embroidered with jewels. But it was not her clothes, nor even her elaborate headdress, again encrusted with precious stones, which so impressed him that, according to those who witnessed it, he stepped forward to meet her, his eyes alight with joy.

The French historian Monstrelet wrote that 'she was very handsome, of high birth, and of the most engaging manners.'[2] Others described her as a tall girl, 18 years old, slim and fair-haired, who blushed prettily as Henry stepped forward to greet her in welcome.

Catherine, for her part, was profoundly relieved to find that her future husband was nothing like the brute she had been led to expect by her ladies. Much whispering and nodding of heads had gone on as they dressed her in the richly embroidered robes. Some had been sympathetic, believing that their poor little princess was being traded for political reasons; others were convinced that this marriage was the first stage to captivity, shut up in that great tower in London, from which few, if any, emerged alive. From all that was said, she expected a stern warrior scarred by the wounds of war, but instead she found a slim, athletic man whose long face and aquiline nose gave him a stern countenance, but whose hazel eyes lit up with pleasure at the sight of her.

Though he had seen her portrait, Henry probably expected to some extent to see a replica of her mother: dark-haired, squat and stout, with a voice that grated on the ear. Instead he found confirmation of all that his ambassadors had promised in the young woman whose soft sweet voice had only a slight French intonation as she spoke in halting English.

The meeting with Catherine was the only happy event of that conference, which ended in stalemate as far as Henry was concerned. While he did agree to withdraw his claim to the sovereignty of France, on condition that he kept his recent conquest of Normandy and the lands agreed to by the Treaty of Brétigny, Isabeau and Burgundy haggled over Catherine's dowry. They eventually consented to a sum of 800,000 crowns but insisted that 600,000 crowns should be deducted as the amount never recovered from the dowry of her sister Isabella when she had returned to France following the death of her husband King Richard. Also, still unaccounted for, was the jewellery that Isabella had possessed.

Henry and Burgundy had a private meeting to try to settle these differences but, discovering that he was already in touch with the Armagnacs (or dauphinists, as they now were called), Henry turned in fury upon Burgundy, who spat insults on him in return.

The only result of the conference at Meulan, on which so much money had been spent, was that John the Fearless, Duke of Burgundy and Charles, Dauphin of France signed a treaty of mutual support on 11 July 1419. This alliance, made on a causeway at Pouilly-le-Fort, near Melun, seemed to signify the end of an era of dispute. With the warring factions united, it seemed that King Henry's hopes of winning France had finally come to an end.

9

The Royal Captives

The English invasion of France, particularly its effect upon the dissident factions in that country, had been keenly observed through the reports of ambassadors by the Duke of Albany, then regent of Scotland. Albany, insisting that he had no money to pay the ransom the English demanded, had made certain that his nephew, King James, would remain in captivity in England for fourteen years. Efforts to gain his freedom had proved futile. On succeeding his father, Henry V had been quite happy to keep him as a political prisoner, who might prove useful as a bargaining chip at some future time.

That was soon to come.

The Aulde Alliance, a treaty of mutual support, had joined Scotland and France for 115 years since 1295. Since then, French rulers had used Scotland much as a whipping boy, promising money and men for war against England, to the ultimate benefit of France. Albany, now nearly 80, had long sat on the fence, waiting to see whether the Armagnacs or Burgundians were worth supporting, particularly which party would pay most for mercenary soldiers, before tying his colours to the mast.

In July 1418, two Scottish bishops sent to France, had returned with letters from Queen Isabeau and Burgundy asking Albany for help in the war with England. The following year, when it seemed probable that the fall of Rouen would unite the French factions to expel the enemy, another

Scottish delegation visited John, Duke of Burgundy, in Provence. But, only two months later, it was the catastrophic news of the culmination of the feud between John the Fearless and the dauphin which would bring negotiations to an end.

In Scotland, the Duke of Albany saw his chance to deliver a blow to England by supporting the Armagnacs and the Dauphin of France. A few Scottish men, looking to gain financial reward and enrich themselves with plunder, were already in the service of the dauphin. In May 1419, Sir William Douglas of Drumlanrig joined them with 150 men-at-arms and 300 archers. Following this, an embassy was sent from France to Albany, who played his cards cunningly, treating with both the Burgundians and the Armagnacs, much in King Henry's style. Henry became more aware of what the Scots were planning when, on 22 July, some citizens of Bordeaux managed to write to him, telling in great secrecy that the King of Castile, an ally of the dauphin, was not only preparing to besiege their town, but had sent forty ships to Belle-Île, off the coast of Brittany, to take men on board and sail to Scotland to transport an army to France.[1]

The message arrived in time for the Duke of Bedford to warn the sheriffs of Devon and Cornwall to try to intercept the Castilians as they sailed north. Whether they actually reached Scotland is not clear, although, on 5 September 1419, Henry received an appeal for help from the people of Bayonne which confirmed his enemy's intention of sending Castilian ships from Belle-Île to Scotland. The origin of the vessels, transporting the forthcoming expedition to Scotland, is unknown.

What is known is that an army of 6,000–7,000 men, commanded by John Earl of Buchan, Albany's second son, who was Constable of Scotland, and the latter's brother-in-law, Archibald, Earl of Wigtown, heir of the powerful Earl of Douglas, defeated an attempt by the Bretons to beat them back to sea, landing at La Rochelle before the end of October. They received a rapturous welcome from the dauphin who, calling Buchan 'another Messiah', loaded him and the other leaders with honours and rewards.

The Scots contingent, sent to defend the Loire Valley, made themselves extremely unpopular by stealing everything they could find. Dubbed 'sacs à vin' and 'mangeurs de mouton', they were hated by one and all. Despite their unruly behaviour, the arrival of the Scottish contingent in France was a cause of grave concern to Henry, who wrote to the Bishop of Durham:

'Windsor Castle', by E.W.
Haslehust, 1866. (Windsor
Castle, 1910)

Leeds Castle, Kent. (Courtesy
of William Bray and The Leeds
Castle Foundation)

John the Fearless (1371–1419)
Duke of Burgundy, oil on panel
(fifteenth century). (Louvre, Paris/
Bridgeman Images)

Portrait of Richard II 'The Westminster
Portrait', 1390s. (Westminster Abbey,
London/Bridgeman Images)

Effigy of Henry IV (1367–1413) on his tomb in Canterbury Cathedral (fifteenth century). (Canterbury Cathedral, Kent/Bridgeman Images)

King Richard resigns the crown. (Courtesy of the Bibliothèque nationale, Paris)

White Hart, from 'The Wilton Diptych'
c. 1395–99, egg tempera on oak (verso),
Master of the Wilton Diptych (fl.
c. 1395–99). (National Gallery, London/
Bridgeman Images)

S. Harding Del. d Sculp.

QUEEN KATHARINE.
Henry V.
From a Curious Limning in a M.S. Prayer Book, in the Possession of
M.r Edwards Bookseller Pall Mall.

London Pub. Sep. 1. 1792. by E & S. Harding Pall Mall.

A stipple engraving, probably of
Catherine de Valois, by Silvester
Harding. Published in 1792 by E. &
S. Harding, after an unknown artist.
(Copyright the National Portrait
Gallery, London: NPG D9396)

Charles of Orléans and his two younger brothers receiving instruction. From a manuscript of Sallust's *Jugurtha*. (Bibliothèque nationale. Mss. lat. 1747, fol. 1)

King Henry arrives at Troyes. (Courtesy of the Bibliothèque nationale, Paris)

Portrait of Philip the Good (1396–1467) Duke of Burgundy, Weyden, Rogier van der (1399–1464). (Musée Communal, Bruges/ Bridgeman Images)

Portrait of Henry V (1387–1422) oil on panel (see 106922) (fifteenth century). (National Portrait Gallery, London/ Bridgeman Images)

Portrait of Isabella of Portugal, *c.* 1450, oil on panel, Weyden, Rogier van der (1399–1464). (J. Paul Getty Museum, Los Angeles/Bridgeman Images)

Royal Ms 16 F II, f.73: Tower of London and shipping, with Charles, Duke of Orleans seated in the Tower writing, from *Poems of Charles Duke of Orleans c.* 1500 (vellum) (sixteenth century). (British Library, London/copyright British Library Board. All Rights Reserved/Bridgeman Images)

THE TOWER OF LONDON.

The Tower of London. (From *An Escape from the Tower: A Story of the Jacobite Rising of 1715*, 1896)

Joan of Arc at the Siege of Orléans. (Courtesy of Bibliothèque nationale)

I would that ye … set a good ordinance for my North Marches, and especially for the Duke of Orléans and for all the remnant of my prisoners of France, and also for the King of Scotland; for as I am secretly informed by a man of right noble estate in this land that there has been a man of the Duke of Orléans in Scotland and accorded with the Duke of Albany … that there should be found ways to the having away specially of the Duke of Orléans, and also of the king … Wherefore I will that the Duke of Orléans be kept still within the castle of Pontefract, without going to Robertes place or to any other disport, for it is better he lack his disport than we were deceived.[2]

Convinced as he was, almost to the point of being paranoid, of connivance between the Scots and the French to free his most important prisoners, whose ransoms promised such great gain, Henry wrote again to the Chancellor on 1 October, ordering him to keep special watch over the dukes of Orléans and Bourbon:

For their escaping, and principally the said Duke of Orléans, might never have been so harmful, if any of them escaped nor prejudical [sic] unto us as might be now, if any of them escaped, and namely the said Duke of Orléans, which God forbid.

Robert Waterton's personal friendship with Charles of Orléans must have been reported to him. So he exhorted the chancellor to enquire 'if Robert of Waterton use any reckless governance about the keeping of the said Duke' and if so to write to him about it 'that it be amended':

for no trusting, fair speech nor promise that might be made unto him, nor for any other kind of cause, be so blinded by the said Duke that he be the more reckless of his keeping.[3]

As a result of this correspondence, Charles of Orléans was removed from Pontefract and the kindly Robert of Waterton, to the care of Sir Thomas Burton, warden of Fotheringhay Castle in Northamptonshire, one of the greatest, most unassailable fortresses in England. Standing on a low hill, the castle looked over the River Nene and towards the parish church of the village of St Mary, where lay the bones of King Henry's brother, Edward, Duke of York, whose body had been boiled down, as was the custom of the time, and brought back to his own green lands after the Battle of Agincourt, where he had been killed. As he looked towards the church across the low-lying fields, Charles may have thought with the wry humour, seen in some of his poems, that, although a prisoner, his life had been spared.

Charles did at least have the company of some of his fellow captives at Fotheringhay for Arthur of Richemont, the Count of Eu and Marshal Boucicaut were all in the custody of Sir Thomas Burton at this time.[4] Held as he was in such a heavily guarded castle, it is difficult to understand why Henry appears to have been convinced that Charles and his fellow prisoners were treating secretly with the Scots. As is shown by the lack of safe conducts, Charles himself received no visitors from France in the year 1419. Constantly worried about money, on 3 September he wrote a long letter to his chancellor, Guillaume Cousinot and his treasurer general, asking them for financial help. Reminding them of previous correspondence on behalf of his financial agent, Jean Victor, he told them how he had been forced to spend so much of his own money towards his debts that he was now himself in need. He asked them to send funds, as quickly as possible, towards the expenses of himself, his young brother John and the other hostages, adding that if they could speed up the ransom to free John, 'he and I will be very grateful to you and very pleased'.[5] Charles ended this long letter by referring to a missive from Cousinot saying that he was sending a servant to him to discuss his wants. Telling him to use all possible means to get a safe conduct from the King of England, 'so that I can send you my wishes about all my needs', he ends by assuring Cousinot that he is 'in good condition and health'.

On 8 June, Henry gave orders that his two most important French prisoners, Charles of Orléans and John of Bourbon, be taken to London by their respective custodians to appear before the king's council, 'for certain reasons particularly moving us', not specifying what they were. Bourbon was then allowed to go to Dieppe under escort, to try and find money for his ransom, and Arthur of Richemont was permitted to return to Brittany to try to persuade his brother, Duke John, whose loyalty was vacillating, to adhere to Henry's cause.

Charles, with his brother Philip fighting for the Armagnacs, was certainly loyal to the dauphin, but the enormous price asked for his ransom still prohibited his release. Another in much the same position was King James of Scotland, known to have been held in Windsor Castle in 1419 on the evidence of a certain Thomas Haseley, who petitioned Henry VI some time later for a reward, claiming that he had frustrated a plot of the Lollard Thomas Payne, and had:

> arested hym ate mydnyght in a place beside your castell at Windsor where atte that tyme was the kyng of Scottes kept as a prisoner to your seid fader and that the same nyght this seid traitour shulde have … goen with the said Kyng toward Scotland in proof whereof I founde in the traitour's purs a cedule wreten of alle places of gistes and loggynges appointed for hem fro Wyndesore unto Edynbourgh in Scotland.[6]

So there was some foundation to Henry's concern that his prisoners should not try to escape, after all. But at least, as far as James was concerned, there could be no hope of his liberation while Henry was campaigning in France and fighting continued on the borders with Scotland. Meanwhile, like Charles of Orléans, he had no alternative other but to continue to endure the frustration of imprisonment while others of less importance were set free. Most insulting of all was the knowledge that his uncle Albany, though claiming he had no money for his nephew's ransom, had volunteered to lend no less than 30,000 livres to the Duke of Burgundy.

The meeting between the dauphin and the Duke of Burgundy took place on 10 September 1419. The place for what promised to be an agreement on the unification of France was the bridge at Montereau, across the Yonne at its conference with the Seine, some 40 miles south-east of Paris.

Both sides were suspicious of the other's intentions, barricades being constructed at either end of the bridge at whose centre, under a covered enclosure, the prince and the duke were to confer. At the appointed time, about five o'clock in the afternoon, the participants arrived. Cautiously, they advanced towards each other, each escorted by ten councillors, their swords in scabbards buckled to their sides, to meet in the centre of the bridge as agreed.

Both parties were anxious, their nerves strung to a pitch. The Duke of Burgundy, bending the knee to the dauphin, was just about to rise when the pommel of his sword got in the way and he put his hand on it. The men standing behind the dauphin thought that he was drawing it. Instinctively then, one of them sprang forward swinging down his axe, striking Burgundy's head such a blow that it split his skull.

The dauphin stood back in horror, clearly bewildered by the shock of what had taken place, while his men rushed upon the Burgundians in what became a free fight. The dauphin was accused of planning the murder, of which he may have been innocent, it was one of his knights, most probably the commander of his army, Tanguy du Châtel, who struck the deadly blow.

Nonetheless, whether or not he was personally involved in causing the violent death of John of Burgundy, a man he had detested from childhood, the act in itself proved to be disastrous for France. The warring parties, who might, had the conference succeeded, have united against the common enemy, were now ever more inflamed by hostility. Later, the Carthusian Prior of Dijon claimed that 'the English entered France through the hole in the duke of Burgundy's skull.'[7]

10

The Treaty of Troyes

K ing Henry was not slow in exploiting the situation to his own advantage. The murder of John the Fearless had left three claimants to the throne of France. The dauphin was now excluded by the horrendous nature of the crime for which, although probably innocent, he was forced to take the blame. Philip, the new Duke of Burgundy, was held to be too young, which left Henry himself, renowned as an able and clever administrator, as the most likely candidate for the crown.

Henry's ambassadors could safely assure the Burgundians that, were Henry to marry Catherine, he would not hand over power to his brother-in-law, the dauphin. Duke Philip would regain the benefices his father had lost during the past two years. Henry would assist him in wreaking vengeance on the killers of his father. And lastly, one of Henry's brothers would marry a Burgundian lady.

On 2 December, at Arras, Duke Philip agreed to support the truce made between Henry, King of England and Charles, King of France. By its terms Henry would marry Catherine and their children would succeed to the throne of France. Catherine would become Queen of England without any dowry from France.

Philip of Burgundy then agreed to support Henry in receiving royal dignity in France and enjoying the benefits entailed. On the death of his future father-in-law Charles VI, the crown would immediately pass to Henry and from him descend to his heirs. All people in France would swear fealty to him and live by his rules. Anyone opposing him would be condemned. Philip then swore that together they would effect the punishment of the dauphin while Henry would help Philip to secure the inheritance of his wife, Michelle, sister of both Catherine and the dauphin. A large deputation of French men then left Arras to join Henry at Rouen.

On 24 December 1419, with the agreement of Queen Isabeau and the government of France, a truce was arranged with England. Most importantly, its terms included the lifting of the economic blockade placed upon Paris in June, which meant that ships could now come up the Seine, held by the English from its mouth at Harfleur, to relieve the near-starving inhabitants of the city.[1]

On Christmas Day 1419, Henry signed the contract with his great seal, confirming the concessions already made to Duke Philip and his council at Arras. He then gave an emphatic assurance of his wish to cement the peace by his marriage to Princess Catherine and that of one of his brothers to one of Duke Philip's sisters. Henry, having promised that he would support the duke's rights in France, Philip agreed, in return, to help Henry secure his privileges in that country. Together they would overcome the dauphin, Henry swearing not to ransom him or any of his collaborators without the agreement of Philip. Philip, Duke of Burgundy, soon to be known as 'Philip the Good', then marched south from Arras to join Queen Isabeau and her pathetic mad husband King Charles at Troyes, arriving there on 23 March 1420.

Henry had already left Paris on 8 May to ride south-east for about 100 miles to the city of Troyes, centre of the great wine growing district of Champagne. He had crossed the Seine and was nearing the town when the young Duke of Burgundy rode out to meet him, clothed in the black of mourning. He bowed from his saddle, at the head of a great cavalcade of citizens and dignitaries eager to pay homage to the king who would soon be their monarch.[2]

Henry reached Troyes on Monday 20 May. The town was crowded and to make room for his entourage, Queen Isabeau and her daughter Catherine moved out of their lodging at the sign of 'La Couronne' a lodging in the marketplace attached to a Franciscan convent nearby. It was Burgundy who took Henry to the king, who greeted him with a few mumbled words. He then knelt before Queen Isabeau, regal in her high, pointed headdress, and full robes, before turning to Princess Catherine to kiss her with great joy.[3]

On the following day, 21 May 1430, the Treaty of Troyes was signed in the Cathedral of Troyes on the terms already arranged. Henry and Isabeau entered the church to meet in the centre of the great aisle. They then walked side by side to the high altar. The articles of the treaty were read, and consent given by both parties, before Henry signed the texts with the seal used by his great-grandfather Edward III to ratify the Treaty of Brétigny.[4]

Enguerrand de Monstrelet, about whom little is known other than that he was born in Picardy, of a family of the minor nobility, continued the work of Froissart in the two books of his *Chronique* which, spanning the period 1400–44, gives 21 May 1420 as the date of the Treaty of Troyes. The principal conditions are couched in the following terms:

> Charles by the grace of God, King of France. To all our Bailiffs, Provosts, Seneschals, and to all our chief officers of justice, greetings. Be it known that in sign of lasting agreement and perpetual peace we have, in this our town of Troyes, just concluded and sworn a treaty between us and our most dear and well-loved son Henry, King of England, heir and regent of France, in his name and our own on behalf of the Crowns of France and England, in token of his marriage to our dearly-beloved daughter Catherine and of other articles made and agreed between us for the welfare and good of ourselves and our subjects and for the security of this country …
>
> ITEM it is agreed that immediately upon our decease and for all time thereafter the crown and sovereignty of France with all rights and appurtenances thereunto belonging shall be transferred in perpetuity to our said son Henry and his heirs.
>
> ITEM Since we are for the most part prevented from attending to the cares and government of our kingdom, the practice of exercising and ordering the public weal shall for the duration of our life be given over to our said son Henry, with the Council of Nobles and wise men who are in obedience.[5]

Henry was therefore to be responsible for the administration of justice in the kingdom and for its defence; he was to have the power to make appointments to vacant places in the national and local government; he was authorised to submit to the king's obedience all places rebelliously held by the Armagnacs; he was to be known in France as 'our very dear son Henry, King of England and heir to France'; only French-born citizens were to be appointed to King Charles's personal entourage; neither Henry nor Burgundy was to enter into any treaty with the man Charles 'calling himself Dauphin' and whom the king does not even here call 'son'.

Perpetual peace was thus to be assured between the two kingdoms. Monstrelet adds that:

> At this time there gathered in Paris many representatives of the three estates of the kingdom of France according to instructions previously issued, and many councils were held ... As a result the gabelle (or salt tax) quarter-taxes and other levies were renewed, with the exception of the tax on grain.

King Henry, meanwhile, finalised negotiations with the French court, which resulted in the arrangement of a formal treaty. By its terms Henry was to marry Princess Catherine, her dowry, disputed by her mother and Burgundy, being finally fixed at 40,000 crowns a year to be paid by the English exchequer. Her parents were to remain king and queen only until her father's death. Then Henry would become King of France, and his heirs would succeed him forever. The dauphin was to be disinherited and Henry, in the meantime acting as regent, would rule the country under French law.

Catherine, in that spring of 1420, was a confused and unhappy young woman. Aggrieved, on the one hand, at the way her brother had been treated, excited on the other, at the thought of being married to Henry whom she had recognised during their brief introduction, if unwillingly, as a virile, charismatic man.

Henry V of England was now King of France, an achievement crowned by the official announcement, made on the very same day, of his betrothal to Princess Catherine with whom, the chroniclers say, he was already deeply in love.

On Saturday 1 June, Henry visited the royal family at their lodgings. Together they attended vespers with Duke Philip, still in mourning for his father, a sombre figure in black.

The following day, Trinity Sunday, 2 June, Henry and Catherine were married in the Troyes parish church of St John. The guests, English and French, and the young Scottish king and his attendants, were dressed in great magnificence. Musicians played: there was feasting and much rejoicing. Only the spectral figure of Philip of Burgundy was again a sharp reminder of the horrific event that had taken place, less than nine months previously, on a bridge over the same river flowing past the town of Troyes.

Immediately following her marriage, Catherine was given her own household, consisting mostly of English men and women. At its head was Margaret Holland, wife of Thomas, Duke of Clarence, the brother who, until Catherine made Henry a father, was her husband's heir. Three high-born French ladies were part of her household entourage, however, with whom, as she left her parents, Catherine could speak in the language familiar to her since birth.

11

Summons for the Scottish King

As mentioned, also in attendance at the wedding was another guest, James, the young King of Scotland, a quietly spoken, rather heavily built young man of 24. During his long years of captivity in the Tower of London and the other prisons to which he had been sent when London became a death trap during epidemics of plague, he had become studious, devoting his time to reading both English and Latin texts, and writing the verses which had won him recognition as a poet by others of a literary mind. James was of middle height and already showing signs of the stoutness which would one day become obesity. Now, at Henry's wedding, a prisoner as well as a guest, James wore a cloak edged with ermine over his doublet. He was robed as befitted his standing as a king, at the cost of the English exchequer.

It was the knowledge that some Scottish soldiers were now reinforcing the garrison of Melun that had prompted King Henry to reimburse himself for the cost of providing for his long-held captive by bringing him to France. In doing so, he reasoned that if Scots serving the dauphin refused to obey their own monarch's orders to surrender to the King of England, they could die as traitors to their country.

Summoned by special messenger, James had reached Southampton by the end of the first week of May 1420. He had already received money from the Duke of Burgundy who, in view of the complaint that he had no rev-

enue from Scotland, had authorised James to take customs from Scottish
merchants. Then in May and again in July, in addition to other gifts of
money to cover his expenses, there are entries amounting to nearly £150
for the purchase of armour, horses, tents, banners and other 'apparatus' for
going to the French wars.[1]

Henry was nothing if not an exhibitionist. Knowing well the effect of
visual splendour on impressionable people, he made sure that James sailed
as a king. Equipped according to his rank, he had voyaged to France with a
small retinue of his own, his ensign flying at the mast. Thus, as a chronicler
some thirty years later was to write:

> was soon armyd Charles King of France Harry the fifte kinge of England
> and the saide James king of Scottes Alle with thayre banners displaied
> in one quarelle ayenste the kingis rebelles and enemies of France thane
> cleped Armenacs.[2]

The festivities following the wedding lasted a mere two days before the
combined English and Burgundian armies left Troyes to march for Paris.
The kings of England and France and the Duke of Burgundy rode together,
the King of Scots somewhere in attendance.[3] Behind them came the Queen
of France and her daughter, the new Queen of England.

Reaching Sens, on the River Yonne, the commanders called a halt until
the dauphinist garrison surrendered. Then the army moved on, following
the Yonne to its confluence with the Seine at Montereau, where John the
Fearless had so recently been hacked to death. Because of the Burgundians'
lust for revenge on the dauphinist garrison of the castle, the ladies were left
well away from the scene of battle.

The siege of Montereau proved to be a test of Henry's strength. Battered
by cannon balls, the walls of the town were further weakened by mines,
exploding in tunnels dug towards the foundations. The besiegers' thirst
for vengeance reached fever pitch on the death of an English knight, and
eighteen French prisoners were hanged in view of the defenders. At last, on
24 June, Montereau surrendered.

The next day, Philip of Burgundy found the grave where his father had
been so hastily buried. The body, carefully exhumed, was discovered to
be fully dressed, the wounds appearing to be fresh. Taken from the parish

church, the corpse of John the Fearless was carried to its final resting place in the Burgundian Charterhouse in Dijon. Henry and Burgundy, accompanied by their entourage, then proceeded down the Seine towards Paris. But, blocking their path to the capital was the fortress of Melun, well fortified and provisioned to withstand a prolonged attack.

Henry knew already that Melun, defended by a large garrison reinforced with Scottish soldiers, would give strong resistance, this being the reason he had summoned James, King of Scotland, to France. In the event, although fierce confrontation was expected, Melun proved to be more resistant than had been assumed.

As the castle withstood the assault of English cannon, mines were again dug to try to penetrate beneath the walls. King Henry himself, Burgundy and the other commanders, struggled with the enemy in hand-to-hand fighting, grappling with mailed fists in the dim torch-lit tunnels. Famously, as they groped like moles along the tunnels, Henry had a close encounter with the Lord of Brabazan, captain of the town.

The siege dragged on. Henry went to Corbeil to see Catherine and her parents, before bringing her father back with him to order his subjects to surrender. Bluntly, and heroically, they refused, as did the men of the Scottish contingent, when ordered to submit by their own king. A prisoner himself, James had little alternative but to obey when told by King Henry to command his countrymen's surrender. The Scottish commander, James's cousin John, Earl of Buchan, responded with open insolence to Henry, proclaiming his refusal to acknowledge any order given under compulsion.[4] At Sens, the Scottish soldiers had been allowed to leave unharmed. But at Melun the siege dragged on, testing both the mental and physical strength of the assailants, to the point where the ethics of chivalry were lost in exhaustion and anger verging on despair. When the men of the gallant garrison finally did capitulate on 18 November 1420, defeated by both hunger and illness, the twenty Scots mercenaries and their captain were executed for having taken arms against their sovereign.[5]

To his credit, Henry recognised the impossible position in which James stood, and did not blame him for failing to force his subjects to surrender. In fact, it seems that some form of friendship developed between the two kings, so different in character but only a few years apart in age. Henry himself, most enigmatic of men, seems to have recognised the steely determination belied by the outward diffidence of his young Scottish prisoner.

Certainly it would seem that, a month later, on 1 December, when Henry made his formal entry into Paris, King Charles beside him, James of Scotland was amongst the many English and French nobles who followed in procession behind them, cheered by the ecstatic people of the city, who loved a spectacle whoever their rulers might be.

In contrast to the colourful sight of the train of French and English nobles following the two kings, was the stark figure of Philip, Duke of Burgundy, riding in full mourning, in solitary sorrow on the other side of the street.

The pageant continued, the joyful atmosphere enhanced by fountains running with wine and rose water. The next day saw yet more festivities as Queen Isabeau and her daughter Catherine, the new Queen of England, arrived in Paris. The citizens rejoiced, believing that war and famine were soon to end. But the price of bread would double by Christmas, and the weather was so cold that rabbits were said to be freezing to death in their burrows. Children were scrambling on the dunghills searching for food, but provisions were readily supplied for the man now calling himself king.

The two royal families, and, it is thought, also the King of Scots, spent the Christmas festival in Paris when, as reported by Monstrelet, the true state of the hierarchy was revealed. While the still ailing King Charles 'was poorly and meanly served' at the Hôtel Saint-Pol, it was impossible to describe the true magnificence in which Henry and Catherine and their courtiers lived in the palace of the Louvre, where much feasting and other celebrations took place.[6]

This was the height of Henry's triumph, when Paris was at his feet. But in the midst of the rejoicing he received an urgent message from England asking him to return. On 27 December, he left Paris for Rouen with Catherine, his brothers and the Scottish King James.

Travelling through the countryside to Normandy, they saw many signs of the ruination of the land wrought not only by the English invasion, but also the civil war between the Burgundians and the Armagnacs, which had resulted in anarchy in so many parts of France. The lawlessness had now reached a point where the collection of revenues had to be enforced by soldiers. Even round Rouen the roads were dangerous. Bands of brigands, most of them mercenary soldiers who had been disbanded, some Burgundian, some Armagnac, some even English, swooped down to rob and kill any travellers who did not take the precaution to protect themselves by riding in groups with armed guards. None of the greater Norman lords had given allegiance to Henry. Nor had the bishops of the province accepted the new dispensation. So many men had left the country in the hopes of gaining plunder in the recent fighting that fields were lying uncultivated and barns were bare of grain, even when they had not been ransacked.

So appalling was the state of many places that the Abbot of Bec had protested that farming was impossible in his area, when the only people left to manage the land were women, children and men too old to steer a plough. The predators were not only human. It was officially recognised that since the English invasion, the number of wolves had increased so greatly in Normandy that they were attacking in packs.[7]

Despite the deprivations of the outlying country, the royal party, accompanied not only by the king's brothers and the King of Scots but by an assemblage of nobles and their squires, arrived to a warm welcome from the citizens of Rouen, who presented gifts to Catherine and openly received them with joy. Travelling slowly due to the short winter days, they had arrived just in time to join in yet more celebrations, it being the Festival of Epiphany (according to the Gregorian Calendar) on 6 January.

From Rouen, in the last week of January of the new year of 1421, they began their journey to England. With them were Henry's brother, John, Duke of Bedford, his cousin the Earl of March and the Earl of Warwick. Travelling through Poix, Amiens, St-Pol and Thérouanne, they reached Calais, where a delegation of merchants and citizens came to meet them bearing yet more fine presents for Queen Catherine before she left her native land. Having boarded the waiting ship, they reached Dover on 1 February with a favourable wind.

Their welcome was ecstatic. Crowds waited their arrival, amongst them some of the barons of the Cinque Ports, who, at sight of the royal standard, waded into the sea to carry their king, now also regent of France, and his bride, of whose beauty so much had been heard, on their shoulders through the surf to the shore.

12

The Hero of England's Return

Engeland went mad for her soldier king. After a short stay at Canterbury, Henry went on ahead to prepare the welcome for Catherine as she entered his capital city. The couple were reunited at Eltham Palace before the royal party progressed to London, going through villages and hamlets where people lined the road, the women dropping curtsies, the men raising hats and caps, all of them cheering as their rulers passed. All of the royal party must have compared the people of the south of England with those in the French province of Normandy such a short way across the sea. Historians of the time have told how the English were both healthier and taller than the French, who, particularly the poorer people, showed the effects of famine caused by the incessant wars in their lack of height and thin frames.

Rapturous as was their welcome in the country, it was nothing to their reception in the City of London. There the merchants, headed by Richard Whittington, four times Lord Mayor of London and now, in his late seventies, still a member of Parliament, had outdone themselves in financing a celebration of pageantry such as had never been seen. Giants, made of some material like papier-mâché, guarded the gates, bowing to the queen as she entered, heraldic lions rolled their eyes, minstrels played and choirs sang in welcome and, best of all, wine flowed through the conduits to the joy of the population, most of whom were soon cheering in drunken joy.

The streets themselves were strewn with ivy and branches of evergreen trees. Bunting festooned the fronts of houses from whose windows people craned to get a better view.

Catherine, amazed and a little bemused by such a welcome, was cheered all the way to the Tower of London, that grim stone edifice of which she had heard so much, both from James of Scotland, so long a prisoner within its walls, and others. Today, however, the royal apartments had been made ready to receive her. Fires heated the rooms scented with rose petals and lavender, fresh linen covered the beds, and comforts of every sort were provided on Henry's instruction.

The next day, Catherine was driven to the Palace of Westminster in a magnificent coach pulled by a great team of horses and escorted by a phalanx of nobles and heads of the city guilds, the latter resplendent in white robes with red hoods, each craft distinguished from the others by embroidery.[1]

Then, on Sunday 23 February the bells of the city peeled out in clamorous joy as the Archbishop of Canterbury, Henry Chichele, crowned Catherine Queen of England at Westminster Abbey, so recently restored to its full glory by Richard Whittington under Henry's direction.

The coronation was followed by a most lavish banquet in Westminster Hall. Henry, as ordained by protocol, was absent and the new queen sat with the archbishop on her right and 'at the Quenes borde the day of the Coronacon ... On the lyfte hand of the queen the kyng of Scottes yn a State'.[2]

James was immaculately dressed for the occasion. From the royal wardrobe he had received a doublet of cloth of scarlet, and a cape of fur, most probably ermine, trimmed as befitted his rank. About the same time, he was given two tunics decorated with his coat of arms, two standards beaten similarly, two pennons beaten with his badges, four shirts and 'pillowsleaves' (sleeves were then separate items to the shirts).[3]

Among those gathered within the great hall of Westminster were Henry's brothers, the bareheaded dukes of Bedford and Gloucester, together with all the most highly born lords and ladies of the land.

That King James was placed beside Catherine would seem to be an indication of Henry's personal liking for the shy, quietly spoken young man. It may even have been at Catherine's request that he was seated beside her. Some sources claim that she begged her husband to release James and allow him to return to Scotland. Henry's father, King Henry IV, had made no idle boast when he joked that he would teach his Scottish prisoner to speak French. James spoke the language so fluently that he and Catherine could converse together as they sat through the tedium of the banquet.

Was it at this point that James fell in love with her as later evidence suggests? This beautiful, charming young woman who, as the wife of the King of England, was so utterly beyond his reach? Certainly it seems logical to think so. Thrown together by circumstance, they had much in common, both aliens, totally dependent upon Henry of Lancaster for their existence in a country hostile to their native lands.

Fish and shellfish, whelks, porpoises and sturgeons were served, but there was no meat because it was Lent. Three enormous courses were mercifully interspersed with 'subtleties' in whose ingenious designs the London pastry cooks had outdone themselves.

The coronation over, it would seem to have been at this time, when Henry and Catherine were living briefly at Westminster Palace, that a refugee arrived at Dover begging to be given asylum. Catherine was ecstatic for it proved to be none other than her childhood friend and former-sister-in-law, Jacqueline of Hainault, whose marital problems, long the talk of the courts of Europe, had already reached London through travellers crossing the Channel from France.

Jacqueline of Hainault, daughter and heiress of William III, Duke of Bavaria, had first met Catherine after her betrothal, as a child of 5, to Catherine's elder brother John, Duke of Touraine. How well Catherine remembered those family visits to Jacqueline's home in the legendary castle of Le Quesnoy, where Jacqueline's father, who treated John as a son, greeted them so warmly. She and John had been so happy together, but had had to adapt to changed circumstance when, six months after they were married (by special dispensation of the pope due to their close relationship), John's elder brother Louis, Dauphin of France, had died suddenly, supposedly broken-hearted by the defeat of Agincourt, and John had found himself the dauphin and future King of France.

Jacqueline, with her haughty bearing, had seemed born to be a queen, though with her high colour and large features, she was no great beauty. But then fate, having appeared to favour them, had struck with devastating cruelty when John had died of the dreadful wasting disease of tuberculosis, at the age of only 19, just a year after the dauphin. Further tragedy had then followed when Jacqueline's father had died only two months later, in June 1417, leaving her alone and widowed, sovereign of Holland, Hainault and Zeeland.

Jacqueline's sorrow at the loss of the two people closest to her was worsened by the attitude of her uncle, the Duke of Bavaria, who claimed both Holland and Zeeland as his own, as male heir. There was civil war. Vulnerable and unable to cope with a rapidly deteriorating situation, Jacqueline had been saved, or so it had appeared, by her other uncle and guardian, John the Fearless, Duke of Burgundy, who had arranged a marriage to the Duke of Brabant, believing that he would ensure her protection. Brabant, much older than Jacqueline, had proved to be incompetent to the point of imbecility when, in 1420, he actually ceded Jacqueline's property to the Duke of Bavaria for twelve years. Landless and furious, Jacqueline turned to Robessart, Lord of Escallion, the one man in her court she believed she could trust.

Together they had made their plans. Already, on 1 March 1421, King Henry had granted a passport to Jacqueline and her mother to visit her estates in Ponthieu, which included the right to go to Calais. She had told her mother at Valenciennes that she would be away for a few days while she went to Bouchain – probably on the excuse of business or of seeing a friend. Subsequently, she had set off in the right direction from Valenciennes, but shortly thereafter Robessart had met her with a company of about sixty armed men. Together they had ridden on to Calais, a journey that took two days. Arriving there, Jacqueline guessed from their welcome that they were expected. From Calais she had sent messages to Henry to ask his permission to cross the Channel to England. Would he or would he not allow her to come?

She had climbed to the battlements every day, gazing across a narrow sea that was sometimes rough, sometimes calm, looking for a sign of a ship returning with the fateful news. At last it came. Her heart soared with happiness. Henry sent her a warm welcome. She was going to escape.

To her joy, when she landed at Dover she had found that the king had sent his brother Humfrey, Duke of Gloucester, Warden of the Cinque Ports to meet her, an honour she knew had been given to the Holy Roman Emperor Sigismund some five years before.[4]

For Humfrey, much occupied as he then was in instructing the barons of the Cinque Ports to assemble a fleet of fifty-seven ships to transport his brother's army to France, it was just another duty. But for Jacqueline, if rumour be true, it was something else. Three years earlier a match had been suggested between her and John, Duke of Bedford, elder of the king's two younger brothers, but negotiations had fallen through. Disappointed, Jacqueline had then been told of the younger brother, better looking and less serious. Now, as he stood before her, a tall young man with fair hair, a cloak falling from his shoulders over a corselet of steel, she may have decided that all she had heard of him was true.

Jacqueline had grown up with John of Touraine at Le Quesnoy. She had grown to love him but as a sister rather than a wife. She had nursed him through the long days of his illness when, towards the end, as the knowledge of death came upon him, he had clung to her, begging her to help him, helpless as a small child.

In contrast, the young man before her moved with the boundless energy of the leopards she had read about. She may have watched, her heart beating faster, as he strode about the quay, shouting directions at the men who were plainly his servants, as to how to load the few possessions she had brought with her into panniers carried by mules. This done, he turned towards her with a brief, yet to her mind, perhaps, captivating smile, to help her to mount the side-saddle carried by the quiet palfrey he had found for her. On its back she travelled on to London where, in the Palace of Westminster, she curtsied deeply first to Henry and then to Catherine, who took her by the hands to raise her to her feet and embraced her with great joy. Risking the anger of Burgundy, Henry gave generous hospitality to Jaqueline of Hainault, largely to please Catherine, who is known, in return, to have given him £1,333 to further his forthcoming campaign.

Following her coronation, Catherine went with Henry on a progress through the kingdom. The aim of this was primarily to allow people to see them but, also, on a purely commercial basis, it was to thank the wool merchants and others for the money already contributed and to ask them for further loans. Behind the royal party came the commissioners, giving receipts for advances from both lay and clerical contributors throughout the country. Many gave joyfully to their idolised king, but others resented what the contemporary chronicler Adam of Usk described as 'grievous taxation of people … unbearable, accompanied with murmurs and with smothered curses among them from hatred of the burden'.[5]

Henry rode on through the West Country and Catherine then joined him at Coventry before the middle of March, and it seems to have been then that the heir to the throne was conceived. Together they went on to Leicester, where King James of Scotland is known to have been with them for the festival of Easter, that year on 23 March. The wardrobe accounts show payments for the carriage of various forms of 'harness' for the king and queen and the king of Scots from London to Leicester, while the Issue Rolls show that James spent 50s 1d at Leicester on Maundy Thursday.[6]

The fact that he travelled with Henry and Catherine on their triumphal tour of the Midlands is further indication of the royal couple's apparent affection for the young Scotsman in their power. It was a friendship soon to be tested, however, even if he found James to be good company. Henry had no scruples about using him as a bargaining chip in the ongoing negotiations concerning his release.

At the end of May arrangements were made with the Earl of Douglas, that 200 Scottish knights and 200 mounted archers should join Henry's army in France. In return, James would be sent back to Scotland within three months of the end of Henry's forthcoming expedition to France, on the pledge that he produce hostages and marry Joan Beaufort, niece of the increasingly powerful Henry Beaufort, Bishop of Winchester, who now lent Henry £18,000 to further his campaign.

From Leicester they travelled on to Nottingham, Pontefract and York, small market towns in those days when the whole population of England was just over 2 million strong. Henry went on to Beverley alone. He was just on the point of leaving the town when a messenger arrived, riding in frantic haste from London, bringing him terrible news.

His army had been totally and unexpectedly defeated at Baugé, a town 20 miles from Angers. Thomas of Lancaster, so recently made Duke of Clarence, had misjudged the strength of the joint force of French and Scottish soldiers commanded by the earls of Buchan and Wigtown. On Good Friday, which fell that year on 21 March, Clarence had encamped in the little town of Baugé when a Scots prisoner revealed that the main force of the combined enemy army, in all about 5,000 strong, was nearby.

Clarence, wanted to attack at once but was faced with the problem of Easter Sunday's proximity, two days away. Fighting was prohibited on this most sacrosanct of days. Unfortunately, nearly all his archers had been allowed to go out foraging but, shouting to the Earl of Salisbury to follow him with all those he could muster, Clarence had set out to attack a greatly superior force of men with only 1,500 men of his own.

A hundred Scottish soldiers had held a bridge against his advance as their full force formed into battle order. Once across the bridge, Clarence had been unhorsed by a Scottish soldier whose lance had broken in his hand. Lying helpless on the ground, Clarence had been killed by another Scot who, proclaiming his triumph, had raised his victim's golden coronet on the point of his lance.[7]

To the French prisoners held in England, the news of the English defeat at Baugé had the thrill of an electric shock. So many English men of rank had been taken. The 18-year-old Earl of Somerset and his brother Edmund, sons of the now widowed Duchess of Clarence by her first marriage to the Marquess of Somerset, were amongst them, as was the Earl of Huntingdon.[8] The French prisoners must have hoped it was a good chance for exchange.

Charles of Orléans's sister Margaret and his 11-year-old daughter Jane certainly believed this to be so. On 1 April, just a week after the battle, they and the Chancellor Guillaume Cousinot sent letters to the dauphin at Tours, beseeching him to write to the Scottish lords who had taken the prisoners to suggest a possibility of exchange against the ransoms of Charles and his younger brother, John of Angoulême. Only 12 when he was sent to England as one of seven hostages (the others being members of Charles's household) to guarantee his brother's debt to the Duke of Clarence, John was now 19.

Three weeks later, on 21 April, Chancellor Cousinot of Orléans went, on Charles's orders, to see the dauphin and the Scottish lords to beg them again to agree to the proposals. At the same time, again on Charles's instruction, a messenger was sent to the Duchess of Clarence and the Duke of Exeter, both in France, to suggest the exchange of Thomas Beaufort – thought to have been an illegitimate son of the duchess of whom she was particularly fond – for John of Angoulême.

It was all to no avail. In no way would Henry even consider the release of Charles of Orléans who, as first cousin and heir of the French king, was the trump card in his hand. Though Charles was given some freedom and treated in a manner befitting his rank, he nonetheless had to endure the frustration of knowing that his sister Margaret had been given in marriage by the dauphin to the brother of the Duke of Brittany – the privilege of bestowing her hand should have been Charles's own. More galling still, his daughter Jane was formally betrothed to the Duke of Alençon – son of and reputedly as handsome as Charles's great friend killed by Henry's henchman at Agincourt – to whom she had first been promised by Charles himself when she was only four months old.

It was useless appealing to Henry. Overcome by anxiety at the defeat of his army, he was also convulsed with grief over the loss of his brother, for whose death he felt partly responsible. Thomas, next in line to the throne, had been closest to him in age, his confidante and companion throughout so much of the French campaign. Just three months ago he had seen him at the Christmas celebrations in Paris, so much alive and with further triumphs ahead, as it had then seemed. His wife, the former Margaret of Holland, was now Catherine's chief lady-in-waiting. Henry would have to face telling her that Thomas had died.

Nonetheless, it was typical of Henry's iron resolve that he mentioned the tragedy to no one until the following day. Then, tight lipped, he said to those around him that he must return at once to France.

But before he went he found time to do two things, which a man with so much on his mind might well have been excused for putting off. First, he arranged an income of £100 a month for the Countess of Hainault, as long as she stayed in England. Then he found time to go to Windsor for the Chapter of the Garter on St George's day. There, in the chapel founded by his great-grandfather Edward III in the Lower Ward of Windsor Castle, making public display of the fact that he held him innocent of his countrymen's part in the tragedy of his brother's death, Henry laid his sword on the shoulder of the young man who knelt before him as he was knighted: James King of Scots.[9]

13

Return to France

On 10 June 1421, James sailed with Henry from Dover to Calais.
Once again he was accoutred from the royal wardrobe, as is shown
by the Exchequer Rolls.[1] Immediately prior to their departure, safe
conducts were issued to several Scotsmen 'to go to England and return'.
Amongst them was the Earl of Douglas, who 'for his love and affection to
and with the consent of James, King of Scots, given at the Earl's request',
swore to serve Henry for life from the following Easter 'against all enemies
by sea and land except for the King of Scots, with a force of 200 knights
and squires and 200 mounted bowmen in return for an annuity of £200
for his men and free shipment.'[2] Having obtained the allegiance of one of
the most powerful men in Scotland, Henry agreed to the temporary release
of James, on their return from the expedition on which they were about
to embark.

Reaching Calais in June, the English king found the situation in France
to be critical. The defeat of his army at Baugé had reawakened French
nationalism. The spell of Agincourt was broken. Brittany, after much
wavering, had joined the dauphin, and Paris itself was divided between the
Armagnac and Anglo-Burgundian parties.

The situation in France presented a new challenge for Henry, who was
still seething with anger over the death of his brother, though he now knew
that Thomas had acted rashly, ensuring his own untimely end. Once in

the country, Henry immediately began to reassert his authority by launching a renewed campaign. In one of his first actions he gave proof of what appears to have been his growing regard for James, placing him, together with his own younger brother, Humfrey, Duke of Gloucester, in charge of the siege of Dreux, the town originally fortified by the Romans about 35 miles west of Paris.

The castle, a formidable building surrounded by a double moat, stood well above the town. From the heights, its cannons rained down stones and balls of iron upon the besiegers, in open defiance of their assault. Plainly it was Gloucester, the experienced soldier, rather than James, who saw the possibility of attacking the castle from an adjoining vineyard, which he recognised as the weak point of its defence. By mining the vineyard under the protection of his guns, he managed to drive off the French defenders from a position from where it was possible to attack the town itself.[3] But in the end it was hunger, caused by the poor harvest of the previous summer, followed by a winter of intense cold during which English foraging parties had stripped the country of food, that forced this town on the border of Normandy to capitulate.

Following the surrender of both the town and castle of Dreux in the second week of August, James went with Henry to lay siege to Beaugency, whose town was taken, though the castle defied attack. Unwilling to waste more time in subduing a fortress of little importance, Henry took James with him and moved on to his major project, the attempted capture of the dauphinists' greatest stronghold, the city of Meaux, whose strategic position in the Marne Valley blocked the passage of the Anglo-Burgundian army towards the Netherlands.

The siege of Meaux, beginning on 6 October 1421, as he himself had anticipated, was to prove the greatest test of Henry's ability as a general. Defying him in command of the garrison was the Bastard of Vaurus, a man of well-known ferocity. Soon the attackers found that they faced not only the city's strong defences, but the late autumn weather as well. First there was rain, so cold and heavy that even the knights were constantly miserable and chilled, water seeping through their armour. Continually, persistently, the rain fell, until in December the Marne flooded, making it almost impossible for wagons carrying supplies and munitions to move.

Foraging was difficult and dangerous. Parties of French cavalry in the surrounding districts drove off English soldiers searching for food. Inevitably there was hunger: rations had to be shortened and the weakening men succumbed to disease. Typhus fever, the scourge of all armies, typhoid and above all dysentery began to debilitate and diminish the ranks. Henry himself was affected and it may have been here, during that long winter that weakened the constitutions of even the strongest of men, that he contracted the illness, believed to have been dysentery, that would ultimately cause his death.

Morale throughout the army was at a low ebb when a courier arrived from England with the news that at Windsor, Queen Catherine, her labour assisted by the presence of Our Lord's foreskin – that holy relic known as the silver jewel, sent specially from France – had given birth to a son. All over London bells rang out in a joyous cacophony of noise, while the mayor ordered 'Te Deums' to be sung in every church.

Though he believed Windsor an unlucky place to be born,[4] Henry was overjoyed. Not only did he now have an heir to the throne of England but his claim to the kingdom of France had just become more secure.

Because of his vital importance as commander of his army, Henry could not leave the subjection of Meaux, a city of such critical importance to his renewed campaign against the dauphinists in France. He did not return to England to attend the christening of his son. In any case, he could not have travelled back to England in time to be present at the ceremony, children being baptised either immediately or within a few days of their birth due to the high infant mortality rate at that time. In his absence, Henry's uncle, Henry Beaufort, the Bishop of Winchester and his brother, John, Duke of Bedford were the boy's godfathers, while Catherine's former sister-in-law, Jacqueline, Countess of Hainault, living with her at Windsor, was his godmother, and held him at the font.

Meanwhile, as Henry had foreseen, the Siege of Meaux dragged on interminably. Though he supervised every detail of the ongoing struggle to force the garrison into surrender, Henry, typically punctilious in every aspect, found time to arrange the establishment of his own household for the man who technically remained his prisoner, King James of Scotland.

James's bodyguard, consisting of four esquires, two valets and ten archers, was commanded by a knight named Sir William Meryng. The costs of various officers and esquires, in continuous attendance from 1 October 1421 to 9 September 1422, 'for the safe custody of the body of the same King of Scots under the governance of the King of England' involved the payment of £544 5s 1/2d, to John Waterton clerk of the king's kitchen.[5]

That Henry's largesse was not entirely free from exploitation is shown by his issue of safe conducts to other Scottish noblemen, who were directed to come from Scotland to the Tower of London and thence to the presence of the kings of England and Scotland.[6] Plainly he expected James's subjects to obey their sovereign's call to arms. No Scottish soldiers appeared. The Earl of Douglas did, however, send his secretary, William Fowlis and Sir Alexander Seton to confer with James, then at Rouen, in February.

Three months later, on 10 May 1421, Henry achieved his greatest tactical triumph when the city of Meaux surrendered after seven months of siege. The brutal Bastard of Vaurus was among those executed on charges of treason to the French crown.

Shortly after this victory, Henry sent his youngest brother Humfrey back to England, to take control of the country so that their other brother, John of Bedford, whom he had left behind as regent, could come out to join him in France. Humfrey, it seems, went with alacrity, eager to renew his acquaintance with Jacqueline of Hainault, whose great inheritance in Flanders – the wealth of which had become clear to him during his time in France – was something to which he now aspired.

14

Last Battle of the Soldier King

As the terms of the surrender of Meaux were being completed, Catherine embarked at Southampton to sail to France with her brother-in-law John, Duke of Bedford and about 1,000 soldiers to reinforce the army. Henry could not spare the time to go and meet her, so he sent James of Scotland to Rouen to await her arrival there. Catherine was now the mother of a 5-month-old son, the future Henry VI, whom she had left behind in England with his nurse, Elizabeth Ryman, in the safety of Windsor Castle. Landing at the English-held port of Harfleur, on 21 May, she travelled up the Seine to Rouen, a distance of some 60 miles.

Her happiness at seeing James who, from the time they had spent together, it must be assumed she regarded as a close friend, can be imagined. That there was no thought of intimacy between them at this point, if indeed there ever was, is indicated by the lack of rumours that gossip mongers, eager for scandal, would otherwise most certainly have got around.

From Rouen, still following the Seine, James escorted Catherine and her entourage, which included two English widows and some young ladies of high birth, towards Paris. At Mantes, she was greeted with the ringing of bells and with gifts of silver cups, bought at great cost from Paris. Finally reaching Vincennes, she was reunited with both Henry and her mother Isabeau on 26 May.

On the 30th they entered Paris, two ermine cloaks carried before Catherine as a sign that she was Queen of France. That James rode with them in procession is attested by Sir Thomas Myrton, who had been appointed his chaplain and would join him with a safe conduct from England to France on 8 July.[1] Again there was much rejoicing, the citizens honouring both Henry and Catherine with a performance of *The Mystery of the Passion of St George*. Henry and Catherine celebrated Witsun in Paris, probably staying at Vincennes.[2]

As before, the King and Queen of England were lodged in great splendour in the palace of the Louvre, while her parents again occupied their increasingly dilapidated quarters in the Hôtel Saint-Pol.

Monstrelet recorded the changes that were taking place. Decrying the abasement of the King and Queen of France, he claimed that the English thought only of power and pomp. Many Frenchmen were horrified by the way in which their king was being overruled, apparently deprived of all authority. Moreover, the decision to raise taxes caused 'much murmuring, but no rebellion since Henry was a man whom most people feared'.[3]

Henry's triumph at Meaux, eclipsing the disaster at Baugé, had once more established his reputation as the greatest military commander of his day. But two-thirds of France remained unconquered and the dauphinists, under Jacques d'Harcourt, were well ensconced in fortresses at the mouth of the River Somme. On 12 June, the French and English courts moved, first to St-Denis and then to Senlis, the small cathedral town some 25 miles to the north-east.

It was here, just three months after Henry's triumph over the capture of Meaux, that the illness he seems to have contracted during that siege showed itself in the gauntness of his face and thinness of his body, wasted by a fever the doctors could not relieve. Refusing to listen to their advice that he should rest and delegate command of his army, Henry continued to the newly conquered fortress of Compiègne.

There he was halted by bad news. The main dauphinist army was centred at Sancerre, some 70 miles upriver from Orléans on the Loire. From there Catherine's younger brother, the dauphin Charles, was laying siege to the English-held town of Cosne with a combined French and Scottish army, plainly intending to advance against Philip of Burgundy's capital city of Dijon.

The commander of the garrison of Cosne sent a desperate appeal for assistance, saying that if not relieved by 11 August, he saw no alternative but to surrender. True to his alliance with Burgundy, Henry immediately promised to join the relieving force at Cosne with all of his army.

But Henry was now ill. Returning from Compiègne to Senlis it was obvious, from his appearance, that he was a stricken man. The doctors attending him were too afraid to give him medicines to be taken by mouth, so a new physician John Swanwich, one of the leading medical experts of his day, was summoned from England.[4] On 7 July, Henry moved to the castle of Vincennes where, exhausted and burning with fever, his condition became so serious that the University of Paris organised processions to pray for his recovery.

It was then that this greatest, if most unmerciful, of English kings showed the true valour of his spirit when, unable to mount a horse, he had himself carried in a litter to conduct the relief of Cosne. His illness worsened until, at Corbeil, he was forced to stop. For two weeks he stayed there, getting better, or so it seemed. Hopes were running high until, to the horror of those around him, he had a relapse.

Finally submitting to his weakness at Corbeil, he handed over command to his brother John, Duke of Bedford. But so firm was the French belief that Henry himself would lead his army in the forthcoming battle that, even before the deadline of 11 August, the dauphin had withdrawn the siege.

Knowing he could go no farther, fevered and writhing in pain, Henry asked to be rowed down the Seine to Charenton, from where would ride to Vincennes. This time, nothing would induce him to travel in a litter, those who had the temerity to suggest it were met with a sharp rebuff. The King of England would not submit to the ignominy of travelling in a conveyance designed for women and children.

At Charenton he did manage to mount a horse, but the strain of sitting upright in the saddle proved beyond him. Submitting at last to a litter, he reached Vincennes on 10 August where, after three weeks of agonising and debilitating illness, he died on the last day of the month.

After 600 years, it is impossible to accurately diagnose the illness that killed Henry V. Smallpox has been suggested, likewise typhoid, but the most probable answer is that it was dysentery, an infectious inflammation rampant throughout his army, spread by human contact or contaminated water. The Scottish historian Walter Bower, the Abbot of Inchcolm, records the legend that those with Henry, both French and Scots, believed he was stricken with a disease known popularly as St Fiacre's evil. During the Siege of Meaux, he had ordered the plundering of some land dedicated to St Fiacre, a prince of Scotland or Ireland, thought to have been a monk, which no one dared to touch without incurring his wrath. Told of the possible cause of his illness by his doctors, superstitious as were most people of that time, Henry is claimed to have cried out, 'Wherever I go I am bearded by Scots dead or alive.'[5]

During the last three weeks of his life, when he knew he was dying, he gave instructions to his brother John of Bedford, and the members of his council, who stood around his bedside, as to the future administration of his English kingdom and the districts of France he had conquered. Bedford, who was to be regent of France and governor of Normandy, was also specifically entrusted with the guardianship of the 9-month-old King Henry VI, the son at whose birth Henry had been exultant, but who he had never seen. Some were surprised and others wondered why he made no provision whatever for Catherine, his young French wife.

Catherine was not with Henry when he died. She was at Senlis with her parents. Nor, it seems, was the Scottish King James, who is believed to have been at Rouen with his own household. Told of Henry's death, he rode quickly to Vincennes to lead the great funeral procession back to England.

Henry had always loved pageantry. Never had he known a more clamorous reception than when entering Paris with his bride, in that freezing December cold of 1520. Apart from extolling his own importance as King of England, it was the best form of propaganda at a time when most people were illiterate and every form of communication slow in the extreme. Spectacular as were the demonstrations of welcome on his return to England, both after the triumph of Agincourt and following his marriage to the daughter of the King of France, nothing pulled the heartstrings like the pathos of his funeral cortège.

Because of the distance it would have to travel in the heat of the early September sun and of the time involved, the body was dismembered and the flesh stripped from his bones by boiling. The corpse was then put in a wooden coffin before being placed in a larger one made of lead. Bypassing Paris, the coffin was taken to Saint-Denis, where Henry lay in state in the great church of St Denis, burial place of the French kings.[6]

From Saint-Denis, the cortège was transported in boats down the Seine to Mantes, where a vigil was held the following day, when candles burned as the church bells tolled. Henry's coffin was met by a procession before it was placed in the chapel. Leaving Mantes, preceded by a blaze of light from men carrying forty torches, it was placed in a carriage drawn by four magnificent heavy horses. Above rose a greater-than-life-size effigy of Henry wearing his royal robes, in his right hand a sceptre, in his left a golden apple. A silken canopy was stretched over the image against possible rain.

The cortège moved slowly, the king's replica jolting grotesquely below its cover as the carriage rolled over ruts in the road. Four days into its journey, on 19 September, as it neared Rouen, the people of the city watched from the rooftops as the procession approached, and came out to meet it. In the vanguard walked eighty Englishmen, all dressed in black, together with twenty of the leading citizens, each bearing a large torch. Following were the royal chaplains, all chanting dirges. Into the Cathedral of Notre-Dame went the great procession, amongst them all but the very young remembering the vision of King Henry on his brown horse, his cloak reaching almost to the ground, riding into the city as a conqueror after the capitulation of Rouen, following the long and terrible siege.

That had been less than three years ago, in January 1419. Now his coffin lay in state until, on 24 September, Queen Catherine arrived at Rouen with John of Bedford. With them came no less than eighteen carts carrying her late husband's possessions and four filled with her own.

Leaving Rouen on 5 October, the procession moved on through Abbeville, Montreuil, and finally Boulogne to Calais. Leading it (behind the coffin) was John, Duke of Bedford, eldest of the king's younger brothers, alongside James the King of Scotland. Both wore the deep black of mourning, as did the nobles and members of Henry's household who followed behind the leading pair in order of prestige. In sharp contrast to the sombre mourners, the robes of the clergymen and torchbearers were all of purest white.

Catherine, Henry's young widow, is said to have been amongst a great crowd of people in the rear. Chroniclers do not state how Catherine travelled;

it may have been in a litter pulled by two horses, but being a young woman, it is probable that she rode, either on a pillion or a side-saddle, for at least part of the way.

Reaching Calais in early November, they were forced to wait for a few days because of unfavourable winds. The crossing was made, it would seem without too much difficulty. But this time, as they sailed into Dover, on or about 31 October, there were no men from the Cinque Ports rushing through the surf to carry them ashore.

Instead they proceeded from Dover at slow pace, through the bleak November countryside and the towns of Canterbury, Rochester and Dartford to London, just as Henry and Catherine had done less than two years before. On 5 November, the Mayor of London, aldermen and craft guilds met the funeral procession at Blackheath. With them were several bishops, accompanied by a great number of clergy, chanting the Office of the Dead. Headed by an escort of thirty-one different guilds, all clothed in white and carrying torches, the procession went over London Bridge, then from Eastcheap to Cornhill, then to the Stocks, on to the Great Conduit, and at last to the west door of the great cathedral of St Paul.[7]

The next day, followed by crowds of sorrowing people, the procession reached Westminster Abbey where, on 7 November 1422, Henry V was buried in a magnificent sculpted tomb standing in a prominent place close to that of Edward the Confessor.

The funeral itself surpassed everything that had gone before. Monstrelet the French historian was most impressed, and wrote that 'greater pomp and expense were made than had been done for 200 years, and even now, as much honour and reverence is daily paid to his tomb, as if it were certain he was a saint in Paradise'.[8]

The coffin, covered in black velvet embroidered with a cross of white satin and cloth of gold, was borne at each corner by an earl. Four knights held a canopy above it, as it was carried by another eight chamber knights to a funeral car, drawn by five fine horses, draped with the arms of England, St George, St Edmund and St Edward. In front walked yeomen carrying torches, together with pages and knights, their horses draped in black, bearing the shields of England and France and the king's helm, one holding a battleaxe pointing downwards. Behind came a great troupe of mourners, who included councillors riding horses again covered in black cloth.

Reaching the Thames, the coffin was laid into one of a fleet of barges, waiting to carry most of the great procession upriver to Westminster Abbey.

The next day, Saturday 7 November, a requiem mass was celebrated before Henry was buried with great ceremony. Three of his favourite horses, a knight in full armour riding one of them, were led up to the altar, for this was a soldier's funeral of the greatest warrior that England had ever known.

Catherine, dowager queen at the age of 21, would live in Windsor Castle with the new King of England, her little son, now just 11 months old. Shortly after her arrival there she heard of the death of her father, the mad yet lovable Charles VI who, in his moments of clarity, had given her the affection her mother, self-centred in overwhelming ambition, had never been able to impart. His death meant that little Henry, already the sixth of England, was now titular King of France.

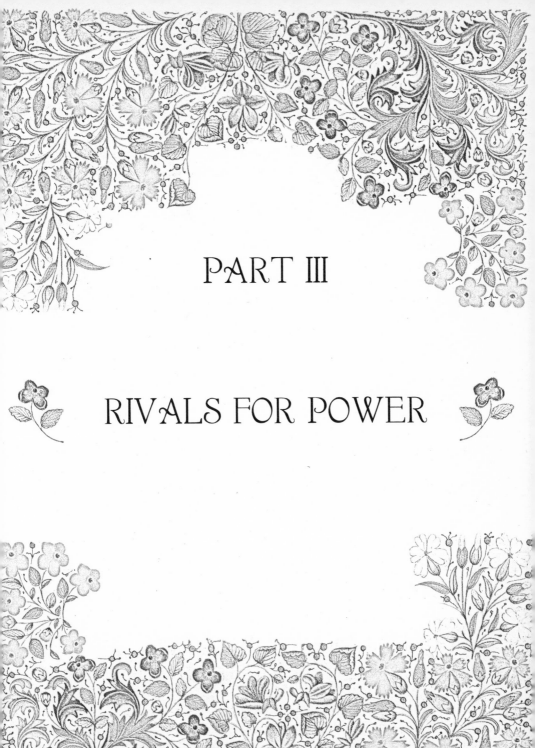

PART III

RIVALS FOR POWER

1

Jacqueline's Story

Couriers were always great conveyors of gossip. For this reason
Catherine must have known of Jacqueline's intention to marry
Humfrey of Gloucester before she had even stepped on England's
shores. She must also have known, for it had been much put about, that
Burgundy, already furious over Henry giving Jacqueline asylum, was now
enraged to the point that diplomatic relations were very severely strained.
Philip of Burgundy was announcing that Humfrey was trying to acquire
lands in Holland to which, through his great-aunt, Jacqueline's mother,
Philip himself made claim.

Jacqueline of course was still married to the Duke of Brabant, over whom
Burgundy had control. By 1420 her attempts to obtain a divorce were still
being debated by Antipope Benedict XIII in Avignon and Pope Martin V in
Rome. Despite being deposed by the Council of Constance in 1417, Benedict
had refused to resign. Now known as the Antipope, he granted Jacqueline
her divorce. The date of her marriage to Humfrey is unrecorded, although
it is known to have taken place after Henry V died on Jacqueline's own
affirmation. Nonetheless, by October 1420, a rumour had reached the Duke
of Brabant that his wife had married Humfrey, Duke of Gloucester and was
already with child. This was proved to be blatantly untrue but, having spent
Christmas together at the monastery of St Albans, they are believed to have
married at Hadleigh in Essex, on or before 7 March 1423.

Meanwhile, robbed of the company of her cousin Jacqueline, Catherine was lonely and still grieving for Henry. She gave all her devotion to their son. The scribes of the court noted, with some surprise, that when called to take part in state audiences, she sat with little Henry on her lap. Such openly displayed affection was unusual, but Catherine had no one else.

At first she had no money, or so it seemed to her. Her dower was settled by Parliament a year after her return. It amounted to 40,000 crowns or 10,000 marks, a larger sum than had been agreed at the Treaty of Troyes, when it had been arranged that, in the event of her becoming a widow, she would receive an annuity of 20,000 crowns. In addition, Henry had given her an income from his Lancastrian estates, as well as the Bohun inheritance of his mother. She was rich, yet she longed for her homeland, particularly in the dark winter months. Spring came so late in England. In France, the mimosa would be flowering by the month of March … after much negotiation, her sister Isabella had been allowed to go home. But Isabella had been childless. Catherine had Henry, her son. To leave England, she would have to part with him. His guardians, appointed by her husband, would never allow him to go to France, still at war with England. Little Henry had been born at Windsor and this, by his dead father's wishes, was where he must live as he grew up.

In the months before he was born, Catherine had explored the great building of which Isabella, after living there for five years, had told her so much. Henry's ancestor William the Conqueror had built his castle on a mound well above the Thames, a site chosen because it guarded the western approaches to London, from which it was only a day's march. In the 1170s, Henry II had rebuilt the Round Tower, the outer walls of the Upper and most of the Lower Ward and the royal apartments in the Upper Ward, securing the castle against attack by substituting stone for wood. Then, nearly 200 years later, Henry's great-grandfather, Edward III, had created the immense St George's Hall for the knights of his newly established Order of the Garter.

The Palace of the Louvre may have been magnificent, but it was nothing in size and strength compared to Windsor Castle, a citadel in itself. At a time when monarchs were expected to live in great grandeur, Windsor outdid the rest.

Set all over were the controllers of the household, responsible for the various departments. Above the stairs were the royal family's own apartments, the chapel, hall, wardrobe, counting house and the chambers, containing their own hall. They dined there, usually about the hour of twelve unless it was a hunting day. This was also where the king's secretary sat with his clerks of the signet as they carefully penned his instructions. Downstairs were the kitchen, the pantry, the still room, where such items as candles and soap and some herbal remedies were concocted, the wine cellars and other domestic offices.

Of first importance in the household was the king's confessor, always a bishop; followed by the Chamberlain of England, who was not always present; the seneschal, or keeper of the household; the keeper of the great wardrobe; the household chamberlain and the king's carvers, who were two or three knights of the chamber; the master of the horse; the controller and the cofferer; the dean of the chapel; the royal almoner; numerous esquires and yeomen of the body in the chamber; and yeomen of the hall. Of a more lowly order were the tasters, used as a precaution to sample the food at a time when poisoning was rife. Still lower in the pecking order were the cooks and the scullions, the washerwomen and the untold number of other servants who carried water, stoked the fires and swept the rooms and corridors of this, the largest house in Europe.

Perhaps Catherine found some relics of Isabella in the royal chambers, the elder sister who had come to live there as a little girl of 7, now nearly a quarter of a century ago. Clothes she had worn may have been left, folded over sprigs of lavender, in the great wooden chests in which such things were stored. Possibly even her doll's house, complete with its little silver furniture, had been left for other children to play with when, at the age of 12, she had returned to France.

2

Invasion of Hainault

A year had passed since Catherine's return to England and arguments over the legality of Jacqueline's marriage continued without any firm decision being reached.

Humfrey of Gloucester, always impatient, decided to win what he considered to be his rightful inheritance, by force of arms. By the end of September 1423, both he and Jacqueline were at Dover receiving an embassy from Mons, the capital city of Hainault, which Humfrey claimed as his own. Decreed Protector of England by his brother's dying wish, Gloucester now left the country in the hands of Henry Beaufort, Bishop of Winchester, Chancellor of the Realm (son of John of Gaunt and Catherine Swynford) despite knowing him to be a rival for power.

On 16 October, Humfrey, now styling himself Count of Hainault, Holland and Zeeland, sailed from Dover with Jacqueline and a fleet of forty-two ships. With a following wind they crossed the Channel to land at Calais the same day.

Hainault was quickly conquered, to the dislike of the citizens who feared that their flourishing businesses might be disrupted by the interference of their new lord. But when John, Duke of Bavaria, Jacqueline's first husband, died of poisoning the next year, Philip of Burgundy, again claiming his right of inheritance as Jacqueline's overlord, invaded her lands. Burgundy then issued a challenge to Humfrey to fight him in single combat, to save many of their subjects being killed, and Humfrey suddenly and unexpectedly returned to England to make arrangements for this contest, or so he claimed.

The duel was fixed to take place on St George's Day, 23 April 1425, when, with a shock that hit like the strike of a cannonball, Humfrey's brother John of Bedford, who was allied to Burgundy, forbade it on the grounds that it would be fatal to their joint effort against France. Pope Martin likewise declined to endorse the combat and finally, by refusing on Bedford's orders to finance the contest, the English Parliament put an end to what would have been one of the greatest trials of chivalry between two of the foremost combatants in Europe.

Subsequently, the English forces left in Hainault were totally overcome. Jacqueline herself was taken prisoner by Philip of Burgundy but, being a tall woman, she managed to escape in men's clothes. She found safety in Gouda, where she once again proclaimed her rights.

Her cause was not lost. Though Humfrey of Gloucester announced that as Lord Protector of England he could not leave the country again, he raised a force, reputedly numbering 1,500 men which, commanded by Lord Fitzwalter, sailed to Holland to Jacqueline's support. In October 1425, her army defeated that of Philip of Burgundy in the Battle of Alphen. Philip, warned of its coming, then tried to defeat the invading English force at sea, but only succeeded in capturing about a third of the army. The rest landed safely to fight Philip at the Zeeland port of Brouwershaven, where they linked up with Jacqueline's men. Initially the English longbowmen triumphed, but then the Burgundian cavalry drove them back into one of the wide Flemish dykes to be drowned or killed.

This was the end for Jacqueline. Her portrait, painted some five years later by an anonymous artist of the Jacoba van Beieren door Hollandse school, shows a tall, rather plain-faced lady with tanned skin. Certainly she had lost the bloom of her youth. Humfrey, whom she loved, but who had married her for her possessions, had most cruelly deserted her. He was living openly with Elizabeth Cobham, one of her ladies-in-waiting, with whom he had become infatuated. Meanwhile, the power of Philip of Burgundy, ominous as a cloud heavy with thunder, threatened to engulf her lands.

Told of Jacqueline's sufferings, Catherine, if only on account of their relationship, must also have been concerned that her sister Isabella's second husband, their first cousin, Charles Duke of Orléans, captured at the Battle of Agincourt, was still held prisoner in England. Treated with all the deference owed to his high rank, Charles was allowed some liberty, if always under supervision. This probably included hunting in the forests round the castles where he was held. The Duke of Bourbon, another prisoner from Agincourt, was allowed to bring his falcons, together with their handlers, from France.

Because of the enormous ransom demanded for his release, Charles of Orléans had been of special value to Henry who, as he lay dying, had specifically instructed his brother Bedford: 'And take care that you deliver not from prison my fair cousin the Duke of Orléans.'[1]

Immediately after his capture, Charles had been held in various royal palaces in and around London. It must have been during his time in the White Tower, where political prisoners were lodged, that he got to know James King of Scotland, whose verses so resembled his own. Also, while there, he had frequent visits from members of his household at Blois, who brought him not only news from home, but clothes and a fine leather dressing case, embossed with his arms, containing two big combs, a mirror and two razors with ivory handles decorated with his arms in enamel. Also delicacies like 3lb of nougat from Lombardy and 7lb of quince marmalade.[2]

Henry had been on the point of departure for his second invasion of France when, 'for certain reasons especially moving us at present', he had ordered Charles to be transferred to the custody of Robert Waterton, one of his most loyal and trusted servants. Waterton was Constable of Pontefract Castle where, on 1 June 1417, the king had ordered him to conduct Charles and hold him for the time being. Pontefract, one of the strongest castles in Yorkshire, its huge keep hollowed out of 50ft of the rock on which it stood, was imbued with a sinister atmosphere. Here, in the depths of the dungeon, Isabella's first husband, King Richard, had died under mysterious circumstances.

Despite his gloomy surroundings, Charles was apparently quite happy there, treated as he was with the deference due to his status. His lack of liberty was made more bearable because Waterton, a kindly man, used to invite him out to his country house at Methley some 6 miles west of Pontefract. Here he was welcomed into the family, as is shown by the presents he gave them, a gold goblet to Cicely, Waterton's wife, and silver necklets to their two children. Specially made in London, these and many other things were paid for through Jean Victor, an Italian merchant in London who undertook all Charles's financial transactions.

Shortly after King Henry's death, Charles had been transferred to the care of Sir Thomas Comberworth, in the castle of Bolingbroke in Lincolnshire, which had once belonged to John of Gaunt and was the birthplace of his son, who had become Henry IV. It was here that Charles heard of the death of Charles VI, the king who had held him at his christening and after whom he had been named. The news was brought from France by three of his officials, who arrived with six servants and twelve horses, bringing a contribution towards the ransom of Charles's younger brother John of Angoulême as well as jewels and silver.

Five months later, in May 1423, two of them came again, this time with word of the Treaty of Amiens, signed on 17 April between England and Burgundy, which proclaimed Henry VI King of France and England. To strengthen the ties of friendship, two marriages were arranged: that of the Duke of Bedford, regent of France, to Anne, younger sister of Philip of Burgundy, and that of Arthur, Count of Richemont, son of the Duke of Brittany, recently freed from imprisonment in England after being captured at Agincourt, to Anne's elder sister Margaret.[3] These alliances, interesting as they were, were of little significance to Charles. There was no word of what he most wanted to hear: his release.

Instead, at a meeting on 26 January 1424, the Council decided that, from the following Easter onwards, the king's prisoners must pay for their own expenses. Brought to London by Sir Thomas Comberworth to be informed of this, Charles was lodged in his keeper's house in the city until 2 February.

Meanwhile, King James of Scotland, Charles of Orléans's companion in captivity for some of the first five years, whose love of poetry Orléans is thought to have inspired, was living intermittently at Windsor while he waited for the completion of the complicated arrangements for his release, which included the provisions of hostages from Scotland.

It would seem that it was on that long, slow journey across France and England in the wake of Henry's coffin, that friendship had developed between Catherine and James. What is more likely than that she should have turned for support to the stalwart figure of the young Scottish king, her companion through both triumph and adversity from the time of their first meeting on that memorable day at Troyes, now nearly three years ago. How much had happened since then!

Whether their relationship developed into love, at that time, or afterwards at Windsor, must remain hypothetical for want of contemporary evidence. Undoubtedly the court gossips would have been agog at any hint of a liaison involving the young and beautiful widowed queen. Only the words of a poem, carefully interpreted, would seem to hold a clue.

3

The Poet King

J ames, King of Scots, like Charles of Orléans, his companion in captivity, became renowned in his own lifetime as a poet. The probability that they were acquainted, if not actual friends while held prisoner in the Tower of London seems borne out by the similarity of their poetry.

Charles of Orléans, already noted as a poet before his capture, was to occupy his time in confinement by writing *ballades*, one of several fixed forms in French lyric poetry, used particularly in the fourteenth and fifteenth centuries, which had developed from the songs of the troubadours. That James was later to write in such a similar form does suggest an affinity between these two prisoners who both found consolation in expressing their longings into words.

The two well-known poems by Charles of Orléans and James's famous epic, found in the appendices of this book, show a very strong resemblance, both in the form of the stanzas and in their exaltation of nature, as to make them comparable as works of men who were not only familiar to each other, but of a similar disposition. While James wrote only a few poems, albeit of considerable length, Charles's output was larger, mainly composed during his twenty-five years of captivity, until his release was eventually negotiated.

Some people believe that 'The Three Estates', a satirical poem attributed to Sir David Lindsay, was in fact written by King James. His greatest known work, however, is the autobiographical allegory called 'The Kingis Quair' (The King's Book). It is written in the style of Chaucer, who by the time of his death in 1400, when James was just 6 years old, was celebrated as the greatest poet of his time. James was clearly influenced by Chaucer's work. The poem begins with him lying in bed, unable to sleep and trying, unsuccessfully, to read Boethius's *The Consolation of Philosophy*. Then he describes what he calls 'myn aventure', remembering how he had sailed to France as a boy:

> Purvait of all that was us necessarye,
> With wynd at will, up airily by the morowe,
> Streight unto schip, no longer wold we tarye,
> The way we tuke, the tyme I tald toforowe.
> With mony 'fare wele' and 'Sanct Johne to borowe'
> Of falowe and frende, and thus with one assent
> We pullit up saile and furth oure wayis went.

Then he tells how he was held 'in strayte ward and in strong prisoun … without comfort, in sorrowe abandoun' and rails against the fate which has robbed him of his freedom.

> 'The bird, the beste, the fisch eke in the see,
> They live in fredome, everich in his kynd;
> And I a man, and lakkith libertee!
> Quhat schall I seyne? Quhat resoun may I fynd
> That Fortune suld do so? Thus in my mynd
> My folk I wold argewe – bot all for noght,
> Was non that might, that on my peynes rought.[i]

Then, as he hears the bell ring for matins, he knows it is time to get up.

> 'My custom was on mornis for to ryse
> Airly as day – O happy exercise,
> By thee come I to joye out of torment!
> But now to purpose of my first entent.'

---

i   Debate.

He continues to describe the beauty and freedom of the birds, asking what he had done to give offence to God 'That I am thrall, and birdis gone at large', swearing that he would serve Him faithfully 'in wele and wo' would He but set him free. Then, suddenly, all else is forgotten as he glances again from the window:

> And therwith kest I doun myn eye ageyne,
> Quhare as I sawe, walking under the toure,
> Full secretly new cummyn hir to pleyne,
> The fairest of the freschest yong floure
> That ever I sawe, me thoght, before that houre;
> For quhich sodayn abate anon astert[ii]
> The blude of all my body to my hert.

He goes into a fantasy world, but then returns to earth.

So who was this lady with whom James, on his own declaration, fell instantly in love? It has long been thought, with good reason, that she was Joan Beaufort, daughter of John Beaufort, Earl and later Duke of Somerset, and niece of the influential Bishop of Winchester. The granddaughter of Henry IV's brother, John of Gaunt, and thus great-granddaughter of Edward III, it was she whom he was ultimately to marry as part of the contract for his release. The reference to 'jonettis' in the chaplet on her head is taken to be an allusion to her name (see Appendix 1, verse 47). This may be so, but no portrait of Joan exists to show whether she was dark or fair. Theirs was an arranged marriage, organised for political reasons to secure James's fealty to the English king. Was it a happy coincidence that he fell in love with her on that May morning, looking down from his window, in what was probably the Norman Tower of Windsor Castle, and seeing her in the garden below? Otherwise could it have been Catherine, known to have been living at Windsor at the time?

The clues provided by James's description suggest that this was so. Catherine is thought to have been tall and fair. James does not mention the height of his idol, but talks of her golden hair and rich attire. Also, most pointedly, he notices her jewellery, her white pearls, the great heart-shaped

---

ii   Astert = rushed.

balas ruby, the colour of fire, that seems to burn on her white throat as a spark of love, and her many emeralds and sapphires.

Would Joan Beaufort, although daughter of one of the most important earls in England, have had such valuable gems? Catherine is known to have had much jewellery in the vastly expensive trousseau she brought with her from France on Henry's insistence. Most notably the plumes, red, white and blue, although not at that time the French national colours, strike a chord with the dauphin's feathers, embellished on the French royal family's shields.

James goes on to describe the lady he witnesses as very high born:

> To hir hie birth, estate, and beautee bryght:
> Als like ye bene as day is to the nyght,
> Or sek-cloth[i] is unto fyne cremesye,
> Or foule doken unto the fresche dayesye.

Then, most significantly, he calls her his queen:

> And to the notis of the philomene
> Quhilkis sche sang, the ditee there I maid[ii]
> Direct to her that was my hertis quene,
> Without in quhom no songis may me glade,
> And to that sanct,[iii] walking in the schade,
> My bedis[iv] thus with humble hert entere
> Devotly I said to this manere[v]

And then again:

> And with the stremes of your percyng lyght
> Conuoy my hert, that is so wo begone,
> Ageyne unto that suete, hevinly sight,

---

i	Sack-cloth.
ii	Which lyrics wrote.
iii	His beloved.
iv	Prayers.
v	In this manner.

That I, within the wallis cald as stone,
So suetly saw on morrow walk and gone,
Law in the gardyn, right tofore myn eye.
Now, merci queen, and do me noght to deye.

Was he describing Catherine, the young French widow of Henry V, whose beauty is known to have enchanted the king at first sight, and with whom, through force of circumstance, James had been so closely involved?

In the absence of further evidence, we shall never know. Only one thing is certain: that according to written records, both James and Catherine are known to have been living in Windsor Castle in the spring and early summer of 1423. The Exchequer Rolls show that James was 'extra hospit-ium regis' in the month of May 1423.[1]

Negotiations for his release were proceeding slowly. On 4 December, the final treaty for his liberation was concluded.[2] James spent the Christmas of 1423 at Hertford with the court.[3] Proof of his expenditure there can be seen in the records of the Exchequer. Because she was still in charge of her son, it must be assumed that Catherine was there as well. Following this, it is probable, if not certain, that she attended King James's wedding to Lady Joan Beaufort.

The marriage, which formed part of the agreement to allow his return to Scotland, took place in the second week of February, probably on the 13th, which was a Sunday, at that time the fashionable day for weddings. The ceremony took place in the church then called St Mary's Oversie, later known as St Saviours, now the cathedral of the present-day diocese of Southwark. Henry Beaufort, Bishop of Winchester, the bride's uncle, who presumably conducted the service, gave the wedding feast at his palace adjacent to the church.

The remission of 10,000 marks of the king's ransom from the royal treas-ury to provide Joan's dowry, at the insistence of the bride's other uncle, Thomas Beaufort, Duke of Exeter, was thought by some to be a clever and to some extent dishonest way of enriching the Beaufort family to the detri-ment of treasury funds.

Whether or not she attended the wedding, Catherine must have been saddened at losing the company of the man with whom she had shared so much triumph and happiness before the devastating sorrow of

Henry's death. She knew that under the circumstances, having to stay at Windsor during the early childhood of her little son, unless in the event of some unforeseen and unexpected occurrence, she would never again set eyes on the young King of Scotland who had been her support through the many struggles of the last three years.

It was only through the couriers who rode back and forth from England to Scotland that Catherine heard how King James had mastered his unruly land on his return. He had avenged himself on his cousins the Albanys, in particular Duke Murdoch who had acted as regent since his father's death and who had withheld his ransom for so long. He had had Murdoch arrested, tried and executed, together with his brothers, only one of whom escaped to Ireland to avoid his family's fate. Even Murdoch's father-in-law, the 80-year-old Earl of Lennox, had lost his head on the block on Heading Hill in Stirling in May 1425.

James, the poet king, the man whose heart beat faster on hearing a nightingale's song, was nonetheless capable of the violence common to most rulers of his time.

4

Mother of the King

Henry V, knowing he was dying at Vincennes, made a will which was subsequently lost. However, in 1978, when the archives of Eton College were being reorganised, a copy of the document, with later codicils, one dated 26 August 1422, just five days before Henry died, was found. This stated clearly that he wished his youngest brother, Humfrey of Gloucester, to be the main guardian and protector of his infant son. His Beaufort uncle, Thomas, Duke of Exeter, youngest son of John of Gaunt and Catherine Swynford (legitimised by Richard II) was to have 'the governance of the child's person' while Exeter's elder brother Henry Beaufort, Bishop of Winchester (the second son of John and Catherine) was to be executor of the will.[1]

But Bedford, the regent of France, would not allow Humfrey to hold the office in England as Henry had decreed. Supported by the body of councillors, consisting of the lords spiritual and temporal in the Parliament, Bedford was able to enforce the implications of the term of civil law, *tutela*, as used by the writer of the codicil, in refusing to allow his younger brother to take precedence in England above himself. Humfrey protested forcibly, declaring that he was being denied the supreme authority of governance to which he was entitled. Although as Protector, Defender and Principal Councillor of the king, he could summon Parliament, his brother denied him the supreme authority, a deprivation he bitterly resented.

On 28 September 1423, the nobles of England swore fealty to the 21-month-old Henry VI, and Parliament was summoned in his name. Despite his uncle Bedford's regency in France, the person and office of the king had been declared inseparable. Thus, even when still a baby in his cradle, the most important acts of state had to be enacted in little Henry's presence. In this instance, in September 1422, the great seal, heavy because it was made of solid gold, had to be ceremonially surrendered in his night nursery at Windsor by his late father's chancellor, the Bishop of Durham, and handed by Duke Humfrey to the keeper of the rolls of chancery for safe keeping.[2] When he was 2½, Henry was thought strong enough to carry the great seal himself.

Even when he was younger – not yet 2 – it was necessary for Henry to attend the second Parliament of his reign. On 13 November 1423, in spite of the cold and darkness of the season, he left Windsor with his mother, in the words of the Speaker of the House of Commons, 'to sit and occupy your own rightful seat and place in your parliament to whom our recourse of right must be to have every wrong reformed'.[3]

As things turned out, they got no farther than Staines before Henry suffered a sudden illness, or what seems to have been a tantrum, for when carried out from the house where they had spent the night, he screamed and kicked and 'would not be carried further'. However, after a quiet day at Staines, those with him were greatly relieved when 'he was glad and merry cheered'. After spending the next night at Kingston, and the following day at Kennington, he rode in state through the city in his mother's arms, apparently a happy little boy. The next day, Thursday 18 November, he was taken in to the Parliament to be seen and to hear the Speaker's loyal address required by protocol, though it meant nothing to him. This done, he then returned, sitting on his mother's knee, via Waltham to Hertford Castle, where they stayed for the festival of Christmas.

Henry was to spend much of his childhood at Hertford. Built before the Norman invasion as a motte and bailey and entered by crossing a drawbridge over the moat, it was afterwards strengthened as a fortress with flint walls and gatehouses. A royal residence since the reign of Richard I, it was also a state prison. John II of France had been held there following his capture in 1359 by the Black Prince.

The castle held poignant memories for Catherine, her sister Isabella having lived there briefly during her marriage to King Richard. This was one reason why she seems to have loved going to Hertford, given to her by Henry as part of her marriage settlement.

Following the festivals of Christmas and Epiphany, Catherine returned to Windsor Castle, the main royal residence, with her household and her little son. Henry had been provided for by the first Parliament of his reign, which allowed 10,000 marks a year for his household expenses. But the council had then decided that 3,000 marks per annum was quite enough for a baby's needs and had purloined the remaining 7,000 to continue the war in France. The 3,000 marks did appear to be adequate in view of what his female staff were paid.

Henry must have known that Catherine was pregnant before sailing for France. At Canterbury, while making the final preparations for his army to embark, he had made a gift of the manor of Old Shoreham for life to Elizabeth Ryman, one of the queen's ladies, to whom he later sent instructions to take charge of his infant son. Little Henry had been left at Windsor with her while Catherine went to join his father in France. Elizabeth Ryman remained in overall charge of the nursery while Joan Astley, his principal nurse, got £20 a year. Matilda Fosbroke, described as a day nurse, was paid £10. Agnes Jakeman, his chamberwoman (presumably a housemaid) and Margaret Brotherman his laundress, both received £5 annually.

It is an interesting point that all these salaries were doubled within the space of two years, an indication of inflation due to the disruption of trade caused by the war. In 1427 another attendant, Margaret Brekenam, asked the council to double her salary of £5 because 'it was insufficient to maintain her honestly in her station' and yet another lady, Rose Chetewynd, was also given £10 'for her good service about his person in his tender age' in 1429.[4]

On 23 April 1424, the council appointed Lady Alice Butler as a governess for Henry. She was 'to train him in courtesy, discipline and other things necessary for a royal person'. She was also given leave 'to administer reasonable chastisement' if and when necessary! Lady Alice, in fact, ran a nursery school. In 1425, when Henry was 4, the council ordered all heirs of the crown's tenants-in-chief of the rank of baron or above, who were in royal wardship during their minority, to be brought up at court with at least one master provided for them at royal expense. Not all Henry's companions were orphans. Nor were they all very young. In 1428, the 17-year-old Duke of York joined their company and at least three other boys, all of them knighted by Henry with a miniature sword at Leicester in 1426, were invited to live at the court, where they and all their servants wore the king's livery. Dame Butler, who was in effect the chief officer, or major-domo of the household, had servants who wore the silver gilt collar of the king's livery, as did those of the household chamberlain.

Henry was again conveyed in state to the Parliament, which opened at Westminster on 30 April 1425. Taken from his mother's carriage at St Paul's Cathedral by his uncle, the Duke of Gloucester and his great-uncle, Thomas, Duke of Exeter, he was set down upon his feet at the west door. From there he toddled into the choir, where he was 'borne up and offered'. Afterwards, 'set upon a courser', obviously a very quiet horse, with men walking beside him to see that he did not fall off, he rode through Cheapside and the City of London to Kennington.

On the day of the opening of Parliament, he was seated on the throne in the Painted Chamber at Westminster to hear the Bishop of Winchester, his great-uncle Henry Beaufort, who was also the Chancellor, preach on the text from the Second Book of Romans, chapter 10: 'Glory, honour and peace to every well-doer.' This choice was inspired by Bedford's victory at Verneuil, on 27 August of the previous year, which had secured little Henry's kingship of France.

5

Rivals in the War for Power

At the age of 4, Henry was too young to know that the mention of peace, even at home, was illusory. Beaufort and Gloucester were now such deadly enemies that the former had been warned to be very careful in London as Gloucester meant to cause him bodily harm, if not to kill him. The loathing between the Burgundians and Armagnacs in France was intense, but that of Gloucester and the Beauforts certainly matched it in virulence.

The bishop had other enemies in London where, as Chancellor, he was blamed for influencing the enactment of several unpopular laws in the recent Parliament. Amongst them was an act, which granted the first levy of tonnage and poundage of the reign on the city merchants, but only on condition that restrictions were put on the movement and activities of alien merchants, a provision he did not enforce.

Humfrey, who had just returned from Hainault, ostensibly to arrange his duel to be fought with Burgundy, was popular in London, where they called him 'the good duke'. He reputedly encouraged the merchants and their adherents to defy Beaufort to the point where a crowd, which had gathered on a wharf by the Thames threatened to throw him into the river 'to have him taught to swim with wings'.[1]

Back in England, Humfrey of Gloucester continued to quarrel violently with Beaufort, to whom he had handed the office of Protector while he was in Hainault. On returning, he found that Beaufort had made good use of his absence to strengthen his own position. Beaufort soon made it plain that he had no intention whatever to relinquish any of his power to his nephew, whom he regarded merely as his assistant, to Humfrey's great humiliation and rage.

Following an outbreak of looting and rioting in London, Beaufort saw his chance to install his own man Sir Richard Wydeville as Keeper of the Tower. Gloucester, then finding himself barred from using his customary lodging in the Tower, on Henry Beaufort's orders, was predictably furious. Publicly he accused Beaufort of usurping the authority of the council, of ignoring the rights of the Protector and Defender of the Realm and of insulting the honour of the City of London. Convinced that Gloucester would defy him by forcing his way into the Tower, Beaufort ordered Wydeville to mount a special guard and to admit 'no one stronger than himself'.

Returning to his inn in Southwark, Beaufort filled the surrounding houses with Lancashire and Cheshire archers.[2] Believing this presaged an attack, Gloucester at once sent a command to the mayor and aldermen of London telling them to be prepared to face an onslaught from the south side of the river. Subsequently the city was heavily guarded with sentries constantly on watch.

It was not until the end of October that swords were actually unsheathed. Both parties, each a large body of armed men, converged upon London Bridge. However, warned of what was happening, the Archbishop of Canterbury, Henry Chichele, and Prince Peter of Portugal, grandson of their mutual ancestor, John of Gaunt, succeeded in persuading them to call a truce.

On 5 November 1425, taking with him Prince Peter and celebrating what he took to be his triumph over his uncle Beaufort, Gloucester paraded his nephew, King Henry, through the streets of London to much popular acclaim. At word of this, Beaufort wrote a desperate letter to the Duke of Bedford, imploring him to come back to England to save him as he lived in constant fear.

Though now aware of the seriousness of the situation caused by the vicious rivalry of these two ambitious men, Bedford was too occupied to come immediately, and delayed his return to January of the following year, 1426.

Coming home then, as a hero after the Battle of Verneuil, he rode through London with Beaufort: Gloucester conspicuous by his absence.

Following this, at a council meeting at St Albans, Humfrey of Gloucester noticeably failed to appear. Nor did he answer a similar summons to Northampton; it was only when ordered by royal decree that, on 18 February 1426, he came most reluctantly to the Parliament in Leicester arrayed in the presence of the little king.

The quarrel by this time was based on who would take charge of the now 4-year-old Henry, who was living with his mother at Eltham Palace, in Greenwich to the south-east of London. In view of their known mutual hatred, Gloucester and Beaufort were instructed to come to the Leicester Parliament with only a small number of unarmed retainers. Once again, poor little Henry had to sit through a sermon from his uncle the bishop, whose text, taken from Ecclesiastes III, was 'Children listen to your father. Do what I tell you if you wish to be safe.'

The king was then removed as Bedford took over as his commissioner. But Henry was again present on 12 March to hear the Archbishop of Canterbury speak on behalf of Beaufort, who denied Gloucester's accusations that he had tried to take the governance of the realm from Henry IV and that he had plotted to assassinate Henry V. The boy, whether or not he understood anything of all this, was then made to declare his acceptance of his great-uncle's innocence on both charges and to watch as the adversaries shook hands.

Beaufort was then discovered to have enriched himself, not only from the customs and subsidies paid at the ports, but by pawning the crown jewels before he was replaced as Chancellor in March 1426. Two months later, at Leicester, the council, headed by the brothers, the dukes of Bedford and Gloucester, contrived a temporary end to the bitter controversy by giving their uncle, Henry Beaufort, permission to make the pilgrimage, which he had long craved. Once safely in France, in St Mary's church in Calais, he was created a cardinal. He thus achieved the exalted position in the Church, which, by compensating, at least in part, for his lack of influence in the governance of England, brought the power struggle to an end. Or so at least it was hoped!

On Whit Sunday 1426, at the Leicester Parliament, Bedford knighted his nephew the king, who in turn made thirty-eight new knights, amongst them his first cousin Richard, Duke of York. Following this, new agreements, settled at Reading in November, included a tripartite family bond and mutual pact, sealed between the king's two uncles and his mother, to defend his interests. This meant that Bedford, having defused the dangerous animosity between his uncle and his brother, was free to return to command the English army in France.

Duke Humfrey then immediately seized on the chance of the departure of both his brother and his uncle to make another attempt to obtain the authority of which he believed he had been robbed. He still craved the governance of the realm, which his eldest brother, Henry V, had clearly intended for him. In the Parliament, which opened in the autumn of 1427, he demanded that a new enquiry investigate the matter and therewith to make a decision on the position he was entitled to hold. Declaring that he would not attend the Parliament, thus thwarting the conclusion of its business, he then announced that he would only return when a clear decision had been reached.

He believed that he had forced an impasse, but using the Archbishop of Canterbury as their spokesman, the councillors replied that in the first Parliament following Henry V's death, Humfrey's claims to the governance of the kingdom had been rejected and his present title devised 'to ease and appease him' and to keep the peace. He attended Parliament, the archbishop added, as Duke of Gloucester only and his powers there were no greater than they would be when the king attained his majority:

> The councillors 'marvelled with all their hearts' that he could not be content with the so recent declaration of the limits of his authority and power … especially as the king had now grown so far in person, wit and understanding, and would take upon himself the exercise of his full royal authority within a few years. Following this a large deputation produced a document requiring Humfrey to agree to this ruling and to obey the king's write by obeying the summons to Parliament.[3]

Gloucester, thus stymied once again, was forced to accept a decision which caused him great bitterness.

Meanwhile, alone in Hainault, Jacqueline was still struggling to cling to the rights of her inheritance against the overriding, all-powerful Philip, Duke of Burgundy. Duke Humfrey of Gloucester, while refusing to leave England, was nonetheless persistently appealing to the Court of Rome for recognition of the legality of his marriage to Jacqueline, which would thereby strengthen his own claim, as her husband, to her provinces in Holland. But, in February 1426, the papal commissioner in charge of the case declared Jacqueline's desertion of the Duke of Brabant to be illegal, and ordered her into the protection of her kinsman Amadeus of Savoy to await Pope Martin's final decision.

Jacqueline was adamant on both counts. Neither would she return to Brabant nor accept the protection of Amadeus of Savoy. On 8 April 1427, she sent two emissaries from Gouda, Lewis de Montfort and Arnold of Ghent, to the council in England. They took with them a letter in which she reminded the council of how Henry V had not only given her sanctuary, but also an income of £100 a month when she had reached his court after escaping from Hainault in 1421. She begged them to urge her husband to help her or, if he could not come himself, to send armed men and archers to her aid.

Her envoys returned with a letter purportedly written by the 6-year-old king. It emphasised the need for peace. To this Jacqueline replied that Burgundy's aggrandisement was making it impossible to deal with him. Again she begged for the help, which she knew she would have received from Henry V, had he only survived.

To everyone's surprise, it was at this point that Jacqueline's former husband, the Duke of Brabant suddenly died. Despite the rumour of his being poisoned, no one, as far as is recorded, accused her of any involvement in the death of this old and rather vacuous man, forced on her as a husband by Philip of Burgundy who had him under his control. His death, whether or not of natural causes, meant that Philip could no longer prey upon Jacqueline on the excuse of doing so on her much-disliked husband's behalf. Instead he repeated insistently that through the right of inheritance, Jacqueline's lands were his own.

Jacqueline, ever more desperate, wrote again to the English council begging for its help. This time Humfrey of Gloucester did make a move to rescue her by asking Parliament for 20,000 marks to help him raise an army for her assistance. His request was debated by the council, which decided that only 9,000 marks should be given to Gloucester. Just under half of it should go towards his salary as Protector, while the rest could be used to raise and equip the force to help his wife's cause. The expeditionary army would go with two purposes, firstly to reinforce the towns still loyal to Jacqueline and secondly to escort her back to England. It was then stated emphatically that the soldiers left in occupation in Holland should only defend Jacqueline's property, not that of anyone else. This was obviously dictated by Bedford, who was struggling to maintain the peace with Burgundy he had achieved with such difficulty.

Gloucester began to raise an army with the Earl of Salisbury's support. But the expeditionary force never sailed. Bedford, well aware of how much Jacqueline's plight excited public sympathy in England, knew that the presence of an invading army in Hainault would provoke Burgundy into forming an alliance with the dauphin as he was already rumoured to have threatened to do. Having told the council that Philip was ready to treat with Gloucester, John of Bedford then wrote to his brother begging him not to risk alienating the very uncertain friendship of Burgundy. As a result of his diplomacy, a truce was signed between Humfrey and Philip in Paris.

Meanwhile, in the following year, 1428, the Pope finally decreed that Jacqueline's marriage to Brabant had been unquestionably legal. She immediately launched an appeal but Humfrey did nothing. Furious and bitterly disappointed, it was nonetheless of some comfort to find that she had support in England.

On 8 March, the Mayor and aldermen of London assembled before Parliament to say that they had received an appeal for help from the lady they still called the Duchess of Gloucester and Countess of Zeeland and Holland. They declared that the nation should rescue her and that they were willing to help in any way they could.

Then, to the amazement and consternation of the august assembly, a gaggle of women appeared. Led by a formidable female from the Stocks Market (a building called after the stocks that stood there on the site of the present Mansion House), they marched up to Gloucester where he stood with two archbishops and several other dignitaries. The lady from the Stocks Market presented them with letters accusing Gloucester of doing nothing to save his wife from her present danger and of leaving her to face her enemies alone while he himself was living in an adulterous liaison with another woman, 'to the ruin of himself, the kingdom and the marital bond'.[4]

Humfrey was indeed living in sin. Eleanor Cobham, Jacqueline's reputedly beautiful lady in waiting, with whom he had so blatantly carried on an affair in front of his wife's eyes, had returned with him to England. She had by this time had two children by him and held him in her thrall, it was claimed, by magic.

Free of his association with Jacqueline, thanks to the papal bull, Humfrey proceeded to marry Eleanor. Later he may have realised her true character, for once she had him in her clutches she proved to be a virago. According to an anonymous contemporary chronicler, Humfrey 'began his marriage with evil and ended it with worse'. Both Monstrelet and the poet Lydgate, mention the pair as incompatible. But much as he may have regretted it, he stayed true to the woman for whom he had deserted Jacqueline in the most hurtful of ways.

6

Childhood of a King

The accounts of the Public Record Office show that though little King Henry and his mother lived mainly at Windsor, they also spent time elsewhere. All great houses in medieval times had to be left unoccupied occasionally to allow them to be thoroughly cleaned. While Hertford Castle was their favourite place to visit they also went to the royal residences of Eltham Palace in Greenwich and Kennington Palace (in what is now the Oval cricket ground), where Geoffrey Chaucer had once famously been Clerk of Works. The hunting lodge at Woodstock was another alternative, as also was Kenilworth, a castle renowned for its magnificence, its tilting yard the scene of many knightly conquests and festivities.

It was at Eltham Palace that the royal family spent Christmas in both 1426 and 1427. John Travail and his London players and another travelling company called the Jews of Abingdon entertained them, with four of the older boys acting interludes. Gift giving took place on New Year's rather than Christmas Day, when little Henry received gifts from his mother and other relations and presumably members of the court.

Several months later, Henry was regally dressed for the occasion on Maundy Thursday, the Thursday before Easter. Wearing a robe down to his feet, he had a gold chain with unicorn and serpentine pendants hung round his neck and a gold collar of esses and broomscods, made by the

London goldsmith John Patyng. Thus attired, he made a Maundy presentation of 2*s* 9*d* each to thirty-three poor men.

In 1428, when their location at Christmas is unknown, Sir John Erpingham gave Henry coral beads and a gold brooch, which had once belonged to his great-great-grandfather King Edward III. Henry gave presents in return. After much consultation with his governess Dame Alice, he presented his mother with a gold ring set with a very fine ruby, which his uncle John of Bedford had given him when in England two years previously. It was a parting present. Henry, now 7 years old, as decreed by the council, was to have his own household. His mother must live without him.

However, they spent the following Easter together at Hertford Castle, where French actors and dancers came to entertain them. On Easter Sunday, Abbot John Wheathampstead led the service in the private chapel of the castle. Then, on the Friday of Easter week, the court moved to the Abbey of St Albans where they stayed until 19 April. This, as Catherine knew, was one of their last times together. She sadly accepted the inevitable separation. Henry was nearly 8 and had to be taught to be a king.

Richard Beauchamp, Earl of Warwick, known as 'the king's master', was appointed to be his tutor. Born in 1382, Warwick was by then 46 and, having married two heiresses, was not only one of the greatest land-owners in England, but one of the most acclaimed. Nonetheless, in his own youth he had lived through great misfortune. When he was born, his father had been high in the favour of Richard II, to the point where the king had been his godfather. But Warwick's father had then been arrested, allegedly as part of the Earl of Arundel's conspiracy to have the king imprisoned. In 1397, when his son was only 5 years old, Warwick had been tried and convicted of treachery and sentenced to life imprisonment in the Tower. Then two years later, when King Richard himself was a prisoner, fate had taken another twist when Warwick had been recalled by Henry IV and restored to his lands and power. His son, Richard, who at the king's coronation had been made a Knight of the Bath, had succeeded to the earldom in 1401 when, in addition to other inheritances, he had received the unusual but special bequest of a bed of silk embroidered with bears and his arms.

Fighting for Henry against the Welsh, Richard Warwick had nearly captured Owen Glendower before, having seized Glendower's banner, being chased out of Wales. Then, following the Battle of Shrewsbury, he had been made a Knight of the Garter by the king. In 1408, Henry IV had given him leave to go on a crusade, first to Rome and then Jerusalem before returning in 1410.

Five years later, he had sailed with Henry V to Harfleur, but the king had sent him back to England in charge of prisoners and spoil. Speaking fluent French, he had been one of the ambassadors sent by Henry from the Siege of Rouen to discuss the terms of both the king's marriage to Catherine and the ensuing truce. Later, after taking the fortress of Melun, Warwick had been one of the commissioners appointed to receive the surrender of Meaux.

So much did Henry V value the integrity of this man, whom, after so much personal experience, he felt he could safely trust, that he told those standing around him as he was dying, that he wanted Warwick to take charge of the education of his son. His instructions were obeyed to the letter. On 8 May, four Knights of the Body and four esquires were ordered to serve the young king, the knights being paid 100 marks a year and the esquires 50. Henry VI had already been given his own doctor, a man called John Somerset who, in addition to his medical qualifications, had previously been master of a grammar school. He was now paid to teach Henry as well as taking care of his health. Henry was also instructed in physical combat, so essential at the time. Warwick bought him small swords and a suit of armour, as the records of the Tower of London show. Now in overall charge of Henry, he could chastise him for being naughty and had the right to move him from one place to another in a time of crisis, such as an outbreak of plague. Large households in those days were always itinerant. Thus it was decreed that while the castles of Wallingord and Hertford would be his summer homes, the young king would live in Berkhamsted and Windsor during the winter months.

Catherine, who did not see Jacqueline again after she left England, found her own problems multiplying as the news of English defeats came from France. Her life changed dramatically in 1428, when her little son was given his own household by order of the law of the land. Shortly after she had gone with him in a grand procession to attend the opening of Parliament, she was told the devastating news.

Little Henry still lived under the care of his governess Dame Alice Butler and nurse Joan Astley. His mother was allowed to see him but only under the auspices of his guardian, the Earl of Warwick. This was when the lonlieness struck. Catherine is said to have more or less retired from public life. She was now in the invidious position of being one of the enemy, as war continued in France. To make things worse, she now had an adversary, dangerous as the assassin hidden behind the curtain, but in this case empowered by right of law.

◦═━═◦

This was the moment when Humfrey of Gloucester, knowing her vulnerability, chose to begin what can only be described as a relentless campaign to victimise the sister-in-law who, from every account of the time, had apparently done nothing to harm him. It can be taken that her friendship and indeed championing of his former wife Jacqueline irked him. Humfrey was a man whose pride precluded any admission of fault. He had also idolised his older brother Henry, who had held off the French attackers with his sword to save his life at Azincourt, and may have considered the idea of Catherine remarrying as a betrayal. These would appear to be the only logical reasons for what amounted to a campaign of hatred against her by the man who, as Protector of England, had the power to destroy his dead brother's isolated widow's chances of future happiness.

That Humfrey of Gloucester was a control freak is nowhere better proved than when Catherine had a chance to marry Edmund Beaufort. Paranoid in his hatred of the Beauforts, and seizing a chance to demean her, Humfrey determined to put a stop to it, whatever the outcome might be. Edmund, Earl and eventually titular Duke of Somerset, was the third surviving son of John Beaufort (created 1st Earl of Somerset by Richard II) and his wife Margaret Holland. On his father's side a grandson of John of Gaunt, and on his mother's, of Joan, the Fair Maid of Kent (mother of Richard II), Somerset was therefore a second cousin of Catherine's late husband King Henry.

It is likely that Catherine already knew Edmund Somerset. Although described as well versed in knightly procedure, he does not seem to have joined Bedford's army in France. Therefore it is probable that, like most high-born young men of his age, he was much about the court. Certainly, if in England, he must have been present at the wedding of his sister Joan to James, King of Scots, which Catherine is known to have attended in February 1424. Edmund was not a rich man by the standards of the time, but was said to be good-looking. Born in 1406, he was four years younger than Catherine but she, at twenty-three, was still at the height of the beauty, which chroniclers so much admired.

Suitable as it would appear to have been, Gloucester put a stop to the marriage. In this case, it would seem that his refusal to sanction an alliance of the king's mother to the Beauforts was not just inspired by personal animosity for Catherine, but by his own conviction that it would increase the Beauforts' power. As Protector of the Kingdom, he used his great influence to make Parliament pass a law prohibiting any person from marrying the dowager queen without the consent of the king and council.

What would seem now to have been Gloucester's irrational hatred and fear of his enemies sprang from the council's decision to limit his own influence. Following King Henry's coronation on 6 November 1429, the Parliament declared the king to be in charge of the government. Despite this obvious idiosyncrasy, the boy being a month shy of 8 years old, it meant that Gloucester's office of Protector was now null and void. Relegated to First Councillor, he was then further humiliated when this same Parliament sanctioned the return of Cardinal Beaufort to the council meetings, judging it both necessary and desirable to the good administration of the realm.

The determination of the Lords of Parliament to limit Gloucester's powers is then shown by the records of the second session, when it was ordained that only men who possessed a freehold worth 40s a year could vote for the knights of the shire who sat in Parliament. This meant that only the richer and more powerful men in England had a voice in how the country was ruled. The less privileged, who were mainly Gloucester's supporters, now lost their authority to take part in elections, thus reducing his own authority.

When the young king went to be crowned King of France in Reims, it was universally realised that no one other than Gloucester, his nearest relation in England, could be regent in his absence abroad. Nonetheless, the precaution was taken of dividing the council into two parts and furthermore it was ruled that no one could be dismissed from it without the acceptance of both sections. Thus secure in the knowledge that Gloucester could not appoint his own followers while he was away, Cardinal Beaufort agreed to escort Henry on his journey. As Warden of the Cinque Ports, Gloucester had arranged the ships for the voyage, and went with his nephew to Canterbury to wish him Godspeed and farewell.

Another event that November, which was later to prove of great significance to Charles of Orléans, was the arrival in England of Isabella, daughter of King John of Portugal, granddaughter of old John of Gaunt, on her way to Flanders to marry Philip of Burgundy, who had lost his wife Anne, sister of John of Bedford.

7

Renewal of War in France

Catherine's ostracism increased as word of the worsening situation of the English forces came from France. In July 1427, the Earl of Warwick had laid siege to the town of Montargis. Situated on the River Loing, bisected by many canals and known as the 'Venice of the Gâtinais', it was the second largest city in northern-central France.

Initially successful, Warwick almost won the surrender of the town, but in a period of heavy rain, the townspeople flooded the water courses and thus drowned many English soldiers. On 5 September, two months after the siege had begun, a French force said to be 1,600 strong and led by two veteran soldiers, John de Dunois and Étienne de Vignolles, known as 'La Hire', stormed into the town and drove Warwick and his army from its walls.

French patriotism revived. Catherine's brother, Charles VII, became more than just a king in name. Monstrelet, writing from the French perspective, says that in 1428:

King Henry gave orders in his council for the gathering of an army of 6,000 chosen men, well tried in war, the greater part of whom were to be sent to France to the assistance of the Duke of Bedford who styled himself Regent of France.[1]

The king, of course, being only 8 years old, was present in name only in the proceedings which resulted in the Earl of Salisbury, one of Henry V's most experienced soldiers, being given the command. Again, according to the same source, an initial force of 3,000 men landed at Calais, whence they marched to Paris. Salisbury followed with the rest of his army, to march through Saint-Pol, Doullens and Amiens, to Paris, where they met with a great welcome from the Duke of Bedford and all the members of the council of France.

Salisbury, on the orders of Bedford and the council, laid siege to the city of Orléans, which had long been the headquarters of French opposition. Climbing up to an upper storey of a tower to make a reconnaissance, he was fatally injured by a piece of flying masonry, dislodged by a cannon ball said to have been fired by a schoolboy, which carried away half his face. Carried to Meung, he died in agony within a week.

The Earl of Suffolk replaced him as captain general of the English forces. Knowing that he lacked both the men and guns needed to storm the city, he attempted to reduce it by starvation, setting up outworks on both banks of the Loire to prevent boats entering with supplies.

John, Duke of Bedford commandeered some four or five hundred wagons from the borders of Normandy and sent them laden with provisions to relieve the English besiegers of Orléans. At much the same time, in February 1429, the Count of Clermont, Charles de Bourbon, assembled a joint force of French and Scottish soldiers at Blois with the object of relieving the beleaguered town. Told of the English convoy of provisions commanded by Sir John Fastolf which was approaching from Paris, Clermont attempted an ambush.

At Rouvry, he and his men must have smelt the fish with which most of the wagons were laden as they drew near. But they were not quite quick enough. The English had time to make a circular barricade with their wagons from which the archers had extra height to send a deadly hail of arrows into the midst of their enemies. Clermont ordered the French to stand back, depending on cannons to make light work of the carts, but the Scots, so famous for their charges, dashed forward into the attack, led by John Stewart of Darnley, the Constable of Scotland.

As the Scots surged forward, the English cavalry, anticipating just such a moment, charged out through a gap between the wagons to slaughter the Scots as they advanced, yelling at a run. John Stewart of Darnley was amongst the many killed in what became known as the Battle of the Herrings, due to the great quantities of fish carried by the wagons at the approach of Lent. As Sir John Fastolf delivered his supplies in triumph, not only the near-starving people of Orléans, but all of the French nation endured yet another blow to their morale.

Desperate to save one of the greatest cities in France, King Charles then sent some of his best officers in command of 1,200–1,400 men to reinforce the garrison of Orléans. Greatly dispirited, he could see no option other than to surrender.

But then, as is so well known, a miracle occurred as a girl of 17 called Joan, dressed like a man, came to see the young king at Chinon, where he was then living. She told him that she had seen visions of saints who promised her that she was the one who would save the king who had been so wrongly driven from his kingdom and reduced to a pitiable state.

With King Charles during this extraordinary interview was the Duke of Alençon, who accepted and believed her from the moment of their meeting. Known to have been a charming man, Joan for her part adored him, always addressing him as 'gentil duc' or 'mon bon duc'. It was to Alençon she told of her four aims: 'to beat the English, to have the dauphin crowned at Reims, to deliver the Duke of Orléans, and to raise the siege of the city.'[2]

'God loved the Duke of Orléans', she said (something she would repeat at her trial), and for that reason she had more revelations about him than about any man alive, except the man she called her king.[3] She went on to assert that God had sent her an angel as a sign of the merits of the king and the good Duke of Orléans, that Saint Margaret and Saint Catherine had told her she would cross the sea within three years to bring the duke back, and that if she was allowed to continue for three years, she would have enough English prisoners to achieve this. Joan, like many others in France, was insensed by the Siege of Orléans. It was in fact against the chivalric law code of the time for an enemy to attack the lands of an absent lord, especially one he held captive, and there was indignation in France that the English should do so. But that an illiterate girl should be aware of this seems so unlikely that one assumes she must have heard it from someone familiar with the laws of chivalry.

The news from France must have greatly raised Charles of Orléans's hopes (who at this time thought to have been in Bourne in Lincolnshire), not only for his own release but for that of the whole of France. Already he knew that his half-brother, John the Bastard of Orléans, and his son-in-law, Alençon, Jane's husband, were fighting with a strange girl who said that she loved him and promised to set him free. Charles had good reason to be both proud of and grateful to his half-brother, his father's natural son, the chubby little boy his mother Valentina had raised as one of her own. Already, in March 1427, he had given him both the County of Porcien in Champagne, to be held directly from the king, and the manor of Champ-le-Roy to the south of his own great castle of Blois. In addition to this, in the following year, when the Bastard had forced the English from Châteaudun in the county of Dunois, the dauphin had created him Count of Dunois in gratitude, a title he seldom used, being happy to be known as 'the Bastard'.[4]

In December 1429, Charles of Orléans at last left Lincolnshire to be transferred to the custody of Sir John Cornwall, whom he had known for many years. Cornwall was in fact his debtor, having lent him money to pay off the Duke of Clarence in 1412 (when the army he had brought to France was no longer needed), and a sum was still owed.

However, Charles was not pressed for repayment, Sir John being one of the men who had most profited from the war. With the money he had gained from ransoms and the sale of ransacked French treasures, he had built a castle at Ampthill in Bedfordshire, standing prominent on a site which could be seen for miles. Charles was there when, in April, word came that young King Henry VI had reached Calais with an army on his way to his French coronation. Here also he heard news of the daughter, now grown up and married, whom he had not seen since she was 6.

It was while waiting for the dauphin's permission to advance against Charles's own city of Orléans that his son-in-law John, Duke of Alençon, took Joan the Maid (as they called Joan of Arc) to meet his young wife Jane who, now aged 20, was just two years older than her. The two young women took to each other immediately, Jane telling Joan how terrified she was for her husband, who had only come out of prison two years before. They had been made to give so much money for his ransom that, forced to sell his great castle of Fougères to his uncle the Duke of Brittany for a knock-down price, Charles called himself 'the poorest man in France'. She would give anything that he might remain with her she said. 'Madam do not fear', answered Joan, 'I will send him back to you safe and sound, and in even better state than he is now.'[5]

Alençon had given Joan a horse after he saw how well she could ride and manage a lance. He was not able to go with her, however, when she finally set out for Orléans, being still on parole, his ransom not yet fully paid. It was therefore the Governor of Orléans who conducted Joan to the south side of the river where Charles's half-brother, the Bastard of Orléans, was to cross the Loire to meet her.

Joan was blaming him for taking her to the wrong bank when the wind changed to allow the crossing, her divine mission being thus confirmed.

Following the relief of Orléans, Joan and her heroic champion the Bastard of Orléans tracked down the dauphin in the castle of Loches. He gave them permission to pursue the enemy and to try to retake the towns of the Loire so recently occupied by the English. This time Alençon went with them on what proved to be a triumphant campaign. In a pitched battle at Jargeau, the English commander, the Earl of Suffolk was captured by the Bastard, who not long afterwards released him on very good terms, fortuitous, as this would prove, for Charles of Orléans.

Catherine, in England, hearing of what had happened, would not have been human had she not secretly rejoiced at the campaign which, as the Maid had prophesised, restored his country to her brother, who was crowned as Charles VII with much ceremony in Reims. But the campaign was not yet over. There was more fighting to come …

Following the success of the French army, Philip, Duke of Burgundy signed a treaty with King Charles, one of the terms being that the town of Compiègne, on the River Aisne, some 40 miles to the north-east of Paris, should be handed over to the duke. When this did not happen, Burgundy ordered John of Luxembourg to reconquer the town.

At about five o'clock in the afternoon of Ascension Day (24 May 1430), Joan the Maid, as always wearing full armour, rode out of Compiègne with John of Alençon and Raoul, Lord of Gaucourt and 500–600 men to confront the advancing Burgundians. Meeting with fierce and unexpected resistance, the French retreated towards the safety of Compiègne, leaving the Maid with the rearguard trying to rally the men. Seeing this, the

Burgundians made a sudden charge and Joan, dragged from her horse by an archer, was taken prisoner.

At the Battle of Verneuil, three months later in August, the dauphin's forces were overcome, despite being reinforced by a strong Scottish contingent. Bedford himself killed the Earl of Douglas and the Scottish king's cousin, the Earl of Buchan, was also slain. Amongst the prisoners taken by the English was John, Duke of Alençon who, despite Joan of Arc's promise to his wife, was to be held in a dungeon for three long years.

8

The Maid of Orléans

Henry VI arrived in France on St George's Day (23 April) 1430. With him went his tutor the Earl of Warwick and his great-uncle the Bishop (now Cardinal) of Winchester, Henry Beaufort. On his landing, his uncle the Duke of Bedford immediately resigned the regency of the country of which Henry was now king. Three months were spent assembling at Calais followed by a whole year at Rouen.

By the time Henry VI landed in Calais, the French had won back so much territory that only Normandy and a few isolated fortresses remained in English hands. However, Cardinal Beaufort had made a rapid visit to Burgundy, just prior to Henry's embarkation, and persuaded Count John of Luxembourg to fight on the English side. This was an unexpected achievement, which turned the tide of the ongoing war, for it was just a month after Henry's arrival, in May, that Joan of Arc was captured by John of Luxembourg at Compiègne. In November, on the advice of Pierre Cauchon, Bishop of Beauvais, the English paid £10,000 (gathered from the estates of Normandy) to John of Luxembourg for the handover of Joan. She was taken to the prison in Rouen.

Her trial was delayed until 21 February 1431[1] and conducted by the Church, Bishop Cauchon and the Vice Inquisitor of France being the judges. But on 23 May, the original seventy charges of heresy were reduced to twelve, and the judges, unwilling to make her a martyr, handed her over to the secular authorities.

Warwick, the Governor of Rouen, presiding over the court, under the overall authority of Cardinal Beaufort, ordered Joan's execution, an act for which he has been consistently reviled throughout the centuries. Nonetheless, as a national leader, she was a threat to England's now tenuous hold on France. Warwick and Beaufort had little alternative other than to condemn her to death, although burning at the stake was horrific even by the brutal standards of the time.

Charles of Orléans's daughter, Jane, must have been saddened and horrified by the killing of the girl she certainly knew personally, if not as a close friend. Nothing records her reaction: indeed she may have been unaware of what had happened, for Jane herself died – for a reason unknown – in that same year of 1431.

Following the death of Joan the Maid, John, Duke of Bedford reasserted the English occupation of France. In defiance of the coronation of Charles VII at the Cathedral of Reims in 1429, Bedford arranged that Henry VI of England should be crowned King of France in the Cathedral of Notre-Dame in Paris, on 16 December 1431.

The English were again in ascendency having retaken so many of their previously held French possessions. In September the council in Rouen ordered that all the revenues from the Norman possessions of both Charles of Orléans and his son-in-law John, Duke of Alençon, belonged to the English king. Constrained as he was by his lack of income, Charles of Orléans was nonetheless to some extent heartened by the continuing attempts of his half-brother, the Bastard. to secure the release of his young half-brother John of Angoulême through an exchange for Thomas Howard, thought to be an illegitimate son of the Duchess of Clarence, captured at the Battle of Baugé in 1421 (now held by Tanguy du Châtel, the Provost of Paris). Taken as a hostage in surety of Charles's debt to Clarence at the Treaty of Buzançais in 1412 when he was only 12, John, after nineteen years of captivity, was now thirty-one.

In gratitude, Charles made the Bastard Count of Périgord and captain of the castle and town of Blois. The Bastard of Orléans then released the Earl of Suffolk, taken at the Battle of Jargeau, on condition that he paid a ransom of 20,000 écus to the Duchess of Clarence as part-payment for freeing John of Angoulême. Suffolk, who was liberated in time to attend Henry VI's coronation in Paris, continued to maintain his strong friendship with the Bastard, whose influence was soon to prove helpful to Charles of Orléans.

In the meantime, in late winter of 1431, Charles had reached the nadir of despair. First came news that his daughter Jane had died. He had not seen her since she was 6 years old, when he had said goodbye to her at Blois before riding off to be captured at Agincourt. Then, while he was still trying to come to terms with the loss of the daughter he had barely known, came word that his wife Bonne, with whom again he had spent so little time, was ill. She was said to be recovering but then he heard that she too was dead.

Again, as when Isabella had died so cruelly in giving birth to Jane, Charles poured out his misery in the *ballades* which are among the most poignant of his works. Many years later, when Jane's widower, John of Alençon was imprisoned, Charles, whose pleas to King Charles VII had saved John from execution, wrote that during his own incarceration he had sometimes wished himself dead. Never had he felt more isolated, without hope of anything better to come.

'Las! Je suis seul,' was his despairing cry. Those whom he loved were gone.

Catherine did not attend her son Henry's coronation, either at Westminster or in the Cathedral of Notre-Dame. Largely forgotten in court circles, she was by then living in Hertfordshire, far from the capital city where the action was taking place. She had fallen deeply and dangerously in love with a Welshman called Owen Tudor. Told by Gloucester that she could not marry Edmund Beaufort, she famously spat back at him: 'Then I shall marry a man so basely, yet so gently born, that my lord regents may not object.'

It has been suggested that Catherine entered a precipitate marriage with Owen Tudor because she was pregnant with a child by Edmund Beaufort. This, however, is pure speculation, probably founded on rumour spread by her enemies at court – even by that prime defamer Humfrey Gloucester himself.

Owain ap Maredudd ap Tewdwr, or Owen Tudor as he was known in England, descended from a daughter of the Welsh prince Rhys ap Gruffudd, was indeed 'gently' born. His father Maredudd ap Tudur (Meredith son of Tudor) and his two older brothers, Rhys and Gwilym, had fought with Owen Glendower in his rebellion against Henry IV in 1400, the year of the birth of his youngest son Owain. When that rising was so barbarously defeated, Maredudd's land was forfeited to the English crown.

Bereft of the income from his former estates, he had moved to London where, for safety, he had changed the name of his surviving son, Owain ap Maredudd, to that of his grandfather, thus making him Owain Tudor. It is interesting that, had he not done so, the surname of the English royal family descended from him would have been Meredith, not Tudor.

The move to London proved a wise one. Owen, as he was known hereafter, became the ward of his father's second cousin Lord Rhys, who saw to it that at the age of 7 he was sent to the court of Henry IV to be a page to the King's Steward. If, as is claimed, he was born in 1400, he must have been 15 at the time of the Battle of Agincourt, where Henry V is said to have knighted him on the field. Following his subjection of Wales, King Henry IV had deprived the Welsh people of many rights, but it is known that after Agincourt, young Owen Tudor was permitted to use Welsh arms in England.

It was after Catherine's return to England, following Henry's death in August 1422, that Owen became the keeper of the queen's wardrobe, a position likened to that of a butler or major-domo in a royal household. As such, he must have been in constant contact with Catherine over domestic matters concerning the servants, the purchase and storage of food, and the replenishment of the cellars where, in anticipation of large and frequent entertainments, quantities of wine were stored.

The legend runs, however, that Catherine fell in love with him when, looking from the window, she saw, what appeared to her to be an Adonis, rising naked from swimming in the Thames. Alternatively, another story tells, that during a festivity of some sort at Windsor Castle, the widowed Catherine was watching the dancing, sitting on a low seat surrounded by her ladies. Owen, perhaps showing off a little, was doing a pirouette when he tripped and fell sprawling into her lap. Embarrassed by his clumsiness as he would have been, this is apparently the moment she fell in love with him. That he was enamoured of her, beautiful woman as she is known to have been, seems certain. No one can have been more delighted than Owen when Gloucester's arbitrary law forbade her intended marriage to Edmund Beaufort.

Her critics made the most of it however, seizing the opportunity to put it about that she could not control her lusts. Her ladies are supposed to have begged her to have nothing more to do with Owen, saying she would demean her dignity by having a liaison with someone they saw as being of low birth. It is also suggested that her love for Owen was the main reason for what seems to have been her sudden decision to leave Windsor and the court.

She chose her time well: Humfrey of Gloucester being too occupied in his intrigues against his arch enemy Henry Beaufort, the Bishop of Winchester, to take notice of what she was about. For a widow to leave court was not unusual. Many chose the sanctuary of a nunnery, the only refuge in those days for women who were unable or unwilling to face the stresses of life in the outside world. Catherine, however, most probably used the excuse of wishing to supervise the running of the estates given to her on her marriage as part of her dower. While this must remain speculation, the one thing that does seem certain is that Humfrey of Gloucester was unaware of her liaison with Owen Tudor at this point. From what is known of his overbearing character, it would seem obvious that, had he done so, although no longer Protector since her son ruled the kingdom in name, he retained enough power, while Henry was in France, to have banished Owen from the scene.

That Humfrey, who had already thwarted her proposed marriage to Edmund Beaufort, was oblivious to her infatuation with Owen, seems proved by the fact that, sometime in 1429, when she went to live in retirement on her estates in Hertfordshire, she took Tudor with her in his capacity as head of her household.

The manor of Much Hadham stood conveniently close to the church. Catherine and Owen are believed to have been married there by her own chaplain or by the resident priest, either in the church itself or in the private chapel, which most houses of such antiquity contained. Nothing remains to prove the marriage, although it was publicly assumed to have taken place. When many years later, Richard III hurled insults at their grandson, calling him a bastard, he had no real evidence of his claim.

Built before the Norman Conquest, the manor was of very ancient foundation. Created originally as the house of the bishops of London, it was either gifted, or lent, to the couple as a place of refuge by a bishop, most likely the Bishop of Ely, within whose diocese it stood. Archaeologists have discovered that the first house was what they describe as an east-to-west hall range with a cross wing on the west. Fronted by a gatehouse, there were stables and other outhouses nearby.

The two eldest of Catherine and Owen's three sons, Edmund and Jasper, are known to have been born at Much Hadham Manor. Then, for some reason they moved to Bishop's Hatfield, perhaps for greater room and comfort as their family grew, where the manor house again belonged to a bishop who had been close to Henry V. It was here that their third son Owen was born.

Catherine's first son, Henry VI, to whom she must have appealed, issued an edict that the legitimisation of his half-brothers was unnecessary, proof that he at least regarded them as being born within wedlock. He also knighted his step-father, made him Warden of Forestries and a deputy lord lieutenant.

9

The Treachery of Burgundy

In Paris, on 17 December 1431, Henry VI of England was crowned King of France. The Cardinal of Winchester performed the coronation, to the great offence of the Bishop of Paris, who claimed this office to be his right. His anger was symptomatic of the growing tide of patriotism spreading through France, where the people were becoming increasingly resentful of English domination.

John, Duke of Bedford, faithful to his dying brother's instructions, knew that maintenance of the English conquests depended largely on the possession of Normandy and the continued alliance of Philip, Duke of Burgundy, sworn at the Treaty of Troyes. The arrangement was already tenuous when in 1432 Bedford's wife Anne, Philip's sister, died and with her, in the words of Monstrelet, 'went a great part of her brother the duke's support for the English cause'.[1] Philip consulted Burgundian lawyers, who obediently told him that while the Treaty of Troyes allowed Henry V to inherit the crown and to pass it on, that did not mean that his son Henry VI could inherit it directly from the now dead Charles VI.

Meanwhile, in Hainault Jacqueline finally submitted to Burgundy, defeated and plainly brokenhearted, for she had truly loved Humfrey of Gloucester, even after realising that he had married her only for her wealth and land. In 1334, knowing now that he would never help her, with the utmost reluctance she finally succumbed to Burgundy's claim to her lands. Acknowledging him as her overlord, she accepted the invalidity of her marriage to Humfrey, Duke of Gloucester as decreed by the Pope in Rome. But, in final defiance, she maintained her titles. She was still Countess of Holland, Zeeland and Hainault, one of the greatest heiresses in northern Europe.

Henry VI, at the age of 13, had not yet attained the seat of power, when in France negotiations for what would be the Treaty of Arras began in August 1435. Offers of reparation made by Charles VII for the part he had played, when still the dauphin, in the murder of John the Fearless, were accepted by the latter's son Duke Philip. At the instigation of Pope Eugene IV, in an attempt to establish peace, a meeting was convened at Arras on 1 July 1435. It was also decided that, if the government in power during the young king's minority in England refused to make peace or accept reasonable offers regarding the return of land, then Burgundy would sign an agreement with King Charles.

The English council, as the French had foreseen, had no right to make any settlement, and could only maintain its king's claim to the throne of France and to the conquests of land made by his father and uncle the Duke of Bedford. Subsequently, once it was seen that the council could make no formal offer, Burgundy signed a separate agreement with Charles VII.

Philip of Burgundy then sent his king of arms of the order of the Golden Fleece to visit King Henry in England with one of his heralds. On arrival, they were treated in a very circumspect manner and sent to lodge in a shoemaker's house in London, where they lived in constant fear, forbidden even to leave their lodgings to go to mass. Once delivered to the treasurer, the letters they brought caused even greater offence. Burgundy addressed Henry as 'King of England, high and mighty prince, dear lord and cousin', the title 'sovereign lord' notably absent.

Henry wept bitterly when told of Burgundy's pact with the French king, tears pouring down his face. Even twenty years later, remembering his 'good uncle of Burgundy's treachery', he could hardly hold back his grief. Humfrey of Gloucester stormed out of the council in a rage and went straight to his barge moored nearby in the Thames.[2]

The king was not the only one who was upset. As the news travelled through London some of the citizens formed themselves into a band and roamed the streets looking for merchants from Burgundy. Some were set upon and murdered before the ringleaders of their assailants were seized on the king's orders and brought to trial and imprisoned.

Shortly afterwards, word came from France that Queen Isabeau, Catherine's mother, chief architect of the Treaty of Troyes, had died in the Hôtel Saint-Pol. Following the death of her husband and her son's ascension to the throne, she had lived there, largely in retirement, for about thirteen years. So ended the life of the woman whose scandalous affair with her brother-in-law, Louis, Duke of Orléans, the man so notoriously murdered on the orders of John of Burgundy, had been the talk of Paris. Small she had always been and reputedly grown stout in later years, but never had she lost the strength of will which, in the days of her power and youth, had so galvanised both her family and the court.

Aged 64 or 65 at the time of her death, Isabeau had outlived five of the six sons and four of the six daughters she had borne. Isabella and Catherine had both been queens of England; Charles, the sole survivor of her six sons, was now, since the defeat of the English armies, the undisputed King of France. A miniature of her funeral cortège in the chronicle of Martial d'Auverne shows her lying in an open coffin, draped in material embroidered with golden fleurs-de-lis as she was rowed up the Seine towards the Basilica of St Denis, burial place of the kings and queens of France.

Catherine, Isabeau's youngest daughter, who had not seen her mother since the day – thirteen years past – when she had left France accompanying Henry's coffin, was pregnant with her fifth child when word came that her mother had died.

On 14 September, shortly after the Treaty of Arras which had categorically denied the right of his nephew to be King of France, John, Duke of Bedford died in France. His life had been dedicated to the service of his brother King Henry and to the son who succeeded him. Then, a few months later, news reached England of another death, that of Jacqueline of Hainault, Catherine's childhood friend who had first married her brother John of Touraine and who would, if he had lived, been Queen of France. Poor and alone, deserted by Humfrey of Gloucester, who had married the mistress he had flaunted before her eyes, Jacqueline had married for the third time, apparently for love. This last husband was Francis, Lord of Borssele, an influential Dutch nobleman with whom she lived happily until her death from tuberculosis in 1436.

This was the year when French and Burgundian forces combined to drive the English out of Paris. On 19 April, marching from Saint-Denis, which was already in their hands, they put scaling ladders against the walls of the city. Up them went the Lord of L'Isle-Adam, Governor of Paris, leading the way with the Bastard of Orléans at his heels. Once within, they were joined by a large number of people who went through the streets shouting, 'Peace! Long live the king and the Duke of Burgundy!' Once they had opened the gates, they were joined by the Constable and many of the French lords with a host of followers, who marched on the Bastille. The English nobles and bishops who had taken refuge in the Bastille were allowed to leave unharmed in their boats waiting in the Seine, near the Louvre. Other towns and fortresses capitulated as the tide of French nationalism, inspired by Joan of Arc, grew with an unstoppable force.

Philip of Burgundy seized the opportunity of his alliance with the King of France to declare war on England. On word of this, Humfrey Duke of Gloucester (now, since the death of Bedford, lieutenant of the king in Calais and the regions of Picardy, Flanders and Artois) at once began preparing to lead an army to defend Calais, most valued of English possessions, which was under siege. King Henry, still fulminating against the treachery of the Duke of Burgundy, went personally to Canterbury to wish his uncle, now a man of 46 but still possessed of some of the good looks for which he was famed, success in relieving the garrison of Calais.

Gloucester landed to find that Burgundy had attacked Calais on 9 June. With an army reckoned to be 30,000 strong, he was confident of an easy victory. Many of his soldiers were Flemings who fought with the object of winning the Company of the Staple of Calais, a group of traders who, in exchange for the collection and payment of taxes, owned the sole rights to participate in the valuable wool trade with England. But the city, well defended and provisioned, refused to surrender. Attempts by the Burgundians to block the harbour failed, allowing Duke Humfrey to sail in to rescue the beleaguered English garrison with a force of 10,000 men. Once Calais was safe, Gloucester raided deep into Flanders, for which success he was high in the king's favour, returning to England in triumph.

10

Betrayal

It was sometime during the summer of that year of 1436 that Catherine herself was overcome by disaster. Humfrey of Gloucester discovered her secret marriage. The identity of whoever it was informed on her remains as much of a mystery as the reasons for the intensity of the malevolence of Catherine's former brother-in-law, still so much in evidence, as he tried to destroy the happiness she seemed to have achieved with her second husband. It has never been fully explained why, since her coming to England, Gloucester had aimed so ceaselessly to cause both harm and disruption to the widow of the brother he had so much venerated. Nor do we know why Catherine's eldest son, the king, now 15, was unable to protect her. Perhaps he was terrified of his uncle, who had inaugurated the legislation preventing the widowed queen from marrying without Henry's prior consent. It is equally possible that he was unaware of his mother's troubles. Later described as mad, Henry had inherited the unbalanced mind of his French grandfather, an infliction which would occasionally deprive him of his reason throughout his life.

It was late summer; the harvest was being cut by men with scythes and carried in horse-drawn carts to the granaries in the farmsteads where it was to be stored. Catherine was heavily pregnant with her fifth child when a posse of soldiers rode up to the gates of the manor of Bishop's Hatfield. In the still, sunlit air she may have heard the captain demanding entrance in the name of the king. She could hardly comprehend what was happening when the officer told her that he bore orders from her son, the king, for her arrest.

The cruelty then shown to her seems incredible, even by the standards of that age. An anonymous scribe of the time, plainly currying favour with Gloucester, wrote that:

> the high spirit of the Duke of Gloucester could not brook her marriage. Neither the beauty of Tudor's person nor his genealogy, descended from Cadwallader kings, could shield either him or Catherine from sharp persecution as soon as the match was discovered.
>
> Her household was dissolved with immediate effect and she was parted from her children, the eldest of whom went to live with Catherine de la Pole, sister of the Earl of Suffolk. Owen was imprisoned in Newgate and Catherine sent to Bermondsey Abbey.

The latter part of this statement at least is incorrect. Owen was only imprisoned at a later date. Sadly, as far as Catherine is concerned, it is true. She was sent to Bermondsey Abbey, the ancient Benedictine foundation in what is now Bermondsey Square in the district of Southwark, and it was here, shortly after her arrival, that her one and only daughter was born.

Historians differ over what happened to the girl, only agreeing that she was named Margaret. One account relates that she died, either at birth or soon afterwards, but others aver that she lived long enough to become a nun, but died while still young. Catherine herself did not survive Margaret's birth. She may have had complications resulting in septicaemia, as was so common in those days, or she may, as was public opinion, simply have died of exhaustion, having lost all will to live.

Knowing she was dying, she made a will addressed to her first son, the king, asking him rather obscurely to carry out her wishes 'in tender and favourable fulfilling of mine intent', begging him to care for the children, his three half-brothers and the newborn daughter for whose welfare she was deeply concerned.

Certainly it is known that King Henry was never to forgive Gloucester for the cruelty he had shown to his mother. At his insistence, Catherine was given the funeral of a queen. She died on 3 January 1437, but her body lay in state at St Catherine's Chapel in the Tower of London until, on 18 February, she was taken to St Paul's Cathedral before being buried in the Lady Chapel at Westminster Abbey. King Henry had an altar tomb built for her on which she is described as the widow of his father, no mention of her second marriage being made.

By coincidence, her death occurred just a month before that of King James of Scotland. Because he blocked his escape route to stop his tennis balls from being lost, he was trapped like a rat in the sewer in which he had tried to flee below the floor of the Black Friars Monastery in Perth. He was stabbed to death by one of a band of enemies led by Sir Robert Graham, who James had arrested on his return from England in 1424. The identity of the lady he loved, who inspired his most famous poem, 'The Kingis Quair', is to this day unknown. Was it Joan Beaufort, the woman he married, as has been generally believed? Or was it the young widowed queen, Catherine, known to have been living in Windsor castle on that morning in May, the enchanting, ethereal French princess Shakespeare called 'Catherine the Fair'?

PART IV

LEGACY

1

The Widower

The full powers of kingship in England were vested in Henry VI at Windsor Castle on 13 November 1437, only ten months after the death of his mother in January of the same year. Had he only obtained authority earlier, he might have prevented her arrest and subsequent banishment from her home.

What happened next is inexplicable given the circumstances. Told of Catherine's death, Humfrey, Duke of Gloucester might well have buried the hatchet. But it was not to be so. The workings of this devious man's mind are difficult to comprehend. Gloucester issued the summons to Owen Tudor to come to Westminster, promising him a safe conduct.

On reaching the city, Owen found what he believed to be a place of sanctuary in Westminster. Ordered to come before the council, he swore he was innocent of any charge, the main one being that of marrying Queen Catherine contrary to the law passed at Duke Humfrey's instigation in 1428, prohibiting the marriage of the dowager queen without the consent of Parliament.

Believing himself acquitted, Owen thankfully left London to ride home for Wales. But he had not gone far with his few men, probably no further than the outskirts of London, before a company of hard-riding soldiers in the livery of Humfrey of Gloucester galloped up from behind with drawn swords to arrest him in the name of his stepson the king.

Cursing himself for trusting Gloucester, Owen was taken back to London as a prisoner. Robbed of all the money he possessed, £137 10s 4d, he was incarcerated in Newgate prison, most dreaded of London's jails. Built at the end of the twelfth century by Henry II, the prison took its name from one of the seven gates built into the Roman London Wall. Although renovated by the executors of Dick Whittington, it was still rat infested and renowned for cruelty.

It was also famous for bribery of jailers, particularly the unlocking of fetters and purchasing of drink and food, which made existence bearable for those who could afford it. Owen Tudor, robbed of every penny, could not benefit from this traffic. Used as he was to sleeping on a feather mattress, protected from draughts by the curtains of a four-poster bed, he now found himself lying without blankets on a pile of evil-smelling straw. Fortunately, still in his thirties, he was strong enough, both mentally and physically, to survive the cold, cruelty and near starvation.

Somehow he escaped the prison in January or February 1438. That this period encompasses the various festivals following New Year may mean that the guards were either drunk, or else bribed with promises of future compensation for turning a blind eye. But he was recaptured, this time by a henchman of Gloucester's – John, Lord Beaumont – and returned to Newgate, probably to be put in irons.

Shut away and helpless in his jail, unless informed by his jailers Owen may not have been aware at first of the dramatic changes that were taking place in the country, where the king was now ruling on his own. It would seem that, still under the influence of Gloucester, Lieutenant of the Kingdom, Henry was unaware of what had happened to the step-father he believed had gone back to Wales.

Owen was left in Newgate for another six months until, mercifully, his imprisonment was discovered and news of it taken to the king. Henry, furious at the way he had been deceived, immediately ordered Owen's release. He was freed on 14 July 1438 and transferred from his dreadful incarceration to Windsor Castle.

Interestingly, the man who rescued him was none other than Edmund Beaufort, Duke of Somerset, nephew of Henry, the Bishop of Winchester, and the man whom Catherine might have married had Gloucester not interfered. It seems likely that Beaufort, through his informants, had discovered Owen's imprisonment and reported it to Henry, in view of the fact that he was placed in Beaufort's charge. It is also known that Owen was released from supervision in July 1439, on the recognisance of £2,000, before being pardoned for all offences on 12 November of that year. Thereafter, he became a member of the king's household for an unspecified time and awarded an annuity of £40.

Henry also showed concern for his half-brothers, left bereft of their parents since their mother's death and their father's imprisonment. The two eldest, Edmund and Jasper, were being cared for by the Earl of Suffolk's sister, Lady Catherine de la Pole, the Abbess of Barking at Henry's expense. Owen, the youngest, was likewise provided for, living in a monastery at Westminster.

Following the death of the Duke of Bedford in September 1435, Richard, Duke of York became Regent of France. The task was hopeless in the face of the renewed French spirit but, together with John Talbot, Lord Shrewsbury, they fought to keep the northern part of Normandy in English hands.

Negotiations for peace continued intermittently, one of the first questions to be settled being that of the release of the Duke of Orléans, who had been held prisoner in the Tower and other fortresses for no less than twenty years, since his capture under a pile of corpses at the Battle of Agincourt in 1415. According to Monstrelet, one of the reasons for such prolonged captivity was that some of the noble gaolers were making good money from his expenses, provided by the English Exchequer.[1]

In August 1432, Charles had been transferred from the care of his austere custodian, Sir John Cornwall, to that of William de la Pole, Earl of Suffolk. This had happened only a short time after Suffolk's return to England. Taken prisoner at Jargeau by Charles's half-brother, the Bastard of Orléans, the two had formed a strong friendship before being given his release. Now much the same companionship developed between Suffolk and Charles of Orléans, who thus began the happiest time of his captivity in the company of one who not only knew and loved France, but was also a man of letters with whom he had much in common. Suffolk's main seat was at Wingfield, on the border between Norfolk and Suffolk, but he also lived much at Ewelme, the Oxfordshire estate inherited by his wife Alice Chaucer, granddaughter of the famous poet.

It was either at Wingfield or Ewelme that Charles met another Alice, first cousin of Suffolk's wife, the young widow of Sir William, also called Lord Moleyns, who had been killed in France in 1428 or 1429. A poem he wrote in English, in which her name appears as an acrostic, seems to suggest that Charles fell passionately in love with her (see Appendix 2). He appears to have wished to marry her but, surprisingly, she turned him down. In the last of seven poems thought to have been written for her, he upbraids her for her heartlessness:

Ye shal be payd after your whylfulnes
And blame nothing but your mysgovernans,
For when good love wold fay had yow avans,
Then went ye bak with wyly frauhynednes.
I knew anon your sotyl wylenes
And your danger, that was mad for ascans
Ye might have been my lady and maitres
For ever mor withouthyn varians;
Biut now my hert yn Yngland or in France
Ye go to seke other nyw besynes.

It would seem that Suffolk put paid to the romance. Alice, though a widow, was very young and he probably foresaw the opposition that the alliance of a royal prince, cousin of the king, to the widow of mere English knight, would cause, at least in France.[2] Charles was removed from Wingfield, to the care of Sir Reynold Cobham of Sterborough Castle in Surrey in May 1436.

A less happy term of imprisonment came two years later, when he found himself transferred to the guardianshp of Sir John Stourton, of Stourton in Wiltshire, a man who had raised over 100 bowmen to take to France. A member of several important embassies to the French, he was keeper of Charles of Orléans at Stourton from 1438 to 1439. Charles later complained of his strictness.[3] Although so nearly the end of his time in England, this period was one he found the hardest to endure. In particular, he loathed the winter as the cold of stone-built castles seeped into his bones. 'En yver, du feu, du feu' ('in winter, some fire, some fire'), he wrote, describing his need for the warmth of open fires.

While the French kings had been apathetic in their efforts to free him, Burgundy pushed the talks forward, not only because of their close relationship but also because, tactfully forgetting the murder of Charles's father, Louis of Orléans, at the instigation of Philip's father, John the Fearless, Burgundy saw reconciliation between them as a way of strengthening his cause.

However, it was not Philip but his wife, the Duchess Isabella, the daughter of John, King of Portugal (who had passed through England so briefly in November 1429 on her way to Flanders to marry Philip), who is known to have been the main instigator in arranging Charles of Orléans's release. Philip's first wife Michelle de Valois, sister of both Isabella and Catherine, had died childless. His second, Bonne, daughter of Philip of Artois, had also died and he had then married Isabella, a formidable lady by all contemporary accounts.

Isabella had herself seen the suffering in Normandy, a land ruined by the ravages of war whose people were abandoning it. To a delegation of the women of Paris, who had come to her to plead for peace, she had said: 'My good friends, it is one of the things of this world that I most desire, and for which I beg my lord day and night, seeing as I do the great need for it.'[4]

Charles had been allowed to go as far as Calais to attend a peace conference in the summer of 1434. But the talks had dissolved into a stalemate so that he had had to return to England seething with disappointment. Frustrated, he felt himself abandoned, but Isabella – a name he loved if only for his first wife still so dear to him after nearly thirty years – fought on with ever-greater determination to win his release.

Philip of Burgundy, trying to re-establish trade with England, made a different approach to the peace problem at Gravelines in January 1439. Henry agreed to release the Duke of Orléans for a fixed period in return for hostages and financial assurance. Cardinal Beaufort then went over to Calais to discuss the possibilities of another conference with Duchess Isabella, who insisted that Charles of Orléans be present.

Subsequently, Charles and Sir John Stourton crossed the Channel to Calais on 26 June. There, to his great joy, Charles was reunited with his half-brother, 'the Bastard', whom he had last seen as a sturdy little boy of 11. Charles was finally able to thank him for all he had done to take care of his lands over the intervening years.

Then, on 13 July, to his even greater delight, he was allowed to meet Isabella, in whom most of his hopes of freedom now lay. Together they talked for hours in the tented camp on the outskirts of Calais, stopping only for wine and sweetmeats. Finally it was Isabella who drew up a plan, if not for peace at least for a long truce, which was taken to England on 5 August by envoys to lay before King Henry. Charles meanwhile remained in Calais with Beaufort who, hearing that people were asking about him, posted extra sentinels to keep close watch.

Waiting with ever-increasing impatience, Charles's hopes were once again cruelly dashed as the envoys returned with the message that the plan was completely unacceptable to Henry. He is unlikely to have been surprised to learn that it was Gloucester who had forced the decision on his young and malleable nephew. Isabella immediately asked for safe conducts to return to Calais to confer with Charles. It was thanks to her that he was at last able to communicate with her husband, writing mainly in the *ballades* at which he was so adept. Returning to England in October, through the auspices of Cardinal Beaufort, Charles at last had an audience with the king. Henry had by then heard from Isabella of the proposed dates for the renewal of the peace conference the following year, to which he quickly replied, longing for the war to end. By then it was quite clear to him that this could never be achieved unless Charles was released. Therefore, at the audience, he gave Charles the wonderful news of the temporary freedom he was to be allowed.

Elated, Charles returned to Stourton to write letters to his friends and relatives, including the queen and the dauphin, asking them for financial support towards his ransom. Eleven of them replied offering substantial sums.

But in England, Humfrey of Gloucester stubbornly opposed Charles's release. He insisted that, in view of the known weakness of both King Charles VII and the dauphin, Charles might be made regent of France. King Henry refused to listen to him, determined to keep his word. It was the release of Orléans which led to the mortal quarrel between King Henry VI and his uncle Gloucester. Henry began to be suspicious of his uncle, believing the insinuations of some of Gloucester's enemies that he was conspiring to kill him. If true, his reasons were obvious. Henry was yet unmarried, and had no children. Humfrey, his only surviving uncle, was thus the heir to the throne.

The king's paranoia increased when Gloucester's second wife, Eleanor Cobham, was accused of planning his death through witchcraft. Normally the punishment for such treachery was drowning or burning at the stake, but thanks to her position, Eleanor was merely made to walk through the streets of 'London like a common prostitute' before being sentenced to life imprisonment under strict supervision in one of the royal castles in 1441.

From that time onwards, Henry had nothing more to do with his uncle, forbidding him to enter his presence. The Earl of Suffolk who, as the Chamberlain, was constantly at Henry's side, had taken his place as confidant.

The Parliament of February 1447 was held in Bury St Edmunds, a stronghold of Suffolk's lands. Riding there from London, Henry was closely guarded wherever he slept, so fearful had he become of Gloucester's intent to murder him. Reaching Bury St Edmunds in safety, on or about 10 February, he found armed soldiers patrolling the streets for his protection.

Gloucester arrived on the 18th, escorted by a retinue of some eighty men. Riding up a side street in the dusk, he asked what it was called and was told that it was the Street of Death. Gripped by a sudden great fear, he rode on straight to his lodgings to be bluntly informed that the king refused to see him. He was arrested shortly after and all his followers dispersed. Three days later, on 21 February, he died.

It was claimed that it was the humiliation at the hands of the nephew he believed he had loyally served that killed him. Otherwise there were whispers. Poison was so easy to procure. Strangulation was suggested but the body bore no marks when examined. Henry had no pity for the man whose cruelty towards his mother had resulted in her early death.

Messengers sent from Burgundy were allowed access to Charles of Orléans to discuss the terms of his release. Firstly, Burgundy asked if he would marry his niece, the widowed Mary, Duchess of Cleves. Secondly, he asked if Charles would sign a treaty of alliance, swearing never to take action against himself or any of his family with the exception of King Charles VII and the dauphin. Desperate to gain his liberty, under any terms, Charles concurred with both propositions. The agreement was reached on 2 July 1440. On his immediate release, the French Crown would pay the English 80,000 *écus*, while Charles, for his part, would find 140,000 at a future time.

Once free, he made a formal farewell to King Henry, and to some of the nobles with whom he had grown familiar as a captive of high rank.

Having sworn to Henry that he would do everything in his power to secure peace between England and France, Charles was granted a safe conduct to sail to Calais. From there, an escort of English knights escorted him to Gravelines where, now speaking better English than French, he arrived to a rapturous welcome both from Philip of Burgundy and his wife Duchess Isabella. In gratitude for her part in securing his freedom, he bent over Isabella's hand saying, 'Madam, I make myself your prisoner.'

In the great celebrations following his marriage to Mary of Cleves, described by the chronicler Olivier de la Marche as 'a very beautiful lady', he was made a Knight of the Golden Fleece of Burgundy, the order founded by Philip's grandfather, Philip the Bold, in 1396.

Returning home to the great castle of Blois, to even greater rejoicing, he found to his great delight that his precious collection of books, mostly rare and expensive acquisitions, had been rescued and moved by Yolande of Aragon to Saumur, to save them from being stolen by the English. Charles loved women. Particularly beautiful ones, as Yolande is known to have been. And women loved him. It was now twenty-five years since that blissful summer of 1415 when Yolande had brought her own children and the pathetic little dauphin Charles, so abandoned by his mother that she had taken him under her wing, to stay with Charles at Blois. How young they had all then been. How totally unaware of the impending cataclysm of Agincourt.

Once back in France, Charles was at first involved in politics, being influential in achieving the Truce of Tours in 1444, which assured a five-year peace between France and England, which proved a prelude to the end of the Hundred Years War in 1553.

Retiring largely from public life, he was much acclaimed both as a poet and scholar. His own major works are the two books produced during his captivity, one written in French, the other in English. Although at 46, he was well past what was then considered to be middle age, he had three children with his third wife Mary of Cleves, two daughters and a son named Louis who, in 1498, would become Louis XII, King of France.

Charles would not be there to see this. Returning from an assembly summoned by Louis XI, to his beloved castle of Blois, he was taken ill at Amboise where, on the night of 4–5 January 1565, he died at the age of 71.

2

The King's Half-brothers

King Henry VI spent the Christmas of 1452 at Greenwich, where his wife Queen Margaret was living at the time. It was here that he held the investiture and knighted his two half-brothers, Edmund and Jasper Tudor who had been living in Wales with their father, Owen Tudor, since the death of their mother, Queen Catherine. To increase their status he gave them earldoms, Edmund became the Earl of Richmond and Jasper the Earl of Pembroke.

The rights of their new ennoblement gave them a sustainable income, due to the newly increased farmland rents. Also, of greater importance to Henry, they had the right to summon men to arms. Owen Tudor, of whom little is known since his becoming a member of the king's household around 1440, is believed to have gone with Edmund to South Wales in the autumn of 1455. Edmund died the following year, after which Owen apparently either lived with, or at least joined forces with, his younger son Jasper, Earl of Pembroke, now a man of substance.

On 8 August 1456, tenants of the Duke of York, in confrontation with King Henry, having raised an army in Hereford, marched on Carmarthen Castle, took it by storm and imprisoned Owen's eldest son, Edmund Tudor, Earl of Richmond. They took Aberystwyth Castle, but Henry then granted both that and Carmarthen Castle to his other half-brother, Jasper Tudor, Earl of Pembroke, before York himself could take them into his possession.

It was now recognised that Henry VI, scholar and lover of the arts, founder of both Eton College and King's College, had inherited the mental instability of his French grandfather, Charles VI. In view of this, his cousin Richard Duke of York seized the chance to put forward his claim that, as the direct descendant of Lionel, Duke of Clarence (second son of Edward III), he had a better claim to be King of England than Henry, descended as he was from John of Gaunt, King Edward's third son.

The rights of the Lancastrians to rule England had been questioned ever since Henry IV usurped the throne of Richard II. For this reason, and because his sanity was doubtful, Henry VI, did not command the trust of all his great subjects. On 9 October 1459, a Parliament was hastily convened to meet at Coventry. Henry's queen, Margaret of Anjou, won a parliamentary attainder against the Duke of York and his confederates, the earls of Warwick, Salisbury, March and Rutland.

The attainted earls then mounted a campaign to capture the king, though at that point they had no thought of deposing him. They encountered the royal army at Northampton on 10 July. After half an hour's fighting most of Henry's closest supporters were killed, and he himself was taken prisoner. Subsequently, for more than a year, the king acted in accordance with the will of the confederate earls.

On 16 October 1460, York's legal council formally submitted his claim in the Upper House to the kingdoms of England and France and to the lordship of Ireland, by right of inheritance superior to Henry VI.[1]

Nine days later, on 25 October, in answer to York's insistent demands, the peers of the realm proposed a compromise to Henry, namely that he should continue to reign until his death or voluntary abdication, but that he would disinherit his own son in favour of York's heirs. Terrified, without his forceful queen to guide him, Henry submitted to their demands.

Queen Margaret, however, did not. From Jasper Tudor's castle of Denbigh, whither she had fled after the Battle of Northampton, she took refuge in Scotland in Lincluden Abbey with the Queen Dowager Mary of Guelders and her young son James III. Margaret was arranging for Scottish help against her enemies when news from England came of her supporters' triumph. On 30 December, her army, led by the dukes of Somerset and Exeter and the Earl of Northumberland, had taken York by surprise and killed both him and the Earl of Rutland, his second son.

On 2 February 1461, Edward of Rouen, eldest surviving son of Richard of York, defeated Jasper, Earl of Pembroke and the Earl of Wiltshire at Mortimer's Cross near Wigmore and drove them back into Wales. Tragically, amongst those taken prisoner in this action was Jasper's father, Owen Tudor, who, knowing he was about to be beheaded, murmured 'that hede shalle ly on the stocke that wass wonte to lye on Quene Katheryns lappe'.[2]

His head was placed on the market cross where a woman, supposedly mad, washed the blood from his face and set 100 candles about him. His body was buried in a chapel on the north side of the Greyfriar's Church in Hereford. He lay there without a memorial until his natural son David, born in 1459 in Pembroke Castle, who was only 2 at the time of his father's death, paid for a tomb. Owen Tudor was not forgotten however. Welsh poets kept alive the memory of the man loved by Catherine, England's fair French queen.

Fortunately, Catherine did not live to see her firstborn son Henry VI murdered in the Tower of London on the night or early morning of 21–22 May 1471, supposedly on the order of York's eldest son, who would thus become Edward IV.

When he died at what is thought to have been the age of 61, Owen Tudor could have had no idea, or even possibly imagined, that his Welsh name would be borne by the most famous dynasty of kings and queens in England. His eldest son Edmund, had a son named Henry by his marriage to Margaret Beaufort, daughter of John Beaufort, 1st Duke of Somerset, who would famously defeat Richard III (brother of the Duke of York who had taken the crown of Henry VI) at the Battle of Bosworth in 1485.

Thus it is that Queen Catherine of Valois is remembered today as the daughter of a king, the wife of a king, the mother of a king and the grandmother of a king. Few can have had a greater effect on posterity than did she.

Envoi

When Catherine's Tudor grandson, Henry VII, became King of England, the Lady Chapel in Westminster Abbey was destroyed to make room for his own magnificent chapel. Catherine's remains were then placed on the right side of her first husband's, where they could still be seen, 'the bones being firmly united and thinly clothed with flesh like the scrapings of fine leather', as Samuel Pepys described them when, on 24 February 1668, he visited the abbey and wrote that he had kissed the lips of a queen.[1] Subsequently, over 200 years later, in the reign of Queen Victoria, in 1878, Catherine was finally buried beneath the altar slab of Henry V's chapel.

Appendix 1

'The Kingis Quair', attributed to King James I of Scotland

This appendix offers selected extracts from the poem's 197 stanzas in 1,375 lines. They epitomise the contradictions of character typical of an age when a man, to maintain his authority, could send his nearest relations to their deaths and at the same time write movingly of 'the lytill squerell full of besyness' and of fish swimming in crystal water over 'gravel bright as ony gold'.

Although an allegory, the poem is also partly autobiographical, for it describes James's sea journey, his imprisonment and the huge excitement of falling in love before he finds himself in a dream country amongst animals known in his day. Finally he dedicates his 'quair', his work, to Gower and Chaucer, the leading poets of his time, whom he plainly held in veneration.

The comparison of King James's verses with those of the Duke of Orléans is interesting for it suggests that, sharing common interests, they may have formed a friendship to distract themselves from the monotony both were forced to endure in those long days of imprisonment in the Tower.

The Kingis Quair

1

Heigh in the hevynnis figure circulere
The rody sterres twynklyng as the fyre;
And, in Aquary, Citherea the clere
Rynsid hir tressis like the goldin wyre
That late tofore in fair and fresche atyre
Through Capricorn heved hir hornis bright,
North northward approchit the mydnyght,–

2

Quhen, as I lay in bed allone waking,
New partit out of slepe a lyte tofore,
Fell me to mynd of many diverse thing,
Of this and that, can I nought sat quharfore –
Bot slepe for craft in erth might I no more,
For quhich as tho coude I no better wyle,
Bot toke a boke to rede apon a quhile.

8

The long[e] night beholding (as I saide),
Myn eyne gan to smert for studying.
My buke I schet and at my hede it laide,
And doun I lay bot ony tarying,
This mater new in my mynd rolling:
This is to seyne: how that eche estate,
As Fortune lykith, thame will [ay] translate.

11

Forwakit and forwalowit, thus musing,
Wery forlyin, I lestnyt sodaynlye
And sone I herd the bell to matyns ryng
And up I rase, no langer wald I lye.
Bot now (how trowe ye?) suich a fantasye
Fell me to mynd that ay me toght the bell
Said to me, 'Tell on, man, quhat thee befell.'

23

Puruait of all that was us necessarye,
With wynd at will, up airly by the morowe,
Streight unto schip, no longer wold we tarye,
The way we tuke, the tyme I tald toforowe.
With mony 'fare wele' and 'Sanct Johne to borowe'
Of falowe and frende, and thus with one assent
We pullit up saile and furth oure wayis went.

24

Upon the wawis weltering to and fro,
So infortunate was us that fremyt[i] day
That maugré, playnly,[ii] quhethir we wold or no,
With strong hand, by fors, shortly to say,
Of inymyis[iii] takin and led away
We weren all, and broght in thair contree,
Fortune it schupe non othir wayis to be.

25

Quhare as in strayte ward and in strong prisoun,
So ferforth, of my lyf the hevy lyne,
Without comfort, in sorrowe abandoun,
The secund sister lukit hath to twyne[iv]
Nere by the space of yeris twise nyne;
Til Jupiter his merci list[v] advert,[vi]
And send confort in relesche of my smert.[vii]

---

i	Fremyt = unlucky.
ii	Maugré plainly = plainly in spite of.
iii	Inimys = enemies.
iv	Twine = spin.
v	List = choose to.
vi	Advert = direct.
vii	Relesche of my smert = relief of my pain.

26

Quare as in ward full oft I wold bewaille
My dedely lyf, full of peyne and penance,
Saing ryght thus: 'Quhat hav I gilt, to faille
My fredome in this warld and my plesance?'
Sen every wight has therof suffisance
That I behold, and I a creature
Put from all this, hard is myn aventure!

27

The bird, the beste, the fisch eke in the see,
They lyve in fredome, everich in his kynd;
And I a man, and lakkith libertee!
Quhat schall I seyne? quhat resoun may I fynd
That Fortune suld do so? Thus in my mynd
My folk I wold argewe – bot all for noght,
Was none that myght, that on my peynes rought.[i]

29

The long dayes and the nyghtis eke
I wold bewaille my fortune in this wise,
For quhich, agane distresse confort to seke,
My custom was on mornis for to ryse
Airly as day – O happy exercise,
By thee come I to joye out of torment!
But now to purpose of my first entent.'

30

Bewailing in my chamber thus allone,
Despeired of all joye and remedye,
Fortirit of my thocht and wo begone,
And to the wyndow gan I walk in hye
To see the warld and folk that went forby;
As for the tyme, tho I of mirthis fude
Myght have no more, to luke it did me gude.

---

i   Rought = debate.

31

Now was there maid fast by the touris wall
A gardyn fair, and in the corneris set
Ane herber[ii] grene with wandis[iii] long and small
Railit about; and so with treis set
Was all the place, and hawthorn hegis knet,
That lyf was non walking there forby
That myght within scarse any wight aspye,

32

So thik the bewis and the leves grene
Beschadit[iv] all the aleyes that there were.
And myddis every herber myght be sene
The scharp grene suete jenepere,[v]
Growing so fair with branchis[vi] here and there,
That, as it semyt to a lyf without,
The bewis spred the herber all about.[vii]

33

And on the small grene twistis sat
The lytill suete nyghtingale, and song
So loud and clere the ympnis consecrat[viii]
Of lufis use, now soft, now lowd among,
That all the gardyng and the wallis rong[ix]
Ryght of thair song and of the copill[x] next
Of their suete armony; and lo the text:

---

ii	Heber = arbour.
iii	Wandis = palings.
iv	Beschadit = shading.
v	Jenepere = juniper.
vi	Branchis = branches.
vii	'Boughs spread all over the arbour'.
viii	Ympnis consecret = consecrated hymns.
ix	Rong = rang.
x	Copill = couplet.

34

Cantus: Worschippe, ye that loveris bene, this May,
For of your blisse the kalendis[i] ar begonne,
And sing with us, 'Away, winter, away!
Cum, somer, cum, the suete sesoun and sonne!
Awake for schame! that have your hevynnis wonne,
And amorously lift up your hedis all.
Thank Lufe that list you to his merci call.'

40

And therwith kest I doun myn eye ageyne,
Quhare as I sawe, walking under the tour,
Full secretly new cummyn hir to pleyne,
The fairest of the freschest yong floure
That ever I sawe, me thought, before that houre;
For quhich sodayn abate anon astert[ii]
The blude of all my body to my hert.

41

And though I stude abaisit tho a lyte,[iii]
No wonder was: for quhy my wittis all
Were so overcom with plesance and delyte,
Onely throu latting of myn eyen fall,
That sudaynly my hert became hir thrall
Forever, of free wyll; for of manace[iv]
There was no takyn in hir suete face.

42

And in my hede I drewe ryght hastily
And eft sones I lent it forth ageyne[v]
And sawe hir walk, that verray womanly,

---

i   Kalendis = first days of the month.
ii   Astert = rushed.
iii   A little discomposed.
iv   Manace = menace.
v   'Soon after I looked out again'.

With no wight mo,^{vi} bot onely women tueyne.
Than gan I study in myself and seyne;
'A, suete ar ye a wardly creature
Or hevinly thing in likeness of nature?

43

Or ar ye god Cupidis owin princesse
And cummyn ar to louse me out of band?
Or ar ye verray Nature the goddesse
That have depaynted with your hevinly hand
This gardyn full of flouris, as they stand?
Quhat sall I think? Allace, quhat reverence
Sall I minister to your excellence?

44

Gif ye a goddesse be, and that ye like
To do me payne, I may it noght astert.
Gif ye be wardly wight that dooth me sike
Quhy lest God mak you so, my derrest hart,
To do a sely prisoner thus smert
That luftis yow all and wote of noght bot wo?
And therfore merci, suiete, sen it is so.'

45

Quhen I a lytill thrawe had maid my moon,
Bewailing myn infortune and my chance,
Unknawin how or quhat was best to doon,
So ferr I fallyng into Lufis dance
That sodeynly my wit, my contenance,
My hert, my will, my nature and my mynd,
Was changit clene ryght in anothir kynd.

---

vi   Mo = no more.

46

Of hir array the form gif I sall write
Toward, hir goldin hair and rich atyre
In fret wise couchit with perllis quhite
And grete balas[i] lemyng as the fire,
With mony ane emeraut and fair saphire;
And on hir hede a chaplet fresche of hewe,
Of plumys[ii] partit rede and quhite and blewe.

47

Full of quaking spangis bryght as gold,
Forgit of schap like to the amorettis,[iii]
So new, so fresch, so plesant to beholde,
The plumys eke like to the flour jonettis
And othir of schap like to the flour burnettis,
And above all this there was, wele I wote,
Beautee eneuch to mak a world to dote.

48

About her hir nek, quhite as the fyne amaille,[iv]
A gudely cheyne of small orfeverye[v]
Quhareby there hang a ruby, without faille,
Lyke to ane hert schapin verily,
That, as a sperk of lowe, so wantonly
Semyt birnyng[vi] upon hir quhyte throte.
Now gif there was gud partye, God it wote!

---

i   Balas, a ruby orange red in colour.
ii   Plumys = plumes.
iii   Amorettis = love knots.
iv   Amaille = enamel.
v   Orfeverye = delicate gold work.
vi   Semyt birnyng = seemed burning.

53

Quhen I with gude entent this orisoun
Thus endit had, I stynt[vii] a lytill stound.[viii]
And eft myn eye full pitously adoun
I kest, behalding unto her lytill hound
That with his bellis[ix] playit on the ground:
Than wold I say and sigh therewith a lyte,
'A, wele were him that now were in thy plyte!'

54

An othir quhile the lytill nyghtingale
That sat apon the twiggis wold I chide,
And say right thus: 'Quhare ar thy notis smale
That thou of love has song this morowe tyde?
Seis thou noght hir that sittis thee besyde?
For Venus sake, the blissful goddesse clere,
Sing on agane and mak my lady chere.'

He then scolds the nightingale for stopping its song:

57

O lytill wrech, allace, maist thou noght se
Quho commyth yond? Is it now tyme to wring?
Quhat sory thought is fallin upon thee?
Opyn thy throte; hastow no lest to sing?
Allace, sen thou of resoun had felyng,
Now, suete bird, say ones to me 'pepe'
I dee for wo, me think thou gywnis slepe[x]

67

And quhen sche walkit had a lytill thrawe
Under the suete grene bewis bent,

---

vii	Stynt = ceased.
viii	Stound = time.
ix	Bellis = balls.
x	'Die, it seems to me to begin.'

Hir fair fresche face, as quhite as ony snawe,
Scho turnyt has and furth hir wais went.
Bot tho began myn axis and torment:
To sene hir part, and folowe I na myght
Me thought the day was turnyt into nyght.

151

'Now go thy way and have gude mynd upon
Quhat I have said in way of thy doctryne.'
'I sall. Madame,' quod I. And ryht anon
I tuke my leve als straught as any lyne:
Within a beme, that thro the contree dyvine,
Sche, percyng throw the firmamamament, extendit,
To ground ageyne my spirit is descendit.

152

Quhare in a lusty plane, tuke I my way
Endlang[i] a river plesant to behold,
Enbroudin all with fresche flouris gay,
Quihare throu the gravel bryght as ony gold
The cristall water ran so clere and cold
That in myn ere maid contynualy
A maner soun, mellit[ii] with armony,

153

That full of lytill fischis by the brym
Now here, now there, with bakkis blew as lede,
Lap and playit, and in a rout can swym
So prattily, and dressit tham to sprede
Their curall[iii] fynnis as the ruby rede
That in the sonne on their scalis bryght
As gesserant[iv] ay glitterit in my sight.

---

i   Endlang = along.
ii   Mellit = mixed.
iii   Curall = coral coloured.
iv   Gesserant = scale-armour.

154

And by this ilke ryver syde alawe
Ane hye-way fand I like to bene,
On quhich on euery syde a long[e] rawe
Of treis saw I, full of levis grene,
That full of fruyte delitable were to sene.
And also, as it come unto my mynd,
Of bestis sawe I mony diverse kind:

155

The lyuoun king and his fere^v lyonesse,
The pantere like unto the smaragdyne,^{vi}
The lytill squerell full of besyness,
The slaw ase (the druggar^{vii} beste of pyne),
The nyce ape, the werely^{viii} porpapyne,
The percyng lynx, the lufare^{ix} unicorne
That voidis venym with his evour^x horne.

156

There saw I dresse him new[e] out of haunt^{xi}
The fery tiger full of felonye,
The dromydare, the standar^{xii} oliphant,
The wyly fox (the wedowis inemye),
The clymbare gayte, the elk for alblastrye,^{xiii}
The herknere^{xiv} bore, the holsum grey^{xv} for hortis,
The hair also that oft gooth to the wortis,^{xvi}

---

v	Fere = companion.
vi	Smaragdyne = emerald.
vii	Drugger = drudger.
viii	Werely = warlike.
ix	Lufare = lover.
x	Evour = ivory.
xi	Haunt = lair.
xii	Standar = always standing.
xiii	Alblastyre = archery.
xiv	Herknere = quick of hearing.
xv	Holsum grey = grey badger.
xvi	Wortis = vegetable patch.

157

The bugill[i] draware by his hornis grete,
The martrik sable, the foynyee,[ii] and mony mo:
The chalk-quhite ermyn tippit as the jete,
The riall hert, the conyng,[iii] and the ro,
The wolf that of the murthir noght say 'ho',
The lesty bever and the ravin[iv] bare,
The chamelot[v] the camel full of hare.

197

Unto the impnis[vi] of my maisteris dere,
Gowere and Chaucere, that on the steppis satt
Of rethorike quhill thai were lyvand here,
Superlative as poetis laureate
In moralitee and eloquence ornate,
I recommend my buk in lynis sevin,
And eke thair saulis unto the blisse of Hevin. Amen.

---

i   Bugill = wild ox.
ii   Foynyee = beech marten.
iii   Conyng = coney or rabbit.
iv   Ravin = hungry.
v   Chamelot = camlet (a rich fabric).
vi   Impnis = spirits.

Appendix 2

Poems by Charles Duke of Orléans

Rondel

Strengthen, my Love, this castle of my heart,
And with some store of pleasure give me aid,
For Jealousy, with all them of his part,
Strong siege about the weary tower has laid.
Nay, if to break his bands thou art afraid,
Too weak to make his cruel force depart,
Strengthen at least this castle of my heart,
And with some store of pleasure give me aid.
Nay, let not Jealousy, for all his art
Be master, and the tower in ruin laid,
That still, ah Love! thy gracious rule obeyed.
Advance, and give me succour of thy part;
Strengthen, my Love, this castle of my heart.

Spring

The year has changed his mantle cold
Of wind, of rain, of bitter air;
And he goes clad in cloth of gold,
Of laughing suns and season fair;
No bird or beast of wood or wold
But doth with cry or song declare
The year lays down his mantle cold.
All founts, all rivers, seaward rolled,
The pleasant summer livery wear,
With silver studs on broidered vair;
The world puts off its raiment old,
The year lays down his mantle cold.

Alas Mercy, Where Shal Myn Hert Yow Fynd?

Alas mercy, where shal myn hert yow fynd?
Never had he with yow ful aqwaintans;
Now com to hym and put of hys grevans.
Ellys ye be be unto yowr frend unkind!
Mercy, he hath ever yow in hys mynd:
One let hym have sum confort of plesans!
Let hym not dey, but mak at ons amende;
In all hys woo an right heavy penans,
Noght is the help that whyl not hym avans
Slauth hys to me time and ever com behynde.

En Regardant Vers le Pais de France

En regardant vers le pais de France,
Un jour m'advint, à Douvres sur la mer,
Qu'il me souvint de la douce plaisance
Que je soulais au dit pays trouver;
Si commencai de Coeur à soupirer,
Combien certes que grand bien me faisoit
De voir France que mon Coeur aimer doit.

Je m'avisai que c'était non savance
De tells soupirs dedans mon Coeur garder,
Vu que je vois que la voie commence
De bonne paix, qui tous biens peut donner;
Pour ce, tournai en confort mon penser;
Mais non pourtant mom coeur ne se lassoit
De voir France que mon Coeur aimer doit.

Alors chargeai en la nef d'Espérance
Tous mes souhaits, en leur priant d'aller
Outre la mer, sans fair demeurance,
Et à France de me recommander,
Or nous donn' Dieu bonne paix sans tarder!
Adonc aurai loisir, mais qu'ainsi soit,
De voir France que mon Coeur aimer doit.

Paiz est trésor qu'on ne peur trop louer.
Je hais guerre, point ne la dois priser;
Destourbé m'a longtemps, soit tort ou droit,
De voir France que mon couer aimerd doit.

English translation by James Kirkup:

Gazing at the coast of France
the other day, from Dover on the sea,

Recalling the sweet pleasures
I enjoyed once on those shores.

My soul began to
Sigh at the joy it gave to
see her once again –
the France so dear to my heart,
– I knew how foolish it felt

To harbour such sighs
in my heart, now that I know
the way is open
for a true peace, that can bring
nothing but good for us all.

I took comfort in
that thought, And yet my heart still
Was yearning to see
The France so dear to my heart
– So freighted the ship of Hope

with all my desires,
begging them to sail, with no
delay o'er the sea
and remember me to France
that God's true peace soon may come!

I shall know no rest
Until it is granted to me
To behold once more
The France so dear to my heart.
Peace is a treasure beyond price.

I hate war. Never more shall I sing its praises.
Rightly or wrongly,
I have yearned so long to see
That France so dear to my heart!

Notes

Part I

1 The First Daughter
1 Thompson, P.E. (ed.), *Contemporary Chronicles of The Hundred Years War: From the Works of Jean le Bel, Jean Froissat & Enguerrand de Monstrelet*, translated and edited by P.E. Thompson, The Folio Society, London, 1966, p.205.
2 Ibid.
3 Ibid., p.206.
4 Ibid., p.209.

2 Childhood of Fear
1 Thompson, P.E. (ed.), *Contemporary Chronicles of The Hundred Years War*, p.217.
2 Ibid., p.220.
3 Ibid., p.222.
4 Ibid., p.226.

4 A Journey of Diplomacy
1 This would have been 1366 according to the Julian calendar.
2 Hutchison, Harold E., *The Hollow Crown: A Life of Richard II*, Methuen, 1979, p.15.
3 Ibid., p.26.
4 Froissart, J., *Chronicles*, translated and edited by Geoffrey Brereton, Penguin, 1968, p.251.
5 Froissart, *Chronicles*, pp.238–9.

5 The French Bride
1 Froissart, *Chronicles*, p.244.
2 Thompson, P.E. (ed.), *Contemporary Chronicles of The Hundred Years War*, p.245.
3 Ibid., p.462.
4 Ibid.
5 Ibid., p.254.

6 A Poet is Born

1 McLeod, Enid, *Charles of Orleans: Prince and Poet*, Chatto and Windus, 1969, p.18.
2 Bibliothéque nationale, Paris. Mss.fr. 10431:1828, 1829.
3 McLeod, *Charles of Orleans*, p.279.

7 The Little Queen

1 Hutchison, *The Hollow Crown*, p.127.
2 Froissart, *Chronicles*, pp.425–6.
3 Ibid., p.431.

8 The Fatal Challenge

1 Froissart, *Chronicles*, p.432.
2 Hutchison, *The Hollow Crown*, p.195.
3 Ibid., pp.206–7.
4 Froissart, *Chronicles*, p.440.
5 Ibid.

9 Lancaster's Revenge

1 Froissart, *Chronicles*, p.454.
2 Ibid., p.451.
3 Ibid., pp.452–3.

10 'My God! A Wonderful Land is This!'

1 Ibid., pp. 456–7.
2 Froissart, *Chronicles*, p.460.
3 Ibid., p.462.
4 Ibid.
5 Hutchison, *The Hollow Crown*, p.226.
6 Galbraith, V.H., 'A New Life of Richard II', *History* XXVI (1942), 223–39.

11 The Only Chance of Safety

1 The title held by Prince Charles to this day.
2 British Museum, Add. Mss. 38,690, f.9.

Part II

1 Mortal Rivalry

1 McLeod, *Charles of Orleans*, p.60.
2 Ibid., p.61.

2 England 1410–12

1 Lloyd, Sir J.E., *Owen Glendower*, Oxford University Press, 1931, pp.96–8.
2 For a full description of the Welsh rebellion see Hutchison, *Henry V*.
3 McLeod, *Charles of Orleans*, p.69.
4 Ibid., p.71.
5 Ibid.
6 Ibid., p.76.
7 Ibid., p.77.

3 The Cabochien Revolt

1   McLeod, *Charles of Orleans*, p.90.
2   Ibid. p.99.

4 The Price of a Bride

1   Hutchison, H.F., *Henry V*, Eyre and Spottiswoode, 1967, p.92.
2   Monstrelet, *The Hundred Years War*, The Folio Society, p.37.
3   McLeod, *Charles of Orleans*, p.116.
4   Stat.12 Richard II c.6 and ii Henry IV c4; Rot. Parl.III, 643.
5   Allmand, Christopher, *Henry V*, Methuen, London, 1992, p.73.

5 Invasion

1   Thompson, P.E. (ed.), *Contemporary Chronicles of The Hundred Years War*, p.267.
2   British Museum, Add.Ch. 2607, 4321, 4322.
3   Allmand, *Henry V*, p.86.
4   Shakespeare, *Henry V* (IV.3, II.16–8).
5   Allmand, *Henry V*, p.91.
6   Vickers, K.H., *Humphrey, Duke of Gloucester*, Create Space Independent Publishing Platform (19 February 2014), p.30.
8   Ibid., p.131.

7 The Conqueror

1   McLeod, *Charles of Orleans*, p.199.

8 A Princess Lovely to the Eye

1   Kingsford, C.L., *Henry V*, New York/London, 1901, p.249.
2   Hutchison, *Henry V*, p.272.

9 The Royal Captives

1   Beaucourt, G. du Fresne de, *Histoire de Charles VII*, Paris, 1888–94, I, 791–2.
2   McLeod, *Charles of Orleans*, p.150.
3   Ibid.
4   Ibid., p.151.
5   Ibid., p.152.
6   Balfour-Melville, E.W.M., *James I, King of Scots, 1406–1437*, Methuen, 1936, p.77.
7   Hutchison, *Henry V*, p.183.

10 The Treaty of Troyes

1   Hutchison, *Henry V*, p.185.
2   Ibid., p.187.
3   Ibid., p.188.
4   Allmand, *Henry V*, p.144.

11 Summons for the Scottish King

1   Balfour-Melville, *James I*, p.81.
2   Ibid., p.80.
3   Hutchison, *Henry V*, p.189.
4   Balfour-Melville, *James I*, p.82.
5   Hutchison, *Henry V*, p.191.
6   Monstrelet, *The Hundred Years War*, p.289.
7   Rymer, T. Foedera , *Conventiones, Litterae, etc.*,Vols, 7–10 (London 1709–10) X, p.224.

12 The Hero of England's Return
1   Allmand, *Henry V*, p.156.
2   Balfour-Melville, *James I*, p.83.
3   Ibid., pp.83–4.
4   Vickers, *Humphrey, Duke of Gloucester*, p.77.
5   Hutchison, *Henry V*, p.200.
6   Ibid., p.84.
7   Hearne, T. (ed.) *Vita et Gesta Henrici Quinti*, 1727. Wrongly attributed to Thomas Elmham. Probably written 1445.
8   McLeod, *Charles of Orleans*, p.156.
9   Balfour-Melville, *James I*, p.64.

13 Return to France
1   E.R. 101- 407-4-18.
2   Rymer, *Conventiones, Litterae, etc.*, pp.123–4.
3   Vickers, *Humphrey, Duke of Gloucester*, p.80.
4   Hall, Edward, *Hall's Chronicle; Containing the History of England ...* edited by Henry Ellis, Longman et al., 1809. p.108.
5   Balfour-Melville, *James I*, p.88.
6   Rymer, *Conventiones, Litterae, etc.*, pp.153–4.

14 Last Battle of a Soldier King
1   Rymer, *Conventiones, Litterae, etc.*, p.227.
2   Allmand, *Henry V*, p.170.
3   Monstrelet, *The Hundred Years War*, p.289.
4   Hutchison, *Henry V*, p.212.
5   Walsingham, *The Chronica Maiora of Thomas Walsingham*, p.343.
6   Allmand, *Henry V*, p.174.
7   Ibid., p.176.
8   Hutchison, *Henry V*, p.216.

Part III

2 Invasion of Hainault
1   McLeod, *Charles of Orleans*, p.158.
2   Ibid., p.144.
3   Ibid., p.160.

3 The Poet King
1   Exchequer Rolls. Public Record Office. 407.13, 16–17.
2   Balfour-Melville, *James I*, p.97.
3   Exchequer Rolls. pp.407–14.

4 Mother of the King
1   Wolff, Henry Bertram, *Henry VI*, Methuen, 1981, pp.28–9.
2   Ibid., p.33.
3   Ibid., p.34.
4   Ibid., p.36.

5 Rivals in the War for Power

1   Wolff, *Henry VI*, p.40.
2   Vickers, *Humphrey, Duke of Gloucester*, p.133.
3   Wolff, *Henry VI*, pp.44–5.
4   For a fuller description of this incident and others, see Vickers, *Humphrey, Duke of Gloucester*, pp.127–60.

7 Renewal of the War in France

1   Monstrelet, *The Hundred Years War*, p.294.
2   McLeod, *Charles of Orleans*, p. 174.
3   Ibid., p.172. This and the following statements in this paragraph are Joan's replies of 22 February, 10 and 13 March to the questions put to her during her trial. Mcleod quotes from *Les Deux Proc`es de Jeanne d'Arc, II*, Henri Pion, 1868, pp.56, 110, 121.
4   Ibid., p.173.
5   Ibid.

8 The Maid of Orléans

1   Thompson, P.E. (ed.), *Contemporary Chronicles of The Hundred Years War*, pp.313–16.

9 The Treachery of Burgundy

1   Thompson, P.E. (ed.), *Contemporary Chronicles of The Hundred Years War*, p.317.
2   Ibid. pp.318–19.

Part IV

1 The Widower

1   McLeod, *Charles of Orleans*, pp.150–1.
2   McLeod, *Charles of Orleans*, pp.215–16.
3   Seward, Desmond, *The Hundred Years War: The English in France, 1337–1453*, Penguin, 1999, p.204.
4   McLeod, *Charles of Orleans*, p.203.

2 The King's Half-brothers

1   Wolff, *Henry VI*, p.324.
2   Gairdner, James (ed.), *The historical collections of a citizen of London in the fifteenth century*, Camden Society, 1876, p.211.

Envoi

1   Pepys, Samuel, *The Diary of Samuel Pepys*, 24 February 1668, George, Allen & Unwin, 1929.

Bibliography

Allmand, Christopher, *Henry V* (London: Methuen & Co. Ltd, 1992)

Balfour-Melville, E.W.M. *James I. King of Scots* (London: Methuen & Co. Ltd, 1936)

Beaucourt, G. *du Fresne de. Histoire de Charles VII* (Paris, 1881–91)

Bibliothéque nationale, Paris. Mss.fr. 10431:1828.1829

Bingham, Caroline, *James V, King of Scots* (London: Collins, 1971)

British Museum. Add. Mss.38,690. F.9

Donaldson, Gordon, 'James V–James VI', *The Edinburgh History of Scotland*, Vol. 3 (Edinburgh: Mercat Press, James Thin Ltd, 1965)

E. 407. From Exchequer of Receipt, Issue Rolls

Ellis, Henry (ed.) *The Chronicle of John Hardyng* (In metre). Wrongly attributed to Thomas Elmham, probably written 1445 (London, 1812)

Froissart, Jean, *Chronicles*, Selected, translated and edited by Geoffrey Brereton (Penguin Books, 1968)

Froissart, Jean and Enguerrand de Monstrellet, *The Hundred Years War*, MCMLXVI, translated and edited by Peter E. Thompson (London: The Folio Society, London)

Gairdner (ed.) *The Historical collections of a citizen of London in the fifteenth century* (CS new series, The Camden Society, 1876)

Galbraith,V.H., 'A New life of Richard II', *History*, XXVI (Yale: University Press, 1942) article first published on line 18 December 2007

Hall, Edward, *Hall's Chronicle: Containing the History of England*, edited by Henry Ellis (Longman et al, 1809)

Hearne, T. (ed.) V*ita et Gesta Henrici Quinti* (Oxford, 1727)

Hutchison, Harold F., *Henry V* (London: Eyre & Spottiswoode, 1967)

Hutchison, Harold F., *The Hollow Crown: A Life of Richard II* (London: Eyre & Spottiswoode, 1961)

Kingsford, C.L., *Henry V: English Historical Literature in the Fifteenth Century* (Oxford: Oxford University Press, 1913)

Lloyd, Sir J.E., *Owen Glendower* (Oxford: Oxford University Press, 1931)

Mackie, R.L., *King James IV of Scotland* (Edinburgh& London: Oliver& Boyd, 1958)

McLeod, Enid, *Charles of Orleans, Prince and Poet* (London: Chatto & Windus, 1969)

Nicholson, Ranald, 'Scotland: The later Middle Ages', *The Edinburgh History of Scotland*, Vol. 2 (Edinburgh: Oliver & Boyd, 1974)

Parliamentorum Rotulii, Vol.III. 643.

Pepys, Samuel, *The Diary of Samuel Pepys* (London: George Allen & Unwin, 1929)

Plon, Henri, *Les Deux Prc̀c`es de condemnation, les enquêtes et la sentence de rehabilitation de Jeanne d'Arc*, Manuscrit No. 1119 de l'assemblée nationale édité chez Plon (1955) facsimilé de l'original latin du Proc`es de condamnation de Jeanne d'Arc (1431)

Rymer, T. Foedera, *Conventiones*, Litterae, etc. vols. 7–10 (London, 1709–10)

Seward, Desmond, *The Hundred Years War: 1339–1453* (Library of Congress Cataloguing in Publication Date, 1978)

Vickers, Jean le Bel, *Contemporary Chronicles of the Hundred Years War*, edited by K.H. Humphrey, Duke of Gloucester (USA: privately published, 1907)

Walsingham, Thomas, *The Chronica Maiora of Thomas Walsingham: 1376–1422*, translated by David Preest and introduction by James G. Clark (Cambridge: Boydell Press, 2005)

Wolffe, Henry Bertram, *Henry VI* (New Haven & London: Yale University Press, 1981)

Index